Women and Film Animation

The creations of female animation filmmakers are recognized all over the world while being, paradoxically, unknown to the general public. *Women and Film Animation: A Feminist Corpus at the National Film Board of Canada 1939–1989* brings out of the shadows the work of true pioneers by presenting and analyzing, from a resolutely feminist perspective, the works they have conceived within the National Film Board of Canada (NFB).

This institution has played an essential role in the emergence of animated cinema in Canada, but it is forgotten or ignored that a good part of this vast corpus is the work of women who have worked there not only as assistants but also as directors. These artists have contributed to changing the traditional representations of women in a unique way in both commercial and avant-garde animated cinema. The author accounts for their concerns, their creativity, and their many bright achievements. To do this, she relies on a wide range of critical works in social and cultural history of Canada, in feminist art history, and on multiple studies on animated cinema.

Key Features:

- Provides an interdisciplinary approach that combines concepts from feminist studies, film theory and visual arts for a nuanced analysis of the role of women in animated cinema.

- Discusses historical and sociological background that sheds light on the condition of women.

- Includes a profound analysis of the changes and continuities in the role of women in this industry over time, focusing on the National Film Board of Canada.

- Features previously unreleased archival material and selected excerpts from reviews by the NFB's programming committee, highlighting the impact of production circumstances on the works of specific women animators.

Marie-Josée Saint-Pierre serves as Associate Professor in the Art and Science of Animation Program at Université Laval School of Design. In 2004, she established MJSTP Films, an independent production company specializing in animated documentary. Her notable works include *McLaren's Negatives* (2006), *Jutra* (2014), and *Oscar* (2016). She holds a Ph.D. in Studies and Practices of the Arts, with a specialization in Feminist Studies, from l'Université du Québec à Montréal, and an M.F.A. in Film Production from Concordia University.

Women and Film Animation

A Feminist Corpus at the National Film Board of Canada 1939–1989

Marie-Josée Saint-Pierre

Translated by Raphaëlle Gauvin and Noémie Turmel with
the collaboration of Alexandra Hillinger

CRC Press
Taylor & Francis Group
Boca Raton London New York

CRC Press is an imprint of the
Taylor & Francis Group, an **informa** business

First edition published 2024
by CRC Press
2385 NW Executive Center Drive, Suite 320, Boca Raton FL 33431

and by CRC Press
4 Park Square, Milton Park, Abingdon, Oxon, OX14 4RN

CRC Press is an imprint of Taylor & Francis Group, LLC

© 2024 Marie-Josée Saint-Pierre

ISBN: 9781032694399 (hbk)
ISBN: 9781032685366 (pbk)
ISBN: 9781032694382 (ebk)

DOI: 10.1201/ 9781032694382

Typeset in Minion Pro
by Apex CoVantage, LLC

*Femmes et cinéma d'animation: Un corpus féministe à
l'Office national du film du Canada (1939–1989)
was first published in French by Les Presses
de l'Université de Montréal (2022)*

Contents

Acknowledgements

Fɪʀsᴛ, I ᴡᴏᴜʟᴅ ʟɪᴋᴇ ᴛᴏ thank the two professors who supervised my Ph.D. thesis for their advice, critiques, recommendations, patience, and generosity: Thérèse St-Gelais, main supervisor, head of the Institute of Feminist Research and Studies and full professor for the History of Arts department at the Université du Québec à Montréal, as well as, Louis Jacob, professor for the Sociology department at the Université du Québec à Montréal. My utmost recognition goes to the National Film Board of Canada and its employees who have made the redaction process easier by giving me access to their archives and films. I would also like to thank the institutions that have funded my university studies: the UQAM Foundation for the Graduate Studies Admission Scholarship and the Government of Canada for the Vanier Canada Graduate Scholarship (CGS). On a more personal note, I would like to thank my mother Hélène who was patient enough to read over this book and support me in various instances. I would like to thank the Chaire Claire-Bonenfant, Femmes, Savoirs et Société as well as the Faculté d'Aménagement, d'Architecture, d'Art et de Design (Université Laval) who have contributed financially to the translation of this book from French to English, by Raphaëlle Gauvin and Noémie Turmel with the collaboration of Alexandra Hillinger. Finally, there is Louise Paradis, who worked on the design cover of the book.

Notes

MULTIPLE FILMS MENTIONED IN this document are available for free on the National Film Board of Canada's website: www.nfb.ca. However, geo-blocking systems make access to the website's content limited in certain parts of the world. Readers can visit the NFB's general website to conduct research and view available films.

Introduction

I HAVE BEEN WORKING PROFESSIONALLY in film animation in Québec as director, screenwriter, producer and animator since 2004. I have created many animated short films with my film production company MJSTP Films Inc.[1] Two main themes emerge from my filmography: motherhood (which I tackled in *Post-Partum* [2004], in *Passages* [FR] [2008], in *Femelles* [FR] [2012] and in *Your mother's a thief!* [2018]) and artistic creation (showcased in *McLaren's Negatives* [2006], *The Sapporo Project* [2010], *Jutra* [2014], *Flocons* [FR] [2014], *Oscar* [2016] and *Lauzon's Theory* [2022].[2] My work in film animation is versatile, as I am also associate professor in the Art and Science of Animation Program at Université Laval's School of Design, where I teach film animation theory and directing.

Alas, I found that the feminist-themed films that I have directed have been more difficult to finance and to broadcast. That is why I undertook doctoral studies in the Études et pratiques des arts program at the Université du Québec à Montréal: I wanted to understand the marginal status of animated film and, more specifically, film animation when created by women. Before undertaking doctoral studies, I tried to retrace the pioneers of that scene. Too often, the narratives of Québec cinema remain quiet about them.

Although, the work of women animators from the National Film Board (NFB) of Canada[3] obtained wide recognition around the world and many prestigious awards,[4] the general public is virtually unaware of their work. I felt compelled to give pioneer women their rightful place in history. To avoid their descent into oblivion, documenting the animators' productions and creative processes is vital; so too is analyzing and reaffirming the rights to their feminist discourse and the robust female models within the discipline. These actions are essential for a more accurate representation of their reality.

DOI: 10.1201/9781032694382-1

FIGURE 0.1   *Black Soul.*

My feminist resistance is the result of a realization that dualist conceptions, long described as "natural" by established epistemology and dominant culture, are in fact essentialist and fabricated. Gender studies, which focus on the historical variations of this social construct, have undermined the dominant thought that opposes women's nature to men's. It is by dissociating women from the concept of biological determinism that it is possible to rethink gender relations. To me, feminism is a political position aimed at improving gender relations to achieve equality. Neither universal nor homogeneous, feminist identities and concepts are by no means monolithic. Feminisms, in their various forms, may at times conflict with one another in unavoidable ideological disagreements. This occurs because women constitute a diverse collective, and it would be unproductive to restrict the multiplicity of perspectives concerning the status of women within an inclusive landscape. Feminist trajectories and ideologies in constant motion are influenced by socioeconomic and geopolitical contexts. Feminism therefore faces the difficult challenge of finding individual and collective solutions simultaneously to protect women's personal, economic, social, political and cultural rights. A woman becomes a feminist upon gaiging awarness of the domination and inequality that women are subjected to, but any personal liberation entails not only the transformation of an individual life but also of the society in which women exist.

The lack of historical data on women directors in early cinema does not only concern film animation. Indeed, although there is extensive documentation on Émile Reynaud, the Lumière brothers and Georges Méliès, little was known (until recently[5]) of pioneer women creators like German animator Lotte Reiniger or French director Alice Guy-Blaché.[6] Yet, these two women are essential contributors to the early cinema. What these omissions tell us is that the roots of epistemology theories grow in fertile grounds that fuel power struggles. Such a sparse transmission of knowledge is caused by this exclusion of the vision of others in order to rule and control. More specifically, epistemological constructs too often repeat essentialism linked to androcentrism[7] views that rely on a binary inclusive-exclusive opposition.

Supposed universal values conveyed by prevailing discourses define artistic norms and legitimize the standards of what is valuable and worthy of interest. The realization that women have almost entirely been erased from major narratives is devastating. One of the examples of the oppression of women and cultural minorities is the anonymity of their existence. In film animation history, American "giant" Walt Disney (international) or "genius" Norman McLaren (national) are recognized as figureheads. This recognition of artistic genius denies being selective and pretends to be neutral. The myth of the great artist is a male construct and the vicious circle induced by an overexposure to canons provokes a funnel effect of cultural impoverishment. The obliteration of a feminine memory can only reflect the marginalized role women hold on a social, economic, and political front. Men's selective memory is the common denominator to women's historical invisibility and their exclusion, not only as producers, but also as subjects of knowledge.

The feminist history of art, at odds with the naturalization of dominant knowledge, rethinks the formation of both partial and biased epistemological constructs spread by the perspective of the universal researcher (white, heterosexual, Eurocentric male). The anonymity of women authors puts them in a position of ignorance, since women creators are forgotten, those who follow do not get to tell their own stories given that they do not have any strong female role models with whom they can identify. In addition to being widely cut from historical documents, women have been deprived from their right of speech and from access to artistic creation. There are real political issues related to the integration of women in animation history: by situating themselves historically, they get to rebuild their narratives outside of the masculine authority that regulates the discipline. The history of women is a privileged means to broaden knowledge in the field of film animation.

Although the history of cinema remains rather quiet as to women animators, they were indeed present when directing. Their professional careers have been poorly documented, and few traces of their works remain in the archives. Through power relationships that shape the discourses, film animation history contributed very little to the recognition of women assistants even though they directly and significantly contributed to the creation of animations. For example, Claire Parker and Faith Hubley have both dedicated their careers to assisting their animator husbands without getting fair credit for their work. Looking back on her relationship with her husband, Faith Hubley said: "[he] made me feel very inferior. He was the senior artist and he was ten years older" (Pilling, 1992).

The erasure of women's creations (or those made in collaboration with their partners, husbands, or lovers) is not exclusive to film animation. In the history of art, there are many instances where women sacrificed their personal work for the benefit of their male companion, gave priority to the man's career at their personal expenses or contributed to their spouse's work without obtaining any form of recognition neither historical nor financial. Invisibilizing others is one of the characteristics of male dominance. Hence, in the animation industry, there is a differential power between men and women, one example is the exploitation of women who work for male directors and those who assist their director husbands. The value of women's labor power in the film animation industry cannot be measured when others take credit for it.

Education plays a crucial role in the emancipation of women. For a long time, Disney ran a school in the United States where animation filmmaking was taught and where women were forbidden to attend. A letter addressed to Mary V. Ford in 1938 sheds lights on this reality. The reply that the young woman received after having expressed the wish to study and work within the organization was categorical: "Women do not do any of the creative work in connection with preparing the cartoons for the screen, as that work is performed entirely by young men. For this reason girls are not considered for the training school" (Walt Disney Productions Ltd., 1938, n. p.). Ford was encouraged to apply for the inking and painting on acetate positions.

Thus, at the beginning of animation cinema, when women were not completely excluded, they found themselves in the subordinate role of assisting men who held the high rank of the decision-making hierarchy as creative positions were exclusive to men. In the animation industry, the reproduction of the differential power of exploitation and domination can therefore be witnessed. Sexism is omnipresent. As with domestic work, there is a tendency for men to have women do routine work. For a long time, the function of women in the world of animation mirrored their traditional role in the private sphere, meaning that their responsibility is limited to performing repetitive tasks.

In art, feminist representations are often an act of protest against the "feminine" portrayal of fertile Venus-goddesses-mothers condemned to the ovens of the kitchen. The creations of women animators at the NFB also contribute to the dissemination of a different view of mainstream media production, far from Betty Boop, Jessica Rabbit and other Disney princesses. Therefore, I consider their films as a valid cultural tool since they reveal the condition of women.

Moreover, working for a government institution as a woman creator gives NFB women directors the status of "civil servant filmmakers" (Carrière, 1988) since their artistic creations are entirely financed by the government. This ambiguous status places women directors at the centre of a particular political game because their films are produced within the limits of liberal, egalitarian and institutional feminism. Some politically engaged works present the same socio-economic denunciations of feminist movements. Filmmakers tell the life and memory of women, thereby creating a counter-history in opposition to traditional feminine representations. Film animation can thus be a vehicle for advocacy in which women authors produce political creations that promote awareness and change. It is this feminist creation discourse in film animation at the NFB that I wish to broaden since it presents the world under an innovative and original light.

The social perception of film animation is often that of a commercial activity aimed at children and families, and therefore relegated to the bottom of the hierarchy of the world of arts. This lack of artistic promotion, outside of the restricted circles of enthusiasts and specialized film festivals, is most likely due to Disney's hegemonic influence. Yet, there is an avant-garde animated production, an atypical animated aesthetic which pushes the boundaries of cinematic language. This is precisely the case for the creations discussed in this publication: these films directed by women animators at the NFB and produced without considering commercial pressures have the possibility of opening up to avant-garde production and feminist perspective.

Since the geographical context has a significant impact on the production conditions of women animators (Pilling, 1992), by observing the conditions of creation of women directors at the NFB, it is possible to shed light on the work of these pioneers. The NFB encourages personal discourses that let women animators venture into critical and creative territory. By adopting this narrative strategy, women directors can attempt to subvert the representation of the social domination of women and the oppression of their bodies by targeting their problems, fantasies and desires.[8]

Accounting for women's daily life experiences with animation allows for new spaces of creation and expression for artists. The animation films presented in this book question some stereotypical behaviors that contribute to the domination of women by men. The focus will be put on films where perspective is modified and where inequalities are presented by offering alternatives to the dominant point of view. These films are directed by women that often feel oppressed by society and limited regarding the possibilities for film direction.

Much still must be done for women-directed animated films to be part of the institutions. Seeing as film animation has long been a boy's club in which women did not have access to directing, focus will be given to the socioprofessional trajectories of these women animators in this book. Generally speaking, up until the beginning of the 1970s, the conditions for creation and access to film direction was still unfavorable for women. However, as soon as they started holding positions in that field, echoes of feminist issues become visible in film productions, which shows that there is a real presence of feminist theory in cultural institutions. This book examines the militant feminist perspective in animation that stems from the cleavage between the private and the public spheres. Although the corpus might seem heterogeneous, its homogeneity emerges in the practices of women animators. These productions allow for the understanding of certain aspects of the Québec and the Canadian societies in the period in which they were created. The films' aesthetics, the techniques and the texts all reflect the specific period of their production. The relationship between animation techniques and themes leads to particular aesthetic choices to support the narrative.

The films presented in this book have contributed to changing the traditional representations of gender roles and in exposing their alienating effect in an avant-garde way that is proper to frame-by-frame animated films. Contrary to cartoons, this type of animation is part of the NFB's mandate to promote exploration in artistic creations. This corpus does not find its roots in works from Disney but rather in dadaist, surrealist, expressionist, and, as far as allowed by the limits of the institution, they are personal works. Film animation is a unique communication tool that renders possible—using an atypical angle—the denunciation of certain living conditions of women.

Feminist issues are the cross-disciplinary subject of this corpus: the sexual division in household work, the enslavement of female bodies, the experience of motherhood, the breakdown of the traditional family unit, etc. Animated films are no strangers to the socio-economic contexts from which they emerge. Works that seem to reveal the condition of women and their real oppression by clearly showing that gender divide leads to a social hierarchy were selected. By drawing inspiration from the reality of women in the private and public spheres to create a critical discourse, women directors do not limit themselves to a role of spectators. These portrayals of women by other women give life to female protagonists that no longer hold the position of an object, but rather, that of a subject.

For a more comprehensive examination, this book includes previously unreleased archival material and selected excerpts from reviews by the NFB's programming committees.[9] The juxtaposition of these two sources of information—feminist film analysis and archival research—allows to account for the influence of the production conditions on certain women animators' works. Considering the plurality of perspectives that emerge from institutional animated productions through the axiological cross-referencing of ideologies is at the heart of my perspective as a practitioner. Ideological universes unfold on multiple diegetic levels: that of the animator, the short films, the NFB's and the critical feminist author-practitioners. Women are both producers of knowledge (in filmmaking) and objects of that knowledge (in films).

NOTES

1. Throughout my career, my films have been presented at over 150 festivals and have won over 60 awards worldwide, including two prix Jutra (Jutra award), one prix Gémeaux (Gemeaux award) and one Canadian Screen award.
2. See Appendix A.
3. In order to alleviate the text, the abbreviation "NFB" will be used to refer to the National Film Board of Canada.
4. For example, short films from women animators have won awards such as the Palme d'or at the Cannes Film Festival with *When the Day Breaks* (Forbis and Tilby, 1999), the Golden Bear at the Berlin International Film Festival with *Black Soul* (Chartrand, 2001; see Figure 0.1) or the Academy Award for Best Animated Short Film with *The Danish Poet* (Kove, 2006).
5. Two feature-length films have been dedicated to Alice-Guy Blaché: *Be Natural: The Untold Story of Alice Guy-Blaché* (Green, 2018) and *The Lost Garden: The Life and Cinema of Alice Guy-Blaché* (Lepage, 1995). Two short films have been dedicated to the life and works of Lotte Reiniger: *The Art of Lotte Reiniger* (Isaacs, 1970) and *Lotte That Silhouette Girl* (Beecherl et al., 2018).
6. See Chapter 3.
7. Androcentrism is defined by normal human experience that relies on masculine perception. It is a normative vision that is not always acknowledged as it appears so natural. However, it is fabricated.
8. Women directors often portray women in a way that differs from the male gaze as described in *Visual Pleasure and Narrative Cinema* (Mulvey, 1975) which is widely considered as the founding article of feminist film Studies. According to Laura Mulvey, the stereotypical constructions of characters supported by the symbolic unconscious are the vehicle for projection of male fantasies on the big screen. Films create figures and relationships that reproduce gender relations ideologies. The spectator adopts the male perspective as they must look through the lens of a heterosexual male, the intended audience for whom the film is created, to draw maximum pleasure from their experience. Films put into picture society's androcentric behaviors. In this publication from 1975, Mulvey presents a feminist reading of cinematographic works while referring to Freudian (the gaze) and Lacanian (the mirror) psychoanalyses. According to her, films consist in an activity of voyeurism during which the male gaze is in the active form, whereas the feminine one is in the passive form. By relating to the male protagonist, the spectator projects a double erotic function on the female character. Mulvey also points out that in most American fictional films, the role of the heroine is to generate and justify the male protagonist's actions. Laura Mulvey's vision was subjected to wide criticism, especially due to the *a priori* essentialists that she seems to support. On that aspect, as a reply to her detractors, she wrote, in 1981, *Afterthoughts on* Visual Pleasure and Narrative Cinema *inspired by King Vidor's Duel in the Sun (1946)* in which she nuanced her statements.

9. In the NFB's organizational chart, the programming committee is the decision-making body that gives its approval to produce films. For the time covered in this research (which is no longer the case) meetings took place between the department managers and the filmmakers. All those meetings were documented. The minutes reflect the production conditions to which filmmakers were subjected to. There were numerous minutes. For information purposes, for the French program only, over 400 reports were written between 1970 and 1979.

1

Film Animation, Feminisms and NFB

CHAPTER 1

The Particular Nature of Film Animation

FILM ANIMATION COVERS A particular cinematographic field and defining it is difficult. Too often marginalized in cinematographic studies, film animation should be included without being opposed to live action. Through its many meanings, the etymology of "animation"[1] is broad and may apply to several media. It would be painstaking to try and retrace the advances in animation techniques in the various countries in which it evolved. Since I see film animation as a social practice with specific emergence conditions, I reject a purely technical definition.

The artist who breathes life into the elements of the film occupies a central place in film animation. Paradoxically, animating is creating a series of fixed images, as the illusion of movement can only be obtained at the time of the continuous projection of the images, which were painstakingly created one by one. "The trade of animators consists precisely in focusing on each of these specks of insignificance that are the photograms" (Hébert, 2006, p. 22, our translation). While live action immortalizes movement (mechanical recording), animation creates movement. By building mechanisms to produce images and original movements, animators escape what is observable and what is considered real. It is impossible to draw movement per se, and each animation creates movement according to its internal logic. Technical errors, dust or fingerprints are the traces of the artist's passage in the film. The animator's physical

DOI: 10.1201/9781032694382-3

13

trace and his or her way of inventing movements are directly inscribed in their work.

André Martin emphasizes the importance of the artist in animation, supported by "the talent and temperament of the animators" (Martin, quoted in Clarens, 2000, p. 11, our translation). The animator is more than an artisan that reproduces movement. "In animation, there is a soul. Between the character and the animator, there is not only the effort made to give it movement. Something stays of the warmth that accompanied the evolution" (Martin, quoted in Clarens, 2000, p. 32, our translation). The same observation is made by Donald Crafton (2013) who explains that the spectator does not watch the performance of the animated character, but rather that of the person who breathed life into it. In animation, the artist—the real actor—remains in the shadows, even if the frame-by-frame creation offers a privileged dive into the imagination of its author. The subjectivity of production is inherent to animation work.

Metamorphosis is a fundamental aspect of animated cinema. The possibilities for transforming lines and shapes are endless. "In animation, metamorphosis is first and foremost a figure of time, an effect of time more than movement" (Jean, 2006, p. 58, our translation). The artist does much more than create movement; they can transform it according to their will. Film animation is often an entirely imaginary world that does not wish to replicate reality. It is associated with a dreamlike dimension, encompassing elements such as fantasies or desires. Animation increases the possibilities of cinematographic language tenfold: it allows for anthropomorphism, immortality, insubordination to the laws of physics, corporeality, etc. In the world of frame-by-frame cinema, the relationship between human and object is out of alignment. Anthropomorphism defies the laws of nature and ignores the constraints of reality. In animation, humanizing objects or attributing human traits to animals is common. Animated elements are not subjected to the laws of logic. An animated image offers the spectator a completely unique experience because "there is absolutely no distinction between appearance and reality" (Beckman, 2014, p. 7). In animation, what the spectator believes and what is real, or imaginary intertwine. Film animation is not a genre. It has the same genres as traditional cinema.

Film animation presents unlimited possibilities for technical creation. Even today, we continue to invent new processes and animation techniques are countless: animated drawing on paper and on celluloid, animation without cameras, paint, photographs, watercolors (or other 2D media), animated puppets, pixelation, pinscreen animation, sand animation (or any other stop motion medium), as well as computer animation (2D, 3D and artificial intelligence). Techniques can sometimes be mixed: combined on the same image or during different sequences. Each technique generates a particular aesthetic, and the choice of a technique is often guided by the narrative. Film animation superimposes several artistic codes in the same work.

Constraints in animated production are significant, especially regarding the costs incurred to produce the animation and the time required to build the sequences. "Despite a heavy (or light) technique, the real author is, of course, the one who manages to overcome the material contingencies of image by image to offer a vision of cinema directly linked to the author's imagination" (Denis, 2017, p. 6, our translation). As Marco De Blois (2006) points out, the International Animated Film Association (ASIFA), founded in 1960 in Annecy in France, makes no mention of "cinema" in its definition of animation: "The art of animation is the creation of moving images through the manipulation of all varieties of techniques apart from live action methods" (De Blois, 2006, p. 29). We can understand that position by retracing the origins of film animation.

MULTIFACETED BIRTH WITH A DISPUTED PATERNITY

Humanity has sought, since the dawn of time, to represent itself and its movements through various media. Going back to the prehistoric period reveals the human will to inspire movement into the drawings. On cave walls, paintings already show the succession of movements: running horses or characters hunting. These representations are painted in sequences with subtle alterations of movements (Poncet, 1952) as if the images of the life of Paleolithic men wanted to come alive. There is an undoubtedly a desire to represent life in motion in all periods and in all civilizations: sequences are painted on tableware, sculpted in bas-reliefs or reproduced through various artefacts. In Ancient Greece, sculptures of the Parthenon by Phidias showed the different phases of the movements of a rider and his racing horse (Bendazzi, 2016a).

During the 19th and 20th centuries, many optical toys were invented: zoetrope, kaleidoscope, thaumatrope, phenakistiscope, stroboscopic disk, magic lantern, etc. However, the various toys that recreate the illusion of movement have not yet absorbed the complex technological parameters of the cinematographic apparatus. Donald Crafton, a film animation historian, criticizes univocally reducing optical toys as being at the origin of animation cinema. For animation to be cinematographic, it must be projected with the technical apparatus of cinema. The toy, which is more accessible, physically engages the person in the random visual exploration of the succession of images. The running speed varies from one person to another and does not strictly conform to the rate of 24 images per second as for the projection apparatus in movie theatres.[2] If a technical correlation exists between optical toys and animation, it excludes the cinematographic dimension.

The influence of photographic research on the perception of movements at the end of the 19th century is not negligible either. Edward Muybridge, with *The Horse in Motion* (Muybridge, 1878) was able to prove that, at a specific moment, a racehorse has all four legs in the air. Étienne-Jules Marey also studies human and animal movements with photographic essays that simultaneously present the succession of movements as in *Movements in Pole Vaulting* (Marey, 1887).

Illusionism is at the heart of the precursors of cinema's first experiments, who, as if by magic, give life to motionless things. Through special effects, editing or manipulation of images, directors become magicians. These pioneers record the images one by one and, between some of them, make alterations in the position of the objects. When the photographs are projected one after the other, movement seems to occur like "magic" since there is no visual recording of the human intervention, which caused the displacement of the objects. These filmmakers[3] focus on developing the foundational techniques of special effects artistry. These innovations are specifically geared towards creating special effects, rather than animated films. Therefore, it is not about animation, but rather about experiments, pushing creators to become aware of the importance of changes that take place between the interstices of frames.

Reynaud, a pioneer of film animation, invented the praxinoscope, an optical toy sold throughout Europe in the early 1870s. By modifying his technical device, Reynaud created "optical theatre" and presented his first work on the big screen in front of an audience: *Un bon bock* [FR] (Reynaud, 1892). Unfortunately, "optical theatre" is extremely fragile, which limits its distribution. In addition, Reynaud signed an exclusivity agreement with the Musée Grévin, which prevented him from presenting his discovery elsewhere, in Europe or abroad. The inventor spent several years creating his *pantomimes lumineuses* series, including *Le clown et ses chiens* [FR] (Reynaud, 1892b), *Pauvre Pierrot!* [FR] (Reynaud, 1892a) and *Autour d'une cabine* [FR]

(Reynaud, 1894b). Over 500,000 people attended screenings of Reynaud's *pantomimes lumineuses* between 1890 and 1900 (Bendazzi, 2016a).

Reynaud's technique, which consists of painting each frame individually, is difficult to reproduce. Laboriously, he redraws all the images of the film to completely erase traces of the actual filming. Since there is only one copy of each work (the mechanical reproduction processes of cinema had not yet been invented), this enormously limits distribution possibilities in a society that already values mass production. Disillusioned and at the end of his life, Reynaud destroyed his three "optical theatres" and threw all his *pantomimes lumineuses* in the Seine. Only two reels of his work remain: *Pauvre Pierrot!* [FR] and *Autour d'une cabine* [FR].

The first film animation work was the short *Fantasmagorie* [FR] by Émile Cohl (1908). Cohl initially made a name for himself as a political cartoonist. Later, he worked as a scriptwriter at Gaumont, where he embarked on his cinematic career. Simultaneously, he illustrated all the images for *Fantasmagorie*. Over 700 drawings were needed to create this two-minute film. Cohl photographs each of the drawings individually on cinematographic film. When his drawings are projected one after the other, they begin to move. The premiere of the film took place in 1908 in Paris and obtained immediate international success.

In this film, Cohl exploits the intrinsic qualities of animation: the actions are irrational and unconcerned with the representation of the real world. Cohl records the images by staging himself: the film begins and ends with the hand of the artist who creates it. *Fantasmagorie* and this idea of the artists who put themselves on stage influenced several pioneers of film animation. Blackton's hand breathes life into the drawings in *Humorous Phases of Funny Faces* (Blackton, 1906) and Winsor McCay stages himself in *Gertie the Dinosaur* (McCay, 1914).[4] A differential power exists between the animator and the character they animate; if the hand of the artist can give life to the character, it can take it back just as easily.[5]

COMMERCIAL AND AVANT-GARDE ANIMATION

The transition from individual artisanal creation to teamwork favored mass production and marked the birth of commercial animation in the United States. The cartoon is often associated with the field of comics and caricature. Artists who work in these fields sought to infuse their drawings with vitality and therefore leaped into the world of animation. At that time, the influence of comics was also felt in live action: it would therefore be a simplistic reduction of its influence on film animation (Crafton, 1982). Many illustrators start with lightning sketches[6] and then move on to film animation. The emergence of the cartoon is more correlated by vaudeville theatre: in lightning sketches, the animators perform directly in front of the audience, in a coexistence between the artist who draws (performance-intervention) and the artwork that is created in front of an audience (film animation).

From the beginning of the 20th century, the American film animation industry developed at lightning speed.[7] The animation technique favored by this industry is drawing and painting on acetate, which allows the background to show through the sheet and avoid having to redraw the background with each frame, which greatly shortens the production process. Among pioneer American productions, Dave and Max Fleischer created *Koko the Clown* for the *Out of the Inkwell* series (Fleisher's, 1918). Pat Sullivan and Otto Mesmer invented *Felix the Cat* (Pat Sullivan's Studio, 1919), the first animated character to achieve international recognition.[8] In the 1920s, Disney moved to California and it's on the West Coast that the first fully sound animated short film was created: *Steamboat Willie* (Disney and Iwerks, 1928), in which the iconic Mickey Mouse appears for the first time. The *Mickey Mouse* (Disney and Iwerks, 1928) and *Silly Symphonies* (Disney and Iwerks, 1929) series are released and allow studio workers to develop the expertise needed to produce the first animated feature film in the United States: *Snow White and the Seven Dwarfs* (Hand, 1937).[9]

At the same time, Fleischer Studios created the first female protagonist for an animated series, Betty Boop—a great success. Betty Boop's appearance is close to the pin-ups' aesthetic, massively reproduced icons of popular culture. She is dressed in a short low-cut dress, high heels and garters. She acts sexy and has everything to fulfil heterosexual male fantasies. She is like "a hedonic creature, artificial, inaccessible" (Jean, 2006, p. 99, our translation). According to historian Maureen Furniss:

> Betty Boop was first introduced in 1930—as a dog—in the "Talkartoon" *Dizzy Dishes*, alongside Bimbo the dog. The following year she appeared in her own series—as a woman—and quickly became a star. One of the primary influences of her design was Helen Kane, an American signer famous for her song "I want to be loved by you", which was first performed onstage in 1928 and includes Betty's signature phrase, "boo poop a doop". Betty Boop,

who was primarily voiced by Mae Questel, was unique among female characters of the time, because of her sexualized persona. By 1934, however, Betty Boop had been subjected to censorship.

(Furniss, 2016, p. 116)

Due to American film censorship—the Hays code came into force in 1934—Betty Boop changed: clothes cover a larger part of her body, she now has a little brother and a dog. She becomes a responsible, respectable figure and loses some of her audience. However, the power of Betty Boop should not be neglected, she remains a strong woman all the same: she tries to be elected president (*Betty Boop for President*, 1932) and she owns her own company.

Behind the camera, many women were active in early cinema. "As long as cinema is neither culturally legitimate nor financially profitable, women could find a place in it" (Rollet, 2017, p. 10, our translation). Women creators are not the only ones who are erased. Margaret Winkler, a pioneer in the field of animation distribution, remains too often ignored by historical documentation. After having acquired experience in the Warner Bros. production studios as an executive secretary, Winkler founded in 1921 her own distribution company, specialized in animation, "and went by the initials M.J. to disguise the fact she was a woman (named Margaret) in a field dominated by men" (Furniss, 2009, p. 105). She is responsible for the exclusive distribution of Walt Disney's first works, the *Alice Comedies* series (Disney, around 1920), then she acquires the distribution of *Felix the Cat* (Pat Sullivan's Studio, 1919) and *Out of the Inkwell* (Fleischer, 1918). "What makes Winkler's accomplishment all the more significant is that she not only had an eye for incipient animation talent, but, once these soon-to-be-legendary artists were signed, she seemed to bring out the best in them" (Furniss, 2009, p. 106). Winkler's career is short: only five years. Following her marriage to Charles Mintz, who takes over operations, she is confined to the role of stay-at-home mother:

Her career reflects the opportunities open to women in a field that was not yet solidified as an industry . . . at perhaps no other time in cinema history were women able to command as much power, relatively speaking, as they did during the silent era, through the late 1920s.

(Furniss, 2009, p. 3)

It seems unlikely, indeed, that another woman could have repeated this feat: running a distribution company and bringing together the key talents of that time (Disney, Fleischer and Pat Sullivan Studios).

It should be noted that the public often does not question the content of animated films as they are immediately considered as non-political family entertainment. Yet, film animation can prove to be an important propaganda tool. For a certain time, American and international animation (as well as that produced in Canada) was put at the service of the war effort. Several governments around the world funded animated propaganda films during the First and Second World Wars. In the United States, Max Fleischer was the first to develop animated films for military training after the government realized that the troops retained information better when the messages are conveyed through animation.

Political cartoons proved to be a valuable method of reaching the nation and conveying ideas. The American government mobilized Disney workshops[10] during the Second World War to support the war effort. All employees were registered and closely monitored, even Walt Disney carried permanent identification inside his studios (Solomon [1998], 2009). Although he found the presence of the army in his studios to be an inconvenience, Disney was not against producing propaganda films for the American government.[11] From 1941 to 1945, Disney created many animations for American propaganda and famous characters (Donald Duck, Goofy and Mickey Mouse) were used to convey to the nation the government's views of Nazism, Communism and Patriotism. The propaganda film *Der Fuehrer's Face* (Kinney, 1943) received the Oscar for best animated short film.

A political correlation also exists between the international situation and the initial mandate of the NFB's animation studio. Founded in 1941, the animation department was created to produce animated segments (credits, schemas, maps, etc.) for films that supported the war effort. A propagandist aim is therefore at the origin of the NFB's animation program.

Norman McLaren (1914–1987), a pioneer of animated creations at the NFB, studied at the Glasgow School of Arts. He said he quickly got tired of the immobility of the images he produced: "Everything I was doing was stationary and didn't move. I felt I wanted to work with something that moved" (McLaren, quoted in Saint-Pierre, 2006). John Grierson, the first film commissioner, recruited him to establish the animation department at the NFB. McLaren arrived in Ottawa in 1941[12] and first devoted himself to gathering the technical equipment needed to produce animations. The following year, McLaren recruited young arts students (including René Jodoin and Grant Munro) and trained them in animation, since this form of cinematographic expression was not taught in schools. Norman McLaren's early propaganda works at the NFB are: *Mail Early for Christmas* (McLaren, 1941), *V for Victory* (McLaren, 1941), *Hen Hop* (McLaren, 1942) and *Five for four* (McLaren, 1942).

Propaganda films are not the prerogative of governments; some artists produce animations with propagandist themes on their own initiative. *The Sinking of the Lusitania* (McCay, 1918) is an animated documentary that recreates the sinking of a British ship by a German submarine. This film is considered the first animation of the documentary genre. *L'idée* [FR] (Bartosch, 1932)[13] is a film that influenced several artists. *L'idée* depicts a certain left-wing protest through its criticism of the stereotypical portrayal of the female figure and the myth of femininity. Upon its release, the film "was immediately censored [in Germany] and was not rediscovered until 1945" (Denis, 2017, p. 147, our translation). The feature film *Animal Farm* (Batchelor and Halas, 1954), adapted from the book *Animal Farm* by George Orwell (1945), is another non-governmental denunciatory animation—in this film, the animals revolt against the humans who mistreat them. Thus, it is possible to engage in political animation outside governmental frameworks and to subscribe to "the most extreme position of the avant-garde, that of revolt against all authorities and all institutions" (Bourdieu, 1992, p. 65). This artistic revolution can occur in both form and content.

At the beginning of the 20th century, artists from large cities such as Paris and Berlin became interested in popular culture. Cubism is at its peak. Picasso painted *Les demoiselles d'Avignon* in 1907. Inspired by the photographic works of Edward Muybridge and Étienne-Jules Marey, the controversial Marcel Duchamp painted *Nu descendant un escalier no 2* (1912). This representation is a complete break from classical pictorial traditions, and it depicts the different stages of the movement of a woman walking down a staircase. This artwork expresses what many artists feel: the desire to destroy not only the traditional iconography but also the fixity of images.

Breaking from the commercial productions and—as it was already mentioned—the hegemonic position conquered by the Disney studios for which film animation is first and foremost a commercial activity, the artist of animated avant-garde will offer abstract and non-narrative films; a cinema that explores cinematographic language and that considers itself art. Because it defies the conventions of American cartoons, avant-garde animations are often radical. "We are projected backwards from the paradisiacal visions of Walt Disney, and also from good-natured, competitive and aggressive cartoons" (Carrière, 1983a, p. 44, our translation). *Ipso facto*, artistic avant-garde animation finds itself doubly marginalized, first by the world of art and second by the world of cinema.

In 1924, Fernand Léger, a French painter, co-directed with Dudley Murphy, *Ballet mécanique* [FR] (Léger and Murphy, 1924), an avant-garde short film employing a collage of various live-action techniques (special effects, kaleidoscopic effects and recording at different sample rates) and frame-by-frame recording techniques (cut-out animation and drawn-on-film animation). This experimental film is infused with improvisation and creative freedom. The editing speed, which is sometimes slow, but often very fast, juxtaposes the images to give them a new meaning. Sometimes the images are abstract, symbolic or even reduced to simple geometric shapes, while at other times they are realistic: a woman swinging, a close-up of lips, a corpulent woman climbing a flight of stairs, etc. At that time, *Ballet mécanique* was an innovative cinematographic proposal that influenced the world of film animation and experimental cinema.

After the Second World War, an increasing number of artists work alone. This non-commercial approach allows creators to carry out almost all the tasks of animated film production simultaneously: scriptwriting, animation, direction, cinematography and production. This direct access promotes great creativity and leaves room for spontaneity, experimentation and error (which would be unthinkable with a feature film). "When we step out of the commercially strong currents in the history of animation, we realize that the narrative fragmentation is even greater.... We are no longer subject to what Bazin called the ontological realism of photographic images" (Jean, 2006, p. 111, our translation).

An exemplary case is Alexandre Alexeïeff who had a career in illustration before embarking in animation after seeing *L'idée*. From the start, Alexeïeff dissociated himself from the burlesque characteristics of commercial productions. With Claire Parker, he invented the pinscreen.[14] They worked together on several animated films and the pinscreen technique is at the heart of their artistic project. Their first animation was *Une nuit sur le mont Chauve* [FR] (Alexeïeff and Parker, 1933), they then produced *Le nez* [FR] (Alexeïeff and Parker, 1963), *Tableaux d'une exposition* [FR] (Alexeïeff and Parker, 1972) and *Trois thèmes* [FR] (Alexeïeff and Parker, 1980).

Despite the two wars that crippled the country, Germany remained a heartland for artistic avant-garde and particularly for cinematographic avant-garde. The authenticity of German Expressionism was borne by directors such as Fritz Lang and Paul Wegener. Many talented artists were interested in stop motion cinema and created numerous masterpieces: *Motion Painting No. 1* (Fischinger, 1947), *Lichtspiel Opus I* (Ruttmann, 1921), *Rhythmus 21* (Richter, 1921) and *Diagonal Symphony* (Eggelin, 1925). As we will see later, Lotte Reiniger is a key feminist pioneer. She produced and directed the first feature film in the history of animation: *The Adventures of Prince Achmed* (Reiniger, 1926).

In Czechoslovakia, filmmakers specialized in puppet animation. Trnka, a multidisciplinary artist, made several films after the Second World War. He first worked with celluloids, *The Gift* (Trnka, 1946), and later became interested in puppets and established himself as a leader in this animation technique. *A Midsummer Night's Dream* (Trnka, 1959) and *The Hand* (Trnka, 1965) are examples of his puppet films.

In the United States, Mary Elle Bute and Marie Menken pushed stop motion cinema experimentation forward. Influenced by Kandinsky and Fischinger, among others, Bute produced her first experimental animations in the early 1930s. With *Abstronics* (Bute, 1952) she was the first artist to make video art (Pilling, 1992). Trained as a painter, Marie Menken's first experimental film was *Visual Variations on Noguchi* (Menken, 1945). She experimented with several animation techniques during her career, including collage and non-continuous image recording. Despite being unknown to most, she influenced several visual artists, including the avant-garde filmmaker Stan Brakhage, who directed *Window Water Baby Moving* (Brakhage, 1959) and *Mothlight* (Brakhage, 1963), among others.

Len Lye produced the first film without a camera at the GPO Film Unit in England: he drew on motion picture film for *Colour Box* (Lye, 1935). He abandoned the camera by scratching the film directly to remove the black emulsion in *Free Radicals* (Lye, 1958) and *Particles in Space* (Lye, 1966). There is an affinity between the techniques and aesthetics of Lye and those of McLaren, except that Lye is an independent artist with reduced financial means.

According to Pierre Hébert, many factors favored avant-garde animation, including the democratization and fragmentation of production techniques, the rehabilitation of pioneers, the founding of the Annecy International Animation Film Festival and the International Animated Film Association (ASIFA).

However, the line between avant-garde art and popular cinema is thin. The hegemony of American commercial animation creates a perception of entertainment-oriented film animation: a commercial activity intended for children and families—occupying the bottom of the hierarchy of the world of arts, a "discredit attached to 'popular' success" (Bourdieu, 1992, p. 82). Film animation is probably a victim of this. However, this "popular" art is a legitimate cultural object that deserves to be recognized and studied in the same way as the "learned" arts such as painting or sculpture. Here is an illuminating comparison from feminist animation theorist Amy M. Davis:

> The target audience for Disney films is traditionally seen as the child/family audience, despite the high degree of violence and terror which is typical in Disney films. It is interesting that the same parents who would not think twice about forbidding their child from seeing *Silence of the Lambs* (1991) in which a man kidnaps and murders various women with the intention of making a suit of clothes from their skins would probably also think nothing about allowing their child to see *One-Hundred-and-One-Dalmatians*, in which a psychotic woman is systematically kidnapping the "children" of various families of Dalmatians with the intention of slaughtering them and making a coat from their skin.
>
> (Davis, 2006, p. 26)

The distinction between popular art and high art is by no means obvious and the actual possibility of separating them seems very fragile. The permeability of lines from one to the other allows elite culture to absorb popular culture (and vice versa), which leads to the diversification of interests and practices within cultural groups. Cultural consumption no longer characterizes a social class. "There is a decrease of the symbolic boundaries between social groups and a weakening of the weight of cultural legitimacy in the orientation of individual practices" (Coulangeon, 2004, p. 60, our translation). The theory that the dominant class automatically rejects popular arts and mass culture is no longer valid.

Film animation is often thought to be confined to a ghetto. Indeed, apart from its most commercial manifestations—Disney-and-Pixar-type feature films and television series—film animation is excluded from mainstream cinematographic activities. For example, there are very few animated films in the major generalist festivals, such as Cannes, Venice or Berlin. Similarly, the best animated films—because they are usually short films—almost never hit commercial theatres. As a result, this sector of activity remains completely obscure, even to the most knowledgeable cinephiles.

(Jean, 2006, p. 77, our translation)

Access to animated short films as well as their distribution have always been problematic. Marcel Jean believes that animation filmmakers are victims of ghettoization because they break from narrative cinema: animation filmmakers, who favor the short film format, are not exclusively subject to the narrative rules of commercial cinema. "When looking at the history of film animation, most of the films did not conform to these modes of storytelling" (Jean, 2006, p. 13, our translation). Film animation artists have earned the prerogative to produce films on the fringes of traditional narration and, with the NFB, they find in Canada an institution that produces works without worrying about profits and commercial outlets.

NOTES

1. The term "animation," from Latin *animatio*, designates the action of animating. "Animate" may also serve as an "incitement" or an "inspiration" that provokes the desire to accomplish something. The adjective "animated" is said of a person endowed with life or of a situation imbued with dynamism. *A contrario*, "unanimated" means" "not endowed with life" and the words associated with it are "revive," "resuscitation," "resuscitate" and "resuscitation." The verb "to animate," from Latin *animare* (from *anima*), means "to breathe life into something," "to add movement," "to make livelier" or "to dynamize, stimulate, vivify." Therefore, an "animator" is the person who breathes life into something.
2. It is worth mentioning, however, that it was not until the transition to sound and talking cinema in the late 1920s that films began to be presented at a stabilized speed.
3. In particular, *Le voyage dans la Lune* [FR] (Méliès, 1902), which became famous due to its special effects, its double exposures and its scale models. There is also *The Haunted Hotel* (Blackton, 1907) in which the director instills movement into non-living elements: Objects are autonomous and move by themselves. A similar concept was explored in *The Electric Hotel* (De Chómon, 1908).
4. At the time, when his film was presented in front of an audience, McCay often appeared on stage to interact with the animation, thus extending the vaudeville performance in his cinema. "By depicting themselves at work on

the screen, engaged in their business of making magic, moving drawings, these artists showed themselves impairing the anima—the breath of life" (Crafton, 1982, p. 57).

5. *A Cartoonist's Nightmare* (King, 1935) illustrates this concept well, but in an inverted way because, in this short film, the animator falls in his own film, and he is mistreated by the various characters he animated.

6. Regarding lightning sketches: "There were three irreducible components: an artist, ostensibly the protagonist of the film and invariably played by the filmmaker himself; a drawing surface (sketch pad, blackboard, or canvas), always initially blank; and the drawings, shown being executed by the artist" (Crafton, 1982, p. 50).

7. Two studios were founded in New York: one by American John Randolph Bray (Bray Productions) and the other by American Bill Nolan and the Quebecker Raoul Barré (Barré-Nolan Studio).

8. The distribution of *Felix the Cat* is done outside of cinemas, which means that he is the first marketed animated character with merchandise.

9. Several Disney feature films were produced in the following years, such as *Pinocchio* (Kuske and Sharpsteen, 1940), *Fantasia* (Alger *et al.*, 1940), *Dumbo* (Sharpsteen, 1941) and *Bambi* (Hand, 1942). Significant characters from Disney studios—like Pluto, Goofy and Donald Duck—were created in the 1930s.

10. Other American animation production studios like MGM, Fleischer Studios and Warner Bros were also at the service of the propaganda mission of the American government.

11. Three years after *Snow White and the Seven Dwarfs* (Hand, 1937), two other feature films were released: *Pinocchio* (Luske and Sharpsteen, 1940) and *Fantasia* (Alger *et al.*, 1940). Unfortunately, these two new films were not profitable and Disney was crippled by debt, which would partly explain its non-opposition to the production of cartoons intended for the American government's propaganda effort (Solomon [1998], 2009).

12. It was John Grierson who hired McLaren at the GPO Film Unit where he directed five short films including *Love on the Wing* (McLaren, 1938). See the next chapter on John Grierson's contribution to the founding of the NFB.

13. Bartosch had collaborated on the film *The Adventures of Prince Ahmed* (Reiniger, 1926).

14. The pinscreen consists of a surface made up of thousands of pins that create shadows and contrasts depending on the pressure and degree with which they are positioned. This unique animation technique requires rigorous work and an incredible amount of time to produce an animation.

CHAPTER 2

The National Film Board of Canada

THE NFB IS AN influential vector of Canadian national identities which, since its founding, has been able to accumulate significant cultural capital. Its many missions (educational, political and economic) testify to a notable institutional, social and cultural history. Since its creation in 1939, its mandate has been questioned on several occasions in response to Canada's changing realities: the correlation between the political and socio-economic contexts and the content of production is obvious. Initially dedicated to the official representation of the state, the voice of the institution shifted over time to that of citizen participation (Froger, 2009). One of the NFB's mandates—to build a strong identity by using cinema as an educational tool—still leaves some space for creative freedom, especially in the animation department. Its animated films have also largely contributed to the international reputation of the NFB, and, consequently, to its legitimization with Canadian taxpayers.

John Grierson, the founder and first film commissioner of the NFB, was active in the field of film production in England and Canada for more than five decades. Many regard Grierson as the architect of documentary aesthetics in Britain. At the beginning of his career, he wrote articles as a film critic under the pseudonym *Moviegoer* (Zéau, 2008) and used the term "documentary cinema" to describe *Nanook Of The North* (Flaherty, 1922) in which the director dramatizes the daily life of the inhabitants

DOI: 10.1201/9781032694382-4

of the Canadian Arctic by hybridizing reality and fiction.[1] At that time, Grierson idealized a cinema that shows a certain reality of the lives of ordinary men and women. He believed that the seventh art had a value of truth and could contribute to forging the portrait of a country that was not necessarily real, but that was shaped by the intentions of its author.

Grierson's first production, *Drifters* (Grierson, 1929), is about herring fishermen in the North Sea and the difficulties they face. He produced only one other film in England, *Granton Trawler* (Grierson, 1934), which featured a fishing trawler named Isabella Grier. In 1933, he created the film department within the General Post Office, better known as the GPO Film Unit.[2] He hired, among others, Norman McLaren and Len Lye who will later mark the history of experimental film animation.[3]

In Canada, the nation-building created by the NFB:

> played a pivotal role in unifying and giving identity to a vast, diverse and sparsely populated country. At the time when media representations of Canada were rare or non-existent, the NFB worked to give Canadians the sense that they shared a common national identity.
>
> (Jankovic, 2015, n. p.)

Urbanization, mass communications and the decline of religion in Québec favored the establishment of a national identity in which personal identity is embodied in the community since a nation is an imaginary community (Anderson, 1983).

Following his work at the GPO Film Unit, John Grierson was hired as a consultant by the Canadian government to improve the production and distribution of institutional films: he signed the Report on Canadian government film activities (Grierson, 1938). In his analysis, he concludes that there are four types of governmental cinematographic propaganda: the informative film (for the education sector), the promotional film (for sale purposes), the ministerial film (for the training needs of departments) and:

> the prestige film, intended to convey ideas or to generate loyalty to a country, a ministry or an organization. The film is generally documentary, this means that it translates, in a narrative or dramatic way, certain aspects of the social life and the achievements of the country.
>
> (Grierson, 1938, p. 12, our translation)

In his report on the Canadian government's film activities, Grierson refers to the GPO Film Unit and emphasizes the unique ability of government bodies to infiltrate the education system and produce propaganda films. "Unlike many commercial organizations, it has access to the educational system and can there plant the idea of Canada in terms of both imaginative appeal and curricular information" (Grierson, 1938, p. 13, our translation). He believes the "prestige film"[4] must be further developed, because it is intended for cinemas, it reaches an international audience and it promotes Canada's image. He recommended the centralization of the film services of the Canadian Government Motion Picture Bureau, both for production and distribution, and he suggested hiring permanent staff for administration and temporary staff for the creative aspects.

Following Grierson's recommendations—and convinced of the utilitarian function of cinema and its possibilities to educate the nation—the Canadian government sanctioned the creation of the NFB. The institution was founded on May 2, 1939, with the *National Film Act* and has the objective "to help Canadians in all parts of Canada to understand the ways of living and the problems of Canadians in other parts" (clause 9.A of the *National Film Act*, 1939, n. p.). The NFB is mandated to produce specific documentation: a cinematography that contributes to defining Canadian culture and identity.

> John Grierson . . . put forth an argument to which the Canadian government was not insensitive. "Social" documentary films would be the perfect vehicle for a national art because this genre represents the people without risking degenerating into crowd entertainment or the egotistical expression of artists who only represent themselves.
>
> (Froger, 2009, p. 55, our translation)

Under Grierson's regime, education and propaganda intertwine. School represents the place of establishment *par excellence* of the country's image. The NFB utilizes culture in a nationalist manner, and cinema provides a lens to observe the transformation in the field of education. This transformation shows a shift from originally being under the control of the Church to subsequently falling under the jurisdiction of the State:

> If, until the early 1960s, the Church and the NFB's networks, which provided associations, schools and unions with films from their

catalogue, crossed paths without joining, relations changed and the Church became increasingly interested in the NFB's expertise in social animation. This is one of the most important intellectual crossroads in the cultural history of Québec: the meeting of socio-logical and religious concerns, reconciling modernity and techni-cal progress with the survival of the French-Canadian community and Catholic culture, with the new instruments of social anima-tion linked to the distribution of documentaries.

(Froger, 2009, p. 21, our translation)

Taking films out of the cinema and transforming them into educational art is an advanced form of social education. The intervention of the state in the education system with cinema is a powerful tool to "shape" and instill the dominant ideology in young people. In Québec, if French speakers are strongly influenced by their religious culture, according to Bourdieu (1992), it is, however, practically impossible to create a universal culture if the starting point is religion. The shift in the identity representation of French speakers from the Church to the State in Québec contributes to uni-fying the constructs and knowledge of French-Canadian national culture.

Governments and industry have taken over the essence of the edu-cational process in the name of propaganda. . . . We can say that we have taken education out of the hands of the Church and put it into those of the bureaucrats of public and private enterprises.

(Grierson, quoted in Evans, 1979, p. 6, our translation)

The NFB conveys the ideology of a strong and united identity[5] while developing its own distribution network, alongside commercial cinemas, with the aim of reaching all communities. The institution even offers new methods for the reception of its films: libraries, community spaces and "kitchen screenings." The NFB also uses "travelling" projectionists who are technically independent for the presentation of productions. They promote works through alternative distribution channels to encourage the use of NFB films in communities across Canada. Zéau believes that Grierson's great discovery has been the association of the filmmakers and educators' mandate, thus offering an economic framework to support the documentary cinematographic corpus "that the industry was reluctant to provide" (Zéau, 2015, p. 5, our translation).

With the centralization of the NFB's budgetary staff, the ministries no longer produced films individually, as was the case before 1939. From then on, everyone had to turn to Commissioner Grierson to get the green light to produce films. The commissioner therefore controlled all the NFB's productions. During the Second World War, Grierson also held the position of general manager of Canada's Wartime Information Board, which gave him extraordinary influence over film content and, therefore, over how Canadians perceived the international conflict.

During the Second World War, power relationships in the sexual division of labor were changing. With men having gone to the front, women gained increased access to the labor market to fill the vacancies. As a result, certain positions that were traditionally earmarked for men became available to women.

Women take on jobs which they were considered incapable of doing during peacetime. However, even if they performed the same work as men, their wages remain lower. If the principle of the division of labor according to sex is temporarily erased, the hierarchical principle of the superior value of male labor persists. To exemplify this, it is relevant to look at three[6] productions by Jane Marsh, one of the first women to direct films at the NFB addressing the place of women in times of war. These three documentaries make it possible to capture the Griersonian aim of a cinematographic production space dedicated to state propaganda from a feminist angle.

In the first short film, *Women Are Warriors* (Marsh, 1942; see Figure 2.1), the director deconstructs stereotypes about women's professional abilities. Through archives, women are represented in an atypical way, which contributes to the transformation of gendered social perceptions, but in the direction intended by the war effort: they shoot machine guns, work at the forge, fly planes and engage in military training. Unsurprisingly, the film presents England as a model in the use of women's labor power in times of war. England, Grierson's native land and an allied member of the Commonwealth, rallies housewives to avoid starvation (by assigning them to the fields) and contribute to the war effort (by joining factories). The film offers a certain emancipatory vision of women in the job market (in wartime), but the tone is still a paternalistic and essentializing:

They learned engineering and adapted the production machines,
a skill first acquired at home. . . . Sheet metal riveting makes

FIGURE 2.1 *Women Are Warriors.*

craftsmen of girls who once envied their brothers' toolboxes. . . .
Women learned to turn the domestic needle and thread into tools
of war. . . . Down the long benches of the subassembly room, they
carry on the battle of production, with pliers, gauges of calipers,
one hundredth of small parts are mounted on jigs, by operations
better suited to the dainty hands of women than for the bigger
hands of men.

(Marsh, 1942)

The second film, *Proudly She Marches* (Marsh, 1943a), is a publicity and
propagandist short film encouraging women to join the army. The film

features a certain professional identity of the military woman and her particular contribution to the military. The narration alternates between a male voice and a female voice. There is thus minimal space for the expression of feminist thought in early NFB cinema. In the preamble, the male narrator says:

> In prehistoric time, from the Renaissance to the present day, women have taken their rightful place as the flower and ornament of the human race. . . . Gaiety, affection, daring, modesty, intelligence and the ability to use their intelligence to further enhance their beauty, making them the supreme object of men's admiration, of men's esteem.
>
> (Marsh, 1943a)

Then the female narrator replies: "Ah! Men make me tired. They never give women credit for any common sense at all. Women may be flowers and ornaments all right, but there are a lot more than that these days, believe me" (Marsh, 1943a). The female protagonist expresses an opinion contradicting that of the male narrator. Further on, the female narrator becomes aware of the value of women: "Yes, the more I think about it, the more I'm dead sure that all this talk about women being merely beautiful and little else is just a lot of bunk. Just give us a job and we'll go right to it" (Marsh, 1943a). The female character recognizes her intellectual and physical abilities. She begins to believe in herself: she can, like all other women, fulfil herself in a socio-professional way. In addition to speaking out, she takes a stand: women also have the right to emancipation, recognition and prestige.

The film presents a highly idealized military training process where women experience a frank camaraderie (the narrator specifies that there is no jealousy between them since they all wear the same uniform) and have access to leisure activities (for example, to dances organized with the male soldiers where they will perhaps have the chance to meet their husband). The short film sends the propagandist message that they are participating in a pleasant and emancipatory activity that will give them the opportunity to achieve their full potential, while being more useful to society in times of war. The social hierarchy of sex is explicit: a primary school teacher becomes more useful to her country in the army, because she trains adult men. The professional qualities of women are also portrayed as inferior to those of men: "When she passed her driver's test, Beth took over a full-time job from a man, releasing him for a more important job, perhaps overseas" (Marsh, 1943a). Although women are encouraged to join the army, they remain confined to lower positions compared to those held by men. Some arguments to convince women to enlist carry social representations, clichés, on the body:

> There's nothing like basic training for taking those few extra pounds off your hips, and for showing you what you can best do with your mind and muscles. . . . Well, here go two ornaments of the human race to work.
>
> (Marsh, 1943a)

The third film, *Wings on Her Shoulder* (Marsh, 1943b), is a short film promoting women in Canadian aviation. As in *Women Are Warriors* (Marsh, 1942), it presents active women who contribute to the war effort. Working in uniform, holding various positions, they still have time to have hobbies and entertain themselves. "A young service . . . looking with courage into its future in the sky. Those are the women of Canada's air force. The women who wear wings on their shoulder that made men fly" (Marsh, 1943b).

The propagandist productions produced by Jane Marsh offer a particular vision of the young Canadian woman serving the State in time of war. Thus, it is not the voice of the director that is at the forefront but rather the voice of the Canadian government, which promotes the participation of women in the war effort. The propaganda documentary has a mandate to tell the group what the group should think. The women in Marsh's films embody the official values of the State. The sovereignty of the artist, in this specific institutional context, is subordinated to their mission. Can Marsh, mandated by the State to produce a certain cinematographic discourse, still consider herself an artist? If she had complete freedom in the making of her films, perhaps she would have shown a totally different reality of women in situations of war, such as the void left by the death of a soldier at the front and the consequences for his widow and children. Be that as it may, these supposedly objective cinematographic productions, whether made by a woman or a man, contribute to the promotion of social order.

There is little research on the situation of women within the NFB in its early days. Jocelyne Denault provides some information in the article "*Des femmes devant et derrière la caméra: le cas de l'Office national du film du Canada (1941–1945)*" [FR] (Denault, 1993). The place of women at the NFB mirrors the one they occupy in society, in accordance with an essentialist conception of feminine qualities: meticulousness, patience, submission, etc. They find themselves in positions where they identify the archives, develop film and work on the editing of the films. There are relatively few female directors, and among them, the majority are primarily academics and anglophones.

Nevertheless, a woman runs the distribution division: Helen Watson Gordon. "At barely 30 years old, she is at the head of a team of more than 150 people, the majority of whom, men, are over 40 years old" (Denault, 1993, p. 115, our translation). This is a unique case where a woman holds an executive position with men reporting to her. "The situation of women at the NFB, from 1941 to 1945, is therefore as follows: most women occupy essential positions, but without decision-making power; they have lower wages than men; some are directors, but in limited contexts and for an equally limited period" (Denault, 1993, p. 116, our translation).

During the war, most women are hired temporarily. After the war, men take back their position in the labor market. Women were sent back to the home because the employment sector could not absorb all the adult labor force wanting to work. The global conflict has therefore favored the entry of women into the labor market, but only temporarily. "This reversal proves the theory that women form a potential supply of cheap labor that can be manipulated according to economic circumstances" (Collectif Clio, 1992, p. 271, our translation). Denault and Zéau highlight the difficulty of identifying all the women directors of the time at the NFB, because several films have no credits. "During the war . . . the versatility and anonymity of credits supported submission to the public cause" (Zéau, 2008, p. 67, our translation).

However, during this time period, a particularly important woman worked in the animation department—Evelyn Lambart—who was Norman McLaren's precious collaborator before continuing a career as a solo director. Like McLaren, she was initially placed at the service of the war effort: she worked on the animation of geographical maps for the series of propaganda films *The World in Action*, first broadcasted in 1942. During this period, she directed her first film *The Impossible Map* (Lambart, 1947; see Figure 2.2). According to my research, it is the first animated film directed by a woman at the NFB. In *The Impossible Map*,

FIGURE 2.2   *The Impossible Map.*

Source: Lambart, 1947, © NFB, all rights reserved.

the director represents the earth with a grapefruit and cuts out the 3D shape of the sphere to transpose it into a 2D geographical map.

It is important to note that Alma Duncan and Audrey McLaren also directed an animated film during the same period: *Folksong Fantasy* (1951). In her work, Denault (1996) mentioned that no physical copy of this film exists. However, I was able to view it since it is now available online on the NFB's website. This very literal film visually reproduces folk songs performed by Emma Caslor (*The Riddle Song*, *Who Killed Cock Robin* as well as *The Wee Cooper of Fife*). It combines animation techniques with, among other things, puppets and paper cut-outs, a way of working similar to German pioneer Lotte Reiniger.

Folksong Fantasy is divided into three sections. The first one, *The Riddle Song*, tells the story of lovers who get married and have a baby. The animation, sometimes clumsy and jerky, is reminiscent of puppet theatre. The second section, *Who Killed Cock Robin*, narrates the tragic end of a bird who dies after being shot in the heart by an arrow. Finally, the third section, *The Wee Cooper of Fife*, presents a wife who rebels against her husband. She is reluctant to perform the tasks she has to do in the home: she throws dishes and breaks her loom, which angers her partner. At the end of the animation, the woman finds her place, she sits next to her loom and serves a meal to her spouse: the two protagonists find happiness again. This film coincides with state visions of the traditional assignment to gender roles.

FROM PROPAGANDIST ANIMATION TO ARTISTIC ANIMATION

The propaganda produced by the NFB, under the iron fist of Grierson, is the subject of dispute. *The Royal Commission on National Development in the Arts, Letters and Sciences (1949–1951)* partially redefines the objectives of the NFB. This reorientation, without formal breach of the mandate, transforms the mission of the institution to better meet the needs of the country. The commission made several recommendations for the NFB to continue its work:

> to produce and distribute and to promote the production and distribution of films designed to interpret Canada to Canadians and to other nations. . . . [and to] engage in research in film activity and to make available the results thereof to persons engaged in the production of films.
>
> (*Royal Commission on National Development in the Arts, Letters and Sciences [1949–1951]*, p. 307)

The institution's budget for film distribution is reviewed with an increase in staff and in the number of copies in circulation. The creation of an archival collection also becomes a priority: both for the preservation of NFB productions and for the establishment of a bank of historical archives of events of national significance. This turned out to be a winning strategy: to this day, the NFB sells excerpts from the archives to various productions around the world.

To people who demanded the abolition of the institution alleging unfair competition and who asked for the repatriation of funds to private organizations, the commission responded: "No democratic government can afford to neglect at any time a means of public information so far-reaching and so persuasive as the film. The provision and distribution of films by the national government is as little open to question as the issue of the white paper or the blue book" (*Royal Commission on National Development in the Arts, Letters and Sciences [1949–1951]*, p. 310).

In Québec, the Duplessis government (which had little or no interest in the arts and culture) was very reluctant towards the activities of the NFB and "warned the Québec censors to carefully monitor the NFB films because they could encourage federal centralization" (Véronneau, 1979, p. 9, our translation). Duplessis said of the NFB that it is:

> a real nest of Communists . . . which has often lent itself to tenden-
> tiously Communist and subversive propaganda . . . we need an
> organization in the province that protects our national and reli-
> gious traditions against the dangers of communist propaganda.
> (Duplessis, quoted in Véronneau, 1979,
> p. 9, our translation)

Duplessis' distrust of the NFB is profound. For example, he had the film *Inside Fighting Russia* (Legg, 1942) censored because it showed the success of the Russians in combat (although they were allies in the war against Germany). "Thus, in 1952, when the NFB began to distribute Russian pro-paganda films in Canada, Duplessis hastened to ban the distribution of all NFB films in Québec schools for two decades" (Guévin, 2000, p. 12, our translation). Duplessis did this under the pretense that he must inventory the collection of the provincial cinematheque. NFB productions could still circulate in Québec, but through other distribution channels.

After the Second World War, the NFB continued to offer its artists atypical creative conditions as commercial profits were a secondary con-cern. Because it does not need royalties to pursue its mandate, the NFB has always been able to rely on an independent distribution system, which has allowed it to produce film animation different from that of the United States, which is more concerned with profits and is entirely subject to the laws of the market. Even if the NFB is a State institution, which responds to a nation-building mandate, it can afford to create avant-garde cinema.

NFB films are produced by "sponsorship structures": "those that allow the greatest freedom in order to carry out a project by offering the ani-mator financial security, most often for a short period" (Denis, 2017, p. 33, our translation). However, the structure of these institutions—of which the NFB is a part of—is neither devoid of ideologies nor of various contingencies. That being said, frame-by-frame cinema at the NFB contributes to technical and artistic exploration as studio workers seek new ways to create and explore the language of the seventh art. The institutional desire for international influence, to promote the country and its cinematographic heritage, encourages technical and aesthetic innovation in frame-by-frame production. NFB animated films are recognized by festivals and critics for their great creative innovation. The institution produces low-cost auteur cinema that blurs the boundaries between the arts and cinema. The creative potential seems limitless:

> We always, all our lives, pushed the equipment beyond its limits and damaged it, and then we would have to invent something new. . . . The work was exploratory and originality was valued tremendously. Derivative work was absolutely hated. We didn't do any cell work at all, in fact we were highly contemptuous of Disney.
> (Lambart, quoted in Pilling, 1992, p. 31)

Much like Len Lye's work at the GPO Film Unit in England with *Color Box* (Lye, 1935), McLaren put the camera aside and created animations directly on film. In 1949, Evelyn Lambart and Norman McLaren produced *Begone Dull Care*, an abstract film painted directly on both sides of the film. In works dealing with film animation, the emphasis is often placed on technical innovations. Thus, the discovery of a new animation technique and its application sometimes establishes the reputation of certain animators to whom they confer a unique signature (for example, Alexander Alexeïeff and Claire Parker are associated with pinscreen animation). Norman McLaren technically reinvented himself in almost every one of his films: this creation process is atypical. "Recalling my twenty-five or thirty years of collaboration with Norman McLaren, I am very impressed by the number of techniques he has experimented with. I don't think we've ever made two films with an identical technique" (Lambart, 1975, p. 130, our translation). The myriad of techniques explored by McLaren demonstrates beyond a shadow of a doubt his great talent, but he would never have been able to realize his creations without the prolonged support of the State.

Film animation, as a national educational tool, is a priority for the institution. There is also a pedagogical dimension to McLaren's work, which can make certain realities understood through film animation and inform on the medium itself. "From the 1940s to the 1960s, McLaren constantly sought, through his writings, to democratize animation, making his discoveries public and wanting to do a work of education" (Carrière, 1988, p. 180, our translation). For McLaren, the desire to pass on his knowledge translates into the popularization of his technical knowledge, the logic of frame-by-frame movement and the synthetic sound. McLaren co-directed five educational films on animation production in collaboration with Grant Munro. The films *Animated Motion: Part 1* (McLaren et Munro, 1976) through *Animated Motion: Part 5* (McLaren et Munro, 1978) explain the principles of frame-by-frame motion. Norman McLaren also studied the possibilities of graphic intervention on the soundtrack printing space. By drawing the sounds rather than printing them on 35 mm film, McLaren listed a whole series of shapes representing the musical tones. This process was used for the soundtrack of the Oscar-winning film *Neighbours* (McLaren, 1952). He explained his process of creating synthetic sound in *Pen Point Percussion* (McLaren, 1951). He documented his recording process and visual classification of sound forms in *Workshop Experiments in Animated Sound* (McLaren, 1949).

The francization of the NFB is a major political issue. Indeed, the representations of French-Canadian identity and culture were criticized during the reorientation of the NFB's mandate in the early 1950s. Films produced in French "emphasize too much the picturesque, old-world aspects of French Canada to the comparative neglect of contemporary subjects" (*Royal Commission on National Development in the Arts, Letters and Sciences [1949–1951]*, p. 312). The Commission recommends that "continued attention be given to the production of suitable films produced specifically for French-speaking Canadians" (*Royal Commission on National Development in the Arts, Letters and Sciences [1949–1951]*, p. 313). As will be shown later, the integration of minorities and migrants into the Canadian national identity would become essential for the NFB in the 1970s.[7] The findings of the Commission promote the production of French-language cinema in Québec and outside Québec.

The NFB's move from Ottawa to Montréal was put on the agenda when French speakers started taking on decision-making positions. Many protest that French speakers are mostly confined to subordinate positions; they also criticized the fact that few films have been produced by French speakers. Striving to strengthen the ties with the French-speaking population and to promote the French language and culture within the institution, the move of the NFB was sanctioned and occurred in 1956.[8] This undoubtedly contributed to the legitimization of the NFB in Québec. In addition to encouraging productions in French, the establishment of the NFB in Montréal was a real boost for Québec filmmakers.

During the same period, the evolution of recording devices offered new possibilities of creation. Cameras became smaller and lighter (Sony's Portapak), making it possible to record without a tripod. Also, simultaneous sound recording became a reality. New animation directors were hired in Montréal such as Pierre Hébert, Ryan Larkin and Pierre Moretti. The French section was thus founded in 1959 under the aegis of Fernand Dansereau, Bernard Devlin, Léonard Forest and Louis Portuguais, with Pierre Juneau becoming director of French productions. In 1966, the animation studio was also split in two. René Jodoin became the first director of the French animation department at the NFB. Right away, he oriented production towards artistic exploration:

> Rather than opting for the massive, quasi-industrial production of American-style cartoons geared towards sponsorships, which predominated at that time, René Jodoin resolutely oriented his new studio towards young creators and towards an artisanal conception of cinema, encouraging research, experimentation, improvisation and personal expression. Young filmmakers were therefore craftspeople working directly with the means at hand, aiming to produce autonomous works.
>
> (Bégin, quoted in Carrière, 1988, p. 187, our translation)

René Jodoin prioritized the artisanal side of animation and supervised the production of short films illustrating songs from Québec folklore (just like in the English department). The *Chants populaires* [FR] series produced, among others, *C'est l'aviron* [FR] (McLaren, 1944b) and *Alouette* [FR] (Jodoin et McLaren, 1944). The *Chanson de chez-nous* [FR] series produced films such as *Cadet Rousselle* [FR] (Dunning and Low, 1947) and *La poulette grise* [FR] (McLaren, 1947). The English department produced the *Let's All Sing Together* series. Renowned musicians joined animated productions. The Oscar Peterson Trio created the original music for *Begone Dull Care* (McLaren and Lambart, 1949) and Ravi Shankar created the original music for *A Chairy Tale* (Jutra and McLaren, 1957). Norman McLaren also had a passion for dance and made three films dedicated to this artform: *Pas de deux* [FR] (McLaren, 1967), *Ballet Adagio* (McLaren, 1972) and *Narcissus* (McLaren, 1983).[9]

> Thus, what was initially only a skillful incursion of inexpensive animation technique into cinematographic propaganda (credits, graphics, cartography, etc.) took, that year, the shape of an animation studio made up of a group of about ten filmmakers and a program for the development of various economical and innovative techniques offering an alternative to celluloid.
>
> (Zéau, 2008, p. 66, our translation)

In the 1960s, French animators would explore geometric shapes and produce more minimalist works. René Jodoin directed *Ronde carré* [FR] (Jodoin, 1961) and *Notes on a Triangle* (Jodoin, 1966). These two non-narrative films offer a visual with geometric shapes that transform and dance to the sound of music. He also co-directed, with McLaren, *Spheres* (Jodoin and McLaren, 1969), an animation in which round shapes dance to the rhythm of a Bach composition performed by pianist Glenn Gould. Pierre Hébert directed *Op Hop–Hop Op* (Hébert, 1966), an experimental black and white animation created by removing the black emulsion from the film on which shapes appear furtively.

At the end of the 1960s, under the authority of René Jodoin, an innovative French-speaking legacy was created. "He led, for several years, a young and dynamic core around him" (Beaudet, 1979, p. 4, our translation). It was then that the first women directors in the French program entered the scene.

> The establishment of the French animation studio in 1966, which opened its doors to many through animation internships, made it possible to discover French-speaking women animators. Francine Desbiens and Clorinda Warny—arriving from Belgium—were the first two to join the French animation studio team in 1966 and 1967 respectively. Other women directors were added later as part of training internships: Viviane Elnécavé (1967), Judith Klein (1968), Suzanne Gervais (1969) and Suzanne Olivier (1969).
>
> (Denault, 1996, p. 77, our translation)

To my knowledge, the first film directed by a woman in the French animation studio in Montréal was *Our Sports Car Days* (Elnécavé, 1969;

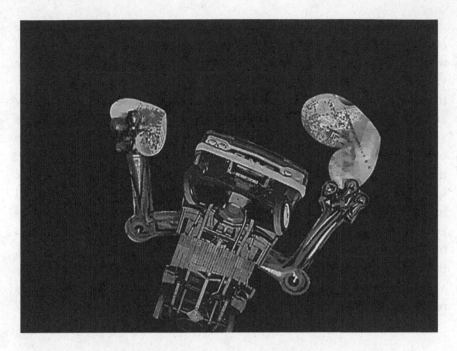

FIGURE 2.3   Our Sports Car Days.

Source: **Elnécavé, 1969, © NFB, all rights reserved.**

see Figure 2.3).[10] This three-minute film unfolds to the rhythm of lively jazz music. The influences of René Jodoin (*Ronde carrée* [FR] and *Notes on a Triangle*) and Norman McLaren (*Blinkity Blank* and *Rythmetic*) are omnipresent. These cut-out papers animations of spherical and rectangular colored shapes explore retinal persistence through the intermittence of completely black backgrounds and animated colored images, which produces a stroboscopic visual pulsation. The shapes are sometimes reminiscent of traffic lights or cars on highways. Two abstract mechanical characters made with magazine clippings seem to be connected by an umbilical cord. This animation is captivatingly fresh and dynamic.

The same year, Francine Desbiens and Michèle Pauzé join Pierre Hébert and Yves Leduc to co-direct *Le corbeau et le renard* [FR] (1969). This collective project offers comic variations on La Fontaine's famous fable, as the final quote clearly shows. As the fox tries to ensnare the crow so that it drops the cheese, the crow says (with a strong Québec accent): "*Voyons estie! Me prends-tu pour un corbeau français?*"[11] (Desbiens *et al.*, 1969).

As for the English animation department, women also made films at the end of the 1960s. Eva Szasz created *Cosmic Zoom* (Szasz, 1968; Figure 2.4) which illustrates the journey of the microcosm of the human cell to the vastness of the universe. Inspired by the book *Cosmic View* (Bocke, 1957), the director created a series of drawings from a live shot of a little boy and his dog in a rowboat. The sequence of images then shows a bird's-eye view that moves further and further away from the protagonists: a map of the city, the province, the country, the earth seen from the universe, the moon, the solar system, the stars, a nebula and the galaxy. The music speeds up and the images are then presented in reverse so that the initial image of the film is quickly showed once again. Szasz then takes the viewers inside the human body: on the hand of the little boy, where there is a mosquito, in the skin, the blood system, the blood cells, the chromosomes, the cells, etc. In this film, Eva Szasz does not do any animation. She makes a series of drawings and creates movements of approach and retreat by recording images with the animation camera.

FIGURE 2.4 *Cosmic Zoom.*

Source: **Szasz, 1968, © NFB, all rights reserved**

Rhoda Leyer directed *Little Red Riding Hood* (Leyer, 1969), in which she reinterpreted Perrault's famous tale. This very minimalist animation is sometimes awkward, and its aesthetic is very particular, halfway between the cut-out paper dolls of the 1960s and antique engravings. Bozenna Heczko created *Pictures Out of My Life* (Heczko, 1973), a film inspired by the drawings and memories of Inuit artist Pitseolak.[12]

THE CASE OF NORMAN MCLAREN AND EVELYN LAMBART

It must be recognized that the fame and success of Canadian film animation are inseparable from the NFB. Norman McLaren became the first NFB director to achieve international recognition. He was a "civil servant filmmaker" (Carrière, 1988) whose artistic creation is entirely financed by the State. He was, however, an atypical example of State film production: his status as an artist and free creator in the animation department is unique. "Norman McLaren is probably the best known of a group of high-quality filmmakers who have had the privilege of developing a continuous body of work over a relatively significant period within the National Film Board's creative community. Attempting to imagine Norman McLaren outside of this community would be a misinterpretation" (Glover, 1975, p. 134, our translation). During his career, McLaren directed more than sixty films. His work was celebrated by critics and acclaimed by film festivals: in 1953, he won the Academy Award for Best Documentary Short Film with *Neighbours* (McLarcn, 1952) and the Palme d'or at the Cannes International Film Festival for Best Short Film with *Blinkity Blank* (McLaren, 1955). Norman McLaren's works are well preserved and easily accessible. However, the duo he formed with Evelyn Lambart illustrates the lack of recognition of women animators. If Norman McLaren is the most significant artist of the NFB in animation, the collaboration with Lambart must be highlighted. The official version of the story focused on the "genius" and success of Norman McLaren. But what about *herstory*?[13]

Lambart spent the majority of the first twenty-five years of her career assisting McLaren (see Figures 2.5 and 2.6). Working on several of his works, she remained in the shadows, unknown, and almost absent from historical documentation.[14] "If scholarly history was written in the masculine gender, it is mainly because it was written by men" (Thébaud, 2007, p. 38, our translation). About her relationship with McLaren, Evelyn Lambart confided:

> Norman had great prestige. I feel that all my life Norman's mantle
> has fallen a bit on me and I think people respect me mainly because

FIGURE 2.5   Evelyn Lambart and Norman McLaren, color test on acetate.

Source: Blouin, 1949, © NFB, all rights reserved.

> I was working with him. Norman was a big figure. Everything that
> we created was so good and won many prizes but working beside
> someone of this stature had certain disadvantages. I often felt very
> insignificant beside him, but he respected me very much.
>
> (Lambart, quoted in Pilling, 1992, p. 32)

In *Eleven Moving Moments with Evelyn Lambart* (McWilliams, 2017),
the director[15] informed us that Evelyn Lambart has been almost deaf since
childhood. From a young age, she was interested in visual languages,
especially in photography. She always wanted to be independent: get an
education, work and never have to get married. After graduating from
the Ontario College of Art, she began her career at the NFB in Ottawa
in 1942 in the lettering department before being reassigned to producing maps. She worked for a monthly propagandist program, *The World
in Action*, a political magazine dedicated to the Canadian contribution
to the war effort. There, she was noticed by McLaren, who entrusted her
with several animation jobs. At that time, under the initiative of Grierson,

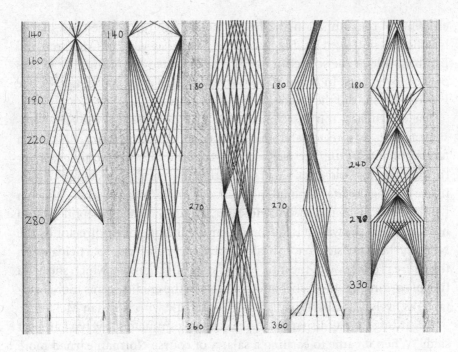

FIGURE 2.6 *Eleven Moving Moments with Evelyn Lambart.*

Norman McLaren founded the animation department, which he directed until 1945. Jim MacKay (1945–1949) then took over his position so that he could devote himself solely to his films. The knowledge she acquired while working at *The World in Action* gave Evelyn Lambart the experience and credibility required to make her first solo animated film: *The Impossible Map* (Lambart, 1947). As previously mentioned, Evelyn Lambart was the first woman in Canada to have directed an animated film at the NFB. Her next solo work is *O Canada* (Lambart, 1957), a short film that uses the travelling technique invented by Norman McLaren in the film *C'est l'aviron* [FR] (McLaren, 1944b).

In 1944, Lambart began assisting Norman McLaren in several of his films. The collaboration lasted until 1965. "Sometimes, I think I'm really a piece of Norman. You can't work that closely with a person for so long and not feel that. We co-ordinated so well together" (Lambart, quoted in Pilling, 1992, p. 31). Lambart's contribution to the work of McLaren is difficult to assess. For *Le merle* [FR] (McLaren, 1959), she cut out the elements of the animation and helped create and record the movements, but she was not given co-director credit. For *Lines Vertical* (McLaren and Lambart, 1960), she scratched the film and created the original drawings of the movements. In *Begone Dull Care* (McLaren and Lambart, 1949; see Figure 2.7), she did the coloring for the animation.

She did the last thirty seconds of the film by herself. If the NFB website cites her as director and animator as an equal to Norman McLaren for *Begone Dull Care*, the fact remains that the film itself only gives her the mention for coloring: "Colors by E. Lambart and N. McLaren". Then, in the closing credits, the final mention is: "By Norman McLaren". Evelyn Lambart's name is not shown. However, an uninformed cinephile would not know that she was subsequently awarded the title of co-director by the NFB on their website. Yet, just like McLaren, she actively participated in the entire production of the film. For other productions for which she has a title of co-director, the distribution of titles in the credits seems more equitable, as Evelyn Lambart shares a single intertitle with Norman McLaren.

Regarding the pay disparity between the two animators, Evelyn Lambart said: "When it came to earning a salary, of course Norman earned more

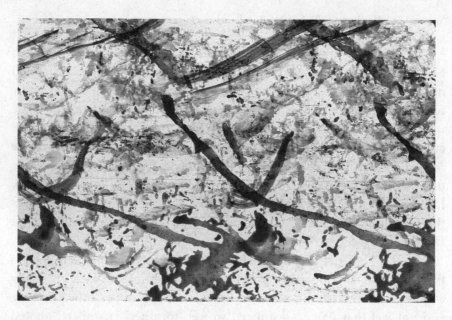

FIGURE 2.7   *Begone Dull Care.*

Source: **McLaren and Lambart, 1949, © NFB, all rights reserved.**

than I did, but then I earned more than some of the other men" (Lambart, quoted in Pilling, 1992, p. 31). Lambart seemed to consider normal the fact that she earned less than Norman McLaren. However, after twenty years, the collaboration deteriorated:

> It was in the early 60s that I started thinking about the idea of doing my own films. Norman was beginning to take interest in ballet films, which didn't hold any interest for me. . . . I felt very lost at that time; I had always worked with Norman and I found it difficult to have to make my own decisions.
>
> (Lambart, quoted in Pilling, p. 32)

In 1965, encouraged by Wolf Koenig, Evelyn Lambart began a solo career. Following in the footsteps of German pioneer Lotte Reiniger, Lambart favored paper cut-out animation technique. Lambart, like Disney, drew inspiration from old tales. These moralistic fables use animals to represent the human condition.

Fine Feathers (Lambart, 1968) is a five-minute-long paper cut-out short film. The animation is felt, well controlled, all with a pleasing color palette. In this film, two birds argue about their physical appearance. The first protagonist, a blue jay, decides to completely modify her body by exchanging her feathers for the branches of a tree. The second protagonist, a loon, creates a necklace with beautiful colorful flowers. But when the loon sees the blue jay, she becomes mad with jealousy and confronts the blue jay by trying to remove her green branches. The loon finds herself a tree and remakes her body with colorful leaves. Both birds seem to decide to alter their physical appearance out of sheer vanity. The loon's jealousy towards the blue jay is only motivated by the desire to steal her appearance. Social pressures are strong on women to meet limited and demanding beauty standards; it is perhaps this social pressure on women's bodies that Lambart wanted to illustrate. At the end of the film, the wind picks up and the two protagonists lose their costumes. It is only by reconstructing their "natural" appearance that they become happy, fulfilled and friends.

Lambart then produced *The Hoarder* (Lambart, 1969), an animation that addresses the disparity in the distribution of natural resources. The protagonist, a bird, wants to have everything for itself. He steals the goods of his fellow citizens to hide them in his cave. He steals from the chick the ladybug and the silkworm he is trying catch to eat. He steals the nest, then the eggs from the mother who broods her eggs. He even goes so far as to steal the sun, which plunges the inhabitants of the forest into darkness and nature dies. By giving back the sun and the other objects that he stole from the community, life resumes and harmony is established. In a somewhat naïve way, this animation can evoke the problem of an inequitable distribution of wealth in a capitalist society.

The following year, she produced *Paradise Lost* (Lambart, 1970). This three-minute-long animation is even darker. In a forest where butterflies and a bird live pleasantly, life is turned upside down when a plane passes through the sky and dumps toxic products on the ground. A cloud of smoke invades the forest. The bird and the butterflies try to escape, but they are overtaken by the pollution. All die, collapsing to the ground, and the leaves fall from the trees to bury them. The animator's message is clear: human inventions cause pollution and destroy nature. Her film is an eco-feminist work.[16]

The magnificent paper cut-out characters of *The Christmas Story* (Lambart, 1974) evolve to the sound of medieval music and resounding trumpets. This animated short film tells the story of the birth of Jesus. The three angels are omnipresent and travel throughout the territory to transmit the Gospel to the shepherds and the three wise men. The three wise men follow a huge twinkling star to the stable where the holy child was born. All offer him sumptuous gifts. The selection of colors is remarkable, and the black background serves to highlight Lambart's protagonists, making them stand out.

Mr. Frog Went A-Courting (Lambart, 1974) is a children's film. Sung by Derek Lamb, this light animation tells the story of a frog who proposes to a mouse after obtaining the consent of its uncle the rat. The viewers attend the reception of this unusual couple and their guests (a flea, a bee, a butterfly and a spider). Even though the film is lighthearted, its ending is cruel: an enormous black snake devours the newlyweds while they are on a boat for their honeymoon.

Lambart's last two productions are inspired by Aesop's Fables. *The Lion and the Mouse* (Lambart, 1976), a very short four-minute film, tells the story of a curious mouse that approaches a sleeping lion. When the mouse touches the lion's paw, the lion wakes up. It roars and the mouse starts shaking. With its sharp claw, the lion pins the mouse to the ground, it is trapped. Yet, the lion decides to free the mouse and it runs for cover. Time passes peacefully until the lion roars again: it is trapped in a hunting net.

The mouse gnaws at the net to free the lion. The mouse comforts the lion, then jumps on its back and the two new friends disappear into the forest.

The Town Mouse and the Country Mouse (Lambart, 1980) compares two opposite lifestyles: a mouse living in the countryside (minimalism) and a mouse living in the city. The country mouse feeds exclusively on the elements of nature and lives plainly. The town mouse has clothes, carries a gun and eats table scraps from humans. The moral of this fable is that it is dangerous to live in the city since the two mice are pursued by a ferocious cat; but fortunately, they manage to escape.

Regrettably, Lambart's films never achieved critical success, as such they remained not only poorly documented but also unknown to the general public. "Marked by discretion, this remarkable woman's career is an example of several animators' journey during the decades preceding 1970" (Roy, 2007, p. 12, our translation). There is a real lack of knowledge of the animations produced by Evelyn Lambart, despite its importance in the history of film animation at the NFB. Today, this forgotten animator is rediscovered and is reinscribed in history, but more for her contribution to the work of McLaren than for her personal work. Although there is a recent interest in her collaborative work with McLaren, her personal work remains marginalized.

The birth of feminist cinema at the NFB occurs at the end of the 1960s: "Before 1967, in Québec, there were practically no films made by women, about women" (Carrière, 1983a, p. 144, our translation).[17] Anne Claire Poirier directed the first feature[18] documentary on women at the NFB *Mother-To-Be* (Poirier, 1968). Despite the openness to the world and the cinematographic revival of the late 1950s, the new documentary wave[19] of live camera remained under the influence of men. Women directors remain on the edge of this cinematographic revival. NFB productions shifted from broadcasting official State speeches to a forum for the voice of the people. Women directors in the 1970s could act as catalysts for the values of certain women. The women directors are not ventriloquists of the State: they offer a unique view of women who have pooled their knowledge. In-house women workers are gaining more and more power and political clout.

NOTES

1. Flaherty's artistic approach is to collect the material *in situ* by living with the people long enough to become immersed in their existence and thus reveal their reality, which is interpreted in the documentary (*mise-en-scène*).

2. The GPO Film Unit mainly produces advertisements and propaganda.
3. *Colour Box* (Lye, 1935) and *Love on the Wing* (McLaren, 1938) are produced at the GPO Film Unit.
4. There are countless internationally recognized artists who were invited to collaborate with the animation departments at the NFB in the 1970s and 1980s, in a desire to boost the prestige of the institution, including, among others, Lotte Reiniger, Alexandre Alexeïef and Claire Parker, Faith and John Hubley, Bretslav Pojar, Paul Driessen and Peter Foldès.
5. In the 1960s and 1970s, French-speaking filmmakers working for the NFB used state resources to portray the realities of modern Quebec. On the brink of the Quiet Revolution, there was a creative revival among these artists, who were increasingly preoccupied with nationalist fervor and who spoke of social change in their films, especially those dealing with the identity of French speakers in Canada. The political context of the early 1970s in Quebec was explosive: people took to the streets and protested. With the October Crisis and the assassination of Pierre Laporte, exceptional provisions were applied to contain and repress the revolt of certain Quebeckers. Pierre Elliott Trudeau, invoking the War Measures Act, sent the army to Montréal and 460 people were arrested and put behind bars. In 1976, the sovereigntist Parti Québécois came to power. Films from Pierre Perrault, Michel Brault and Gilles Groulx sent back to Quebeckers an image of themselves.
6. She also directed *Inside Fighting Canada* (Marsh, 1942) and *Alexis Tremblay: Habitant* (Marsh, 1943c), two productions that were not focused on women.
7. The NFB's mandate of representing ethnocultural communities and national unity is still very present today. "The notion of representativeness has always been the natural vocation and the attempt to square the circle at the NFB: it implies, in the name of responsibility towards taxpayers, that everyone is represented without everything being able to be expressed (Zéau, 2015, p. 11, our translation).
8. There are also regional branches of the NFB, notably in Vancouver, Halifax and Toronto.
9. For its part, the English studio's animated production of the 1950s seemed more focused on the humorous tradition of cartooning as with *The Romance of Transportation in Canada* (Low, 1952). In the 1960s and 1970s, the English-language animated production changed: it abandoned the cartoon aesthetic and turned towards something more poetic. Filmmakers used metaphors to express themselves, as in *Syrinx* (Larkin, 1965), *Cityscape* (Larkin, 1966) and *Walking* (Larkin, 1968).
10. Viviane Elnécavé is originally from Cairo and studied at the École des beaux-arts de Montréal before entering the NFB as an intern with the French team in 1968. The following year, she obtained a permanent position.
11. "What the fuck! Do you think I'm a French crow?" In this excerpt, the crow expresses itself using familiar Québec slang and profanities to mock French nationals.

12. I was unable to watch *Pictures Out of My Life* (Heczko, 1973).

13. "The origin of the pun History-Herstory comes from a presentation by Sheila Ryan Johansson at the annual convention of the American Historical Association (1972)" (Thébaud, 2007, p. 68, our translation).

14. She was credited as co-director and co-animator on five short films she worked on with McLaren: *Begone Dull Care* (McLaren and Lambart, 1949), *Rythmetic* (McLaren and Lambart, 1956), *Lines Vertical* (McLaren and Lambart, 1960), *Lines Horizontal* (McLaren and Lambart, 1962) and *Mosaic* (McLaren and Lambart, 1965).

15. Donald McWilliams also directed the feature film *Creative Process: Norman McLaren* (McWilliams, 1991).

16. "The neologism 'ecofeminism' was used for the first time in 1974 in *Le féminisme ou la mort* by author Françoise d'Eaubonne to establish a connection between Serge Moscovici's political ecology and Simone de Beauvoir's feminist theory" (Ravary-Pilon, 2018, p. 90, our translation).

17. However, at the "Service de ciné-photographie du Gouvernement du Québec, the presence of Dorothée Brisson and, later, Suzanne Caron is noted. These women made films in the mid-1950s. They were the first French-speaking directors from Québec" (Véronneau, quoted in Denault, 1981, p. 43, our translation).

18. *La vie rêvée* [FR] (Dansereau, 1972) was the first feminist fiction feature film directed by a woman in private industry in Québec, but Jean-Pierre Lefebvre was the one who directed the first Québec feminist fiction feature film: *Q-bec My Love* (Lefebvre, 1970).

19. The representations of Québec society in the films produced by the NFB during this period are, however, androcentric and do not correspond to the reality of the social oppression of women. The films offer a masculine vision of Québec society by portraying the experience of men and offering a stereotypical image of women. "The role of women in the political reality of societies has rarely been made visible—we have been made to believe it to be non-existent—because just as in the order of private life, women always perform a role that does not enter historical memory" (Brossard, quoted in Arbour, 1982, p. 3, our translation). The themes studied by the wave of the direct camera are masculine: snowshoe racing in *Les raquetteurs* [FR] (Brault et Groulx, 1958), wrestling in *Golden Gloves* [FR] (Groulx, 1961) and fishing in *Pour la suite du monde* [FR] (Brault et Perrault, 1963). The realities experienced by women in Québec are forgotten by direct cinema. There is, however, an exception: *Le soleil a pas d'chance* [FR] (Favreau, 1975), which offers a feminist look at the situation of the duchesses of the *Carnaval de Québec*.

CHAPTER 3

(Re)presenting Women

F OR A LONG TIME, artistic representations were almost exclusively created through a male vision. Usually, the place of women in these creations is that of the muse, rarely of the author. Feminist film studies have
challenged the iconography traditionally associated with the representation of the feminine with, among other things, the way in which women's
sexuality and daily life are imaged. By reappropriating female experiences
such as motherhood or childbirth, some women directors offer different
visions of the dominant cinematographic discourse. Before analyzing how
feminist artists achieved a collective creative uprising to gain access to
filmmaking at the NFB, it is essential to focus on the evolution of women's
portrayals in films to understand how women artists have reappropriated
this media in a feminist way to showcase a discourse on the fringes of the
dominant circuit.

FEMININE-FEMINIST REPRESENTATIONS OF WOMEN

Feminist art historian Linda Nochlin is a key figure when discussing
the subject of the representation of women and art history. In her article "Women, art and power" (1988), Nochlin analyzes the way in which
women are represented in painting (mainly by men) by recalling the correlation between power and ideologies.

Oath of the Horatii (Jacques-Louis David, 1784) is a painting depicting
Ancient Rome history in which three brothers, accompanied by their wives
and children, swear allegiance to Rome before their father. The men are
standing, strong, muscular, energetic and focused, whereas the women are

DOI: 10.1201/9781032694382-5

passive, seated, submissive and their gaze turned inwards. This representation renews the ideology on the physical strength of men and the weakness of women—a stereotype attributing physical power according to gender.

In Memoriam (Sir Joseph Noel Paton, 1858) illustrates the fragility of women and their inability to defend themselves against violence perpetrated by men. During the exhibition of his work at the Royal Academy of Arts in England, Sir Joseph Noel Paton stated that his goal was to pay tribute to the Christian and heroic qualities of British women in India during the massacre of 1857. How is the heroism of women represented in this painting? As the enemies invade their home, the women kneel in prayer, passive and vulnerable. The painting foreshadows the horror that awaits them: they will most likely be raped and killed. The women are well dressed and make no move to defend themselves. The central female figure holds a bible in her hands: it is her strength. For Linda Nochlin, what is implied here, is that a virtuous woman would never go so far as to raise her hand and use her physical strength even to defend herself. An opposite representation of women is depicted in *And They Are Like Wild Beasts* (Francisco Goya y Lucientes, 1863) as in this painting, the women fight to protect their children. They resort to violence to get justice. "The Spanish mothers who fight so desperately to defend their children, it is implied, are something other than women: they are like 'wild beasts'" (Nochlin, 1988, p. 7).

The Death of Sardanapalus (Eugène Delacroix, 1827) depicts the deployment of the male fantasy that wants to sexually dominate the female body by brutalizing and destroying it. When the painting was exhibited in 1828, the public and critics were appalled. Delacroix openly expressed the heterosexual male fantasy that wants to possess women and subjugate them to satisfy their impulses. By way of comparison, Nochlin offers *Slave Market* (Jean-Léon Gérôme, 1866), a painting in which a naked woman is surrounded by men. Naked and for sale in a slave market, this representation is acceptable—compared to that of Delacroix—because it offers the naked woman as a commodity. As for *Masked Ball at the Opera* (Édouard Manet, 1873), this painting illustrates, according to Nochlin, a "flesh market"; it is the spectacle of female sexuality for sale. She believes the framing, which cuts the bodies, symbolizes the sexual availability of the women of the lower classes for the pleasure of the men of the high classes.

The Artist Sculpting Tanagra (Jean-Léon Gérôme, 1890) presents the male artist in his role as a creator who works with a female nude model. In the painting, he does not touch the leg of the model, but that of the sculpture he creates, with gloved hands. The artist, of advanced age, has the venerable look of a sage with his white hair. He is more reminiscent of a doctor than an artist. His gaze is focused on his work rather than the naked female body beside him. His position of power is justified by the noble cause he pursues: his quest for beauty.

> Modern painting is not exempt from these ideological structures of the gaze of . . . [works], representing female figures in a situation of passivity, based on a sexual politics of the gaze which is at the heart of modern art and, therefore, of the history of modern art. Taking an interest in the gaze from a feminist perspective means examining the dilemma in which women find themselves grappling with this system of representation.
>
> (Zapperi in Rennes, 2016, p. 551, our translation)

As New York feminist group The Guerilla Girls (which promotes arts made by women and non-white people) pointed out: "Do women have to be naked to get into the Met. Museum? Less than 4% of the artists in the Modern Art sections are women, but 76% of the nudes are female."

It is important to note that between 1934 and 1966, the Hayes Code was in force in the United States, therefore film content was closely monitored. Even in the early 1970s, more than half of American productions were created under the constraints of censorship. Representing nudity, seduction, explicit, perverse or extramarital sexuality as well as rape was prohibited. These limits imposed on the representations codify the cinematographic language, producing mainly two antagonistic female identities: the puritan stay-at-home mother and the tempting and sexually active *femme fatale*. It is therefore not surprising that feminists are interested in cinematographic representations since "fiction has been, particularly in Hollywood, a powerful instrument of social and sexual domination, at the same time as the cinema worked on the contradictions engendered by these relationships and their evolution" (Sellier, 2005, p. 71, our translation). In most American films created under the Hayes Code regime, the destiny of the *femme fatale* is either death or domestication by a man since "the film noir *femme fatale* often has an active role as a desiring subject that the film will work to control or destroy. . . . Her active sexuality makes her both fascinating and terrifying for the male protagonists" (Sellier, 2005, p. 76, our translation).

After the Code was abandoned, the female characters became trophy wives or poor damsels in distress and their statuses were determined by their relationships with the male protagonists. The female archetypes are mainly focused on the figure of the mother, the angel, the goddess, the virgin, the whore, the *femme fatale*, the demoness, the bitch, the hysteric, the lesbian and the rival. The "male gaze" (Mulvey, 1975) is omnipresent in cinema and the beauty of female celebrities is overvalued. Actresses become the object of heterosexual men's sexual desires, creating an absence of strong, believable female role models if they are not pleasing to the eye. These unrealistic feminine representations are absorbed by women, polluting their imagination as some define their self-worth in this superficial framework of the cult of beauty in cinema.

In Québec, the clergy initially frowned upon American cinema, believing it to be corrupting and harmful to the nation. The Church tried to limit access to movie theatres by imposing an age restriction and limiting opening hours. The clergy completely censored certain productions or intervened in the editing by cutting certain scenes: it was the "reign of scissors".[1] Later realizing the cinema's possibilities of social animation and education, the Church changed its attitude towards the seventh art, and priests—such as Albert Tessier and Maurice Proulx—made films.

The first women directors in Québec came from religious communities and they mainly produced three types of films (Denault, 1996). First, recruitment films showed the daily life of women in congregations. These representations intertwine documentary and fiction, aiming to depict the personal realization of women in their religious vocation. Second, souvenir films document significant events in the community or are travel diaries set in Japan, China, Korea and the Philippines. Nuns almost exclusively shoot these amateur films, which present their charitable work abroad.[2] Third, prayer films are more creative because they are mystical audiovisual representations created with poetic compositions and landscapes.

Censorship prevailed in Québec until the 1960s, but after the protests of moviegoers against the cuts in *Hiroshima mon amour* [FR] (Renais, 1959), censorship was increasingly called into question. About this event, feminist historian of Québec cinema Julie Ravary-Pilon wrote:

> Faced with the growing frustration of viewers, the Québec government set up a commission in the early 1960s to review the role and powers of the Bureau of Censorship. In 1967, the commission

suggested the complete abolition of the Bureau. Its closure led several filmmakers to explore the limits of what can be projected in terms of sexual mores and nudity without works being censored or labelled as pornographic.

(Ravary-Pilon, 2018, p. 60, our translation)

In this context, new representations of women in Québec cinema are created by men. *La femme-image* [FR] (Borremans, 1960) is a 35-minute independent experimental fiction directed and produced by Guy Borremans. This surreal erotic film explores obsessive love. On its release, it caused a scandal: "First broadcast by its author and then integrated into the circuit of then very active film societies, *La Femme-image* shocked, provoked and shook a few taboos. It contributed, along with other films, to proving that NFB cinema was not the only possible cinema" (Houle et Julien, 1978, p. 102, our translation). According to my research, Borremans shows, for the first time in Québec cinematography, a completely naked woman. His film explores male sexual desire and heterosexual romantic relationships.

Few books study the history of women directors in Québec. Fortunately, *Femmes et cinéma québécois* [FR] (Carrière, 1983a) partially fills this gap by looking at both the creation of women and their representation in cinema. This book covers the period from 1942 to 1982.

Christiane Tremblay-Daviault wrote an article on the period from 1942 to 1960 entitled *Avant la Révolution tranquille: Une Terre-Mère en perdition* [FR]. She noted that a recurring theme in the films of this period is the opposition between life in the city (danger) and life in the countryside (safety). Tremblay-Daviault concluded that the representation of women conforms to the feminine archetype of Mother Earth, submissive, nurturing, virtuous and condemned to the kitchen. She analyzed films such as *À la croisée des chemins* [FR] (Guèvremont et Poitevin, 1943), *Le curé du village* [FR] (Gury, 1949a), *Le gros Bill* [FR] (Bigras et Delacroix, 1949) and *Cœur de maman* [FR] (Delacroix, 1953). She found that these productions pursue clerical aims, shaping women for the gaze of a traditional collective imagination.

However, Tremblay-Daviault observed another tangent: certain female characters stand out from traditional representations. They symbolize the anti-mothers. They are protagonists with negative connotations who act against the social norms of the time: Donalda cannot carry a pregnancy to term in *Un homme et son péché* [FR] (Gury, 1949b), the stepmother kills the child in *La petite Aurore, l'enfant martyre* [FR] (Bigras, 1952), the pianist Nicole Payette seeks emancipation outside her parish in *Le rossignol et les cloches* [FR] (Delacroix, 1952) and Marie-Ange marries a man she does not love solely for his money in *Tit-Coq* [FR] (Gélinas et Delacroix, 1953).

In the same book, Louise Carrière wrote the chapter entitled *Les images de femmes dans le cinéma masculin (1960–1983)* [FR]. With the abolition of censorship and access to foreign cinema, Carrière noted that directors produced emancipated and ingenuous female figures. "These changes were to sound the death knell for the traditional representation of women, the keepers of hearth and home" (Carrière, 1983a, p. 56, our translation). Transgressing prohibitions, these female characters not only smoke and drink alcohol, but they also allow themselves to use foul language and explore their sexuality outside the sacred bonds of marriage:

> Women have opinions, which is something very new on the screen. . . . These women are: Barbara in *The Cat in the Bag*, who would like, somehow, to make Claude aware of his problems; Pierrette in *Mon amie Pierrette* [FR], by Jean-Pierre Lefebvre, who challenges family authority for the first time. . . . Later, Mouffe, introduced in *Jusqu'au cœur* [FR] and *Où êtes-vous donc?* [FR], is looking for her way in the world of advertising, and Geneviève, in *Entre la mer et l'eau douce* [FR], who is fascinated . . . by the artist Claude.
>
> (Carrière, 1983a, p. 60, our translation)

After the abolition of the Bureau of Censorship in 1967, the Québec cinema did not escape the international influence that intertwined sexuality and cinema at that time. This period, nicknamed "Maple Syrup Porn",[3] offered women, undressed for no other reason than the pleasure of the male. Between 1969 and 1971, no less than twelve erotic films were produced in Québec. Including feature films by Denis Héroux: *Valérie* [FR] (Héroux, 1969), *7 fois . . . par jour* [FR] (Héroux, 1971) and *L'initiation* [FR] (Héroux, 1970), and feature films by Claude Fournier: *Deux femmes en or* [FR] (Fournier, 1970) and *La pomme, la queue . . . et les pépins!* [FR] (Fournier, 1974). Sexploitation, a subgenre of exploitation films, features nudity to sell movie tickets. If the production of "films de fesses"[4] exploded, not all directors created this kind of film. In response to the commercial success of *Valérie* [FR] (Héroux, 1969), Jean-Pierre Lefebvre created *Q-bec My Love* (Lefebvre, 1970), the first feminist fiction feature film in Québec.[5] In a memorable scene, the undressed female protagonist holds a circular mirror in front of her genitals in which the film crew is reflected. This powerful and satirical allegory symbolizes this voyeuristic gaze of the spectators by directly returning the *male gaze* to them.

In her analysis, for the period from 1970 to 1982, Carrière separated documentary production from fiction. From then on, television, radio, magazines, advertisements and newspapers were omnipresent in the daily lives of Quebeckers. The influence of American fashion, makeup and cinema was increasingly felt in Canada. Thanks to the NFB's *Premières Œuvres* [First Works] program, Carrière noted that some films escaped commercial representative schemas and presented intellectual works[6] dealing with unhappiness and malaise. However, these films still showed misogyny:

> Women no longer play the role of the mother, but a relative inequality to the benefit of women in terms of their strength of character and their organizational power is established at a first level. In Québec cinema, these "strong women" are almost always represented under the stereotypical features of the waitress, the go-go girl or the semi-prostitute.
>
> (Carrière, 1983a, p. 91, our translation)

These representations are not the ideals to which women aspire. By positioning this type of character as a "strong woman," it helps to hide the oppression that Québec women are victims of. They are naive, simple, superficial and exploited women. Carrière believes that even the work of Gilles Carle does not manage to escape this misogyny:

> With the 1970s and the liberation of women, Gilles Carle carried on. He wanted to introduce the so-called new liberated women of Québec: singers, dancers, sympathetic semi-prostitutes (that is women who benefit financially from their sexual relationships with men). . . . These women are always very young, friendless and available to men. Their main freedom is to choose which man or which men?
>
> (Carrière, 1983a, p. 96, our translation)

The third part of the collective work directed by Carrière and written by Josée Boileau is entitled *Images récentes dans les films à succès* [FR]. For her analysis, Boileau selected three films: *Les Plouffe* [FR] (Carle, 1981), *L'homme à tout faire* [FR] (Lanctôt, 1980) and *Les bons débarras* [FR] (Mankiewicz, 1980). The hit film *Les Plouffe* paints the portrait of a traditional Québec family in which there are three main female characters: la mère Plouffe, Rita and Cécile. La mère Plouffe is represented in a traditional way: pious and completely devoted to her family. She evolves almost exclusively in her kitchen. Rita is an emancipated *femme fatale*, desired by several men, and seen as a whore for her actions. Cécile is a spinster in love with a married man. In *Les Plouffe*, the men are considered heroes and the scenario evolves around them.

L'homme à tout faire [FR] is Micheline Lanctôt's first feature film. Even if the director avoids the ghetto of women who can only speak about men (her main character is male), Boileau noted that "female roles are hardly researched and, admittedly, appear as exact copies of the most typical and pejorative female models" (Boileau quoted in Carrière, 1983a, p. 123, our translation). Some want to seduce, some are naive and others wallow in the comfort of the home, where life revolves exclusively around the husband. It is therefore not because a woman directs a film that she manages to avoid stereotyping her female characters.

Les bons débarras [FR], based on an original screenplay by Réjean Ducharme, offers plausible contemporary female models. Marie Tifo brilliantly plays a single mother dealing with substance abuse issues who struggles to make ends meet. Her daughter Manon, played by Charlotte Laurier, is rebellious. She refuses to go to school and fights with all her might to survive in this difficult world. Both heroines evolve in poverty in an underprivileged neighborhood. Despite her unorthodox maternal ways, the mother profoundly loves her daughter and chooses to make her the priority.

TECHNIQUES ASSOCIATED WITH THE FEMININE SPHERE

The frivolity, servility, docility, fragility and domesticity of women were served excessively. Far beyond the technique of a film, filmmakers offer in a way an aesthetics of hunger. If "The Fairies Are Thirsty",[7] women are hungry. Hungry for positive role models. Hungry to see phallocratic taboos break. Hungry to see the sexist taboos that strike us all die. Hungry to see the mother-whore

stereovision shatter. Hungry to see women faithful to the multiplicity of our existences be embodied. Hungry to finally see the
myths of femininity and virility vanish.

(Lamartine, 1980, p. 32, our translation)

Artistic practices associated with the traditional feminine sphere such
as sewing, pottery, embroidery, weaving and cutting are relegated to the
bottom of the hierarchy of the arts. Evidently, these artistic practices are
almost absent from the history of art and, in the period studied, this hierarchy of disciplines and techniques is widely challenged by feminist art.
By appropriating practices such as knitting, ceramics, lace, tapestry, cutting and writing, women reject the hierarchy of the world of the arts and
speak out. With these materials, which were mostly devalued by institutions, they can create a breach in an area that has long denied them access.
Certain feminist artists claim and revalorize these "minor" media traditionally associated with the private sphere.

Many women . . . have produced very high-quality animated films
in Québec. The recent importance of women in animated film
can be attributed to a certain process of democratization of the
medium. The transition from collective production to artist film,
accompanied by the flowering of various animation techniques,
facilitated the entry of women into animation, a field which, until
the 1960s, was largely reserved for men.

(Levitin, 1992, s. p., our translation)

Bettina Maylone, an animator who has made three films at the
Vancouver animation studio, primarily used the media assigned to the
traditional feminine sphere. In *The Hometown* (Maylone, 1979), the animator used tapestry, embroidery and sewing to depict a personal story:
leaving her native land in the countryside to settle in the big city. The
director interwove the cinematographic techniques of frame-by-frame
cinema with those of sewing. With her needle work, she created representations in a naive style. The textures are varied and the colors are bright.
The hand of the artist embroidering the title of the animation appears on
the screen, thus relaying the process of the animation technique directly
to the animated imagery. She used various textiles, threads and sewing
buttons to represent herself, while evoking urban and rural landscapes.

In *Distant Island* (Maylone, 1981; Figure 3.1), Maylone went back even further in time, to her childhood. She used once again sewing, embroidery and tapestries to illustrate her memories. While doing the narration herself, she remembers the many sailing trips with her parents on magical weekends. During her adventures, she discovers an old, abandoned house in the woods and invents the family that would have lived there through the artifacts that have been left behind.

Her last production at the NFB, *The Magic Quilt* (Maylone, 1985), intertwines live action with the animation technique of sewing. This time, the visual exploration is more advanced because the physical creation of the artist—a huge, embroidered quilt—is the protagonist of the film. Children interact directly with Maylone's work. They are amazed when the elements of the quilt come alive. The two worlds intersect: a felted ball that is thrown by the animated characters of the quilt ends up in the real world in the hands of a little girl who then throws it back into the textile world. The quilt represents Canada, and the children tell the stories of their travels

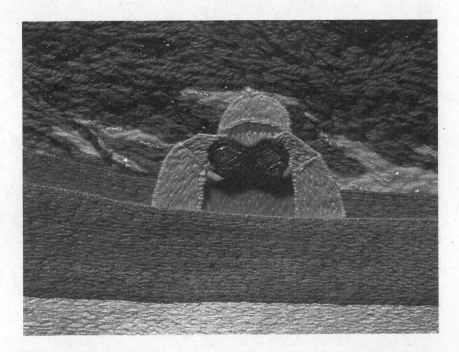

FIGURE 3.1   *Distant Island.*

Source: Maylone, 1981, © NFB, all rights reserved.

across the country. The viewers are exposed to notions of Canadian multiculturalism, the natural beauty of its vast environment and disputes over land ownership.

Directed in 1979 by Mitsu Daudelin, Estelle Lebel and Rachelle Saint-Pierre, *Cogne-Dur* [FR] (Figure 3.2) is another important film which borrows animation techniques associated with the traditional feminine sphere. The film is a ten-minute colored animation produced by Francine Desbiens in which the animators use a visual treatment of hooked rugs. Inspired by *La grande Margaude* [FR], a tale collected by Luc Lacourcière for the folklore archives of Université Laval, this collective creation criticizes the social inequalities of a system stemming from absolute monarchy. It tells the story of the revolt of a people who, by pooling individual talents, take justice into their own hands and annihilate the source of their oppression. Rebuilding the frameworks of society to eliminate gender inequalities, that is the project of the most radical feminists who believe that the current guidelines cannot lead to egalitarian relations between

FIGURE 3.2 *Cogne-Dur* [FR].

men and women. Rosi Braidotti explained the vision of feminism defended by Françoise Collin:

> both an ethical philosophy of human liberation and a political practice aimed at improving the social situation of women by remedying the social and symbolic violence of patriarchy. . . . both sexes need to redouble their ethical and political efforts to rebuild their relationship and transform the public sphere into a commonplace.
>
> (Braidotti, 2015, p. 22, our translation)

Cogne-Dur [FR] is a political film. In this animation, the fight for the liberation of women goes hand in hand with the fight for collective freedom. All evidence indicates that the king, as the owner of the land and the mill, compels the villagers to labor, thereby increasing his own wealth. Nothing suggests that the profits are redistributed to the people. The king has total power, and he takes ownership of the workers' production. The workers are closely watched by a man with a cane—the king's assistant—who dictates work and break times. This injustice in the distribution of wealth generates suffering in the population and contributes to its revolt. Without rebellion, change is impossible. Power is usually transmitted by filial ties, from father to son. For a long time in Québec's labor market, the French-speaking population was exploited by the English-speaking population; this contributed to the rise of nationalist fervor.

In Québec, the expression of individual and collective feminism (whether radical or egalitarian) is inseparable from the nationalist movement. The liberation of women (gender discrimination) and the class conflict (exploitation) are two fundamental considerations. The feminist struggle in Québec unites with the struggle for national liberation. The contribution of feminists to the struggle of women is made with the perspective of a double liberation: gender liberation and national liberation. To achieve collective liberation, one must first go through individual liberation: being a woman, and then being a Quebecker.

Cogne-Dur's four main male characters have individual talents: Vise-Juste [Aim Right] has precise telescopic vision, Tempête [Storm] can produce strong winds, Court-Vite [Run Fast] is faster than his shadow and Cogne-Dur [Hit Hard] has herculean physical strength. By pooling the individual talents of these companions and those of the women of the village, the population succeeds in annihilating the king to correct the injustice of which they are victims. The villagers come together and work to fight against their oppressor.

Even if *Cogne-Dur* [FR] has female characters camped in traditional roles—they take care of the children, bring dinner to the husbands who work on the construction site and sew—they participate in the social life and evolve in the public sphere. For example, they make a cowhide bag using their talent as seamstresses. By creating an object useful for the destruction of the source of their oppression, the value of their work is recognized. By creating the bag—used to carry treasures and food—they contribute, on equal footing with the men, to the collective liberation of the villagers during the looting at the end of the short film.

It is also important to talk about Bruno Edera, a Swiss animation cinema historian who, according to my research, carried out the first international study on female animators: *L'Animation au féminin* [FR] (Edera, 1983). His famous quote *"L'homme raconte une histoire, la femme se raconte"* [the man tells a story, the woman tells her story] (Edera, 1983, p. 73) can be found in this text. The author considered that the media of animation is "the least misogynistic field in the cinematographic and television sphere" (Edera, 1983, p. 73, our translation). Unfortunately, the author did not delve into the causes or the findings drawn from this favorable situation for women creators. Moreover, his perception of women's nature is misogynistic:

> Film animation is well suited to women because of its technical aspects, which are close to what is called "manual work." In particular, we can think of embroidery, which requires a lot of care and patience and can be practiced without taking into account atmospheric conditions. . . . The nature and goals of animation are also, to a certain extent, closer to certain feminine concerns—education and information—than to masculine ones.
>
> (Edera, 1983, p. 73, our translation)

This myth of the "feminine film," a branch of so-called feminine writing, is inscribed in the specificity of the nature of women. It is a vision based on the biological binary opposition and the immutability of the qualities attributed specifically to women. To speak of feminine writing, or of feminine art, is to unduly reduce the voice of women and confine them to their biology. To speak of a typically feminine art only exacerbates the essential-ism of the dominant position. The recognition of women's creations is a continual struggle in all artistic spheres.

Often, women's cinema is associated with a light cinematic art that caters exclusively to women. The trap of essentialization, a phenomenon that locks all women into the same set, unfolds still. This book explores "feminist" films and not "feminine" or "women's" films. A feminist film can be directed as much by a man as by a woman[8] insofar as it advocates gender equality or women's rights. As for "feminine" films, they are more akin to gendered roles and are often perceived as "small films.[9]" There is no homogeneous group of "women": women experience a variety of oppressions and issues, modulated by class, race and sexual orientation. Therefore, from my perspective, there is no such thing as "women's cin-ema": there are only women who create films from their point of view. When it comes to films made by women, some are feminist and assertive, others are not. Women directors are not immune to sexism.

Among feminist filmmakers, there is a desire for a different kind of self-expression, both in terms of form and content: "the visual representation of women is a key issue, as this representation can confront patriarchal domination or radically contradict it" (Des Rivières and Saint-Martin, 1994, p. 3, our translation). Avant-garde cinema, including feminist cin-ema, offers tools to build a narrative subversion. In cinematography, all genres combined, women directors clearly desire to showcase legitimate protagonists who convey their messages by revealing their perspectives. The demands of the second wave of feminism are transmitted through the content of the works. Several women directors are engaged in a quest to raise awareness about the oppression and domination of women. They transpose into the seventh art this new conceptualization of their experi-ence. They want to change things and their weapon is cinema. They use this medium to promote the ideas of the feminist movements such as women's rights, gender equality and access to abortion.

Other filmmakers, such as Carolee Schneemann (Meat Joy, 1964), Annie Sprinkle (*Slut and Goddesses*, 1992) and Émilie Jouvet (*Too Much Pussy! Feminist Sluts, a Queer X Show*, 2010), offered sexualized represen-tations of female bodies by reversing the use of iconography: "by giving it a fundamental political value, because through her body, the performer criticizes the heteronormative order, decompartmentalizing commercial pornography through a discourse held by women, and deconstructing gender identities and gendered sexual practices" (Bilodeau, 2016, p. 164, our translation).

Feminist films propose a political and ideological posture in opposition to the dominant system, in an activist perspective. Feminist films are not exclusive to documentary, feminism can be found in fiction, animation and experimental films. In feminist films, speaking out does not necessarily have to be explicit and activistic. Looking at cinematographic works through a feminist lens allows for the decompartmentalization of the main characteristics of commercial cinema because:

> Any work of art produced by a woman is feminist as far as it combines criticism and creativity. Art demands openness and risk taking; it takes nothing for granted and rests only on the process that produces it. Transformative and rebellious, inspired and contentious, feminist art is another form of structured intensity: it supports the project of creating new beginnings, of giving birth to possible worlds.
>
> (Braidotti, 2015, p. 26, our translation)

However, animation cinema historian Bruno Edera is not wrong when he mentions, in his article, that animation seems to be more welcoming to women who want to make cinematographic productions. As Louise Beaudet, curator of film animation at the Cinémathèque québécoise from 1973 to 1996, points out, the field of animation seems to have been more favorable to women, compared to the documentary and fiction, because:

> the equation film animation = children's cinema and the Disney imagery conveyed by a family-type incarnation, certified as safe with its kilometers on the straight and narrow, far from the sofas of adultery, have ended up being petrified in people's minds. Therefore, what could be more "natural" than to entrust a woman with an area supposedly reserved for kids?
>
> (Beaudet, 1983, p. 214, our translation)

I am often asked why women seem to have had a more direct access to filmmaking in film animation compared to documentary and fiction. Certainly, the emancipation of women through education as well as the democratization of the medium has favored a wider access to animation for artists. However, it is not insignificant that frame-by-frame cinema allows women creators to occupy almost all the positions necessary for the success of their works: scriptwriting, animation, direction, photography and production. Perhaps this is one of the reasons why women have been able to access this field: by working alone on their animated creations, they have been able to break out of the hegemonic and androcentric system governing cinematographic production where they were mostly subjugated to men. Frame-by-frame cinema is perhaps better adapted to the reality of some women, especially those who have chosen to be mothers. My experience is similar, it was possible for me to make eight animated films between 2006 and 2018, while raising my three daughters, because I could practice my art in the comfort of my studio. No matter what time it was, my worktable was there, waiting for me. I had no travel constraints, my work periods molded themselves to the rhythm of my daughters' lives, family obligations and housework. This is a factor that has favored women's access to the production of animated films: the possibility of avoiding certain constraints of film production. The creation of animation can take place entirely in the private sphere.

Lotte Reiniger (1899–1981) is an emblematic figure of the lack of recognition of film animation directors. She reappropriated, in a way, the dining room table to make it an animation bench: she was thus perceived as a craftsperson and not an artist. Yet, Reiniger worked in the field of frame-by-frame cinema for sixty years and made her films in Germany, England, Italy as well as in Montréal. She is the pioneer of silhouette animation, a technique that consists of photographing black cardboard cutouts on an animation table lit by rear projection. Her work is reminiscent of shadow theatre: she called her animation technique *Sihouettenfilm* (silhouette film). As she has made over 70 films, it is surprising that she remains marginalized by historical documentation.

Several works[10] consider that the first animated feature film in the history of this discipline is *Snow White and the Seven Dwarfs* (Hand, 1937). Yet, the feature film *The Adventures of Prince Achmed* (Reiniger, 1926) was produced eleven years earlier. Several factors contributed to the invisibility of this first feature film. In Reiniger's case, her geopolitical situation worked against her since the German film industry of the 1920s was in direct competition with that of the Americans who dominated the market. Hollywood closed its doors to the German invasion. Also, international distribution was interested in commercial cinema and Reiniger produced an artistic feature film with an avant-garde style. Upon its release, *The Adventures of Prince Achmed* was not lauded by German film critics. Distributors were reluctant to circulate it since the technique used was silhouette animation and there were no celebrities in the credits. The lack of distribution on American soil cast a shadow over the film's career, since, at that time, the Americans already held a strong monopoly on distribution both nationally and internationally. It was not until 1942, sixteen years after its first screening, that the film became accessible to the American public.

The controversy over the historical attribution of the first animated feature film to Disney (*Snow White and the Seven Dwarfs*, 1937) rather than to Reiniger (*The Adventures of Prince Achmed*, 1926) could also be explained by the production processes used. Reiniger's techniques involving the cutting of black cardboard silhouettes, the antithesis of the expensive Technicolor processes of the Disney studios, retain an "artisanal" dimension. This production process was devalued by film critics as being reminiscent of arts and crafts. Reiniger's work was deemed "unprofessional" and "feminine". However, this appropriation of a "feminine" technique, transmitted orally from generation to generation, is a feminist gesture of protest:

> The genre of silhouette films also constitutes for Reiniger a kind of feminist validation of women's folk-art form. . . . After the middle of the 19th century, it came to be practiced more and more by women who were not allowed to access to other art training but who learned scissor craft as part of their household duties.
>
> (Starr, [1987] 2009, p. 15)

It must therefore be understood that, in addition to the social, political and economic contexts that influenced women's creative conditions, the accessibility to the media was also a key factor for creation. Reiniger worked with the NFB to create a film:

> The German pioneer, who gave up animation after the death of her husband in 1963, and encouraged by Louise Beaudet of the Cinémathèque québécoise, returned to directing at the NFB in 1975 for *Aucassin and Nicolette*, her penultimate film, directed at the respectable age of seventy-six.
>
> (Carrière, 1988, p. 352, our translation)

The animation *Aucassin and Nicolette* (see Figure 3.3) was adapted from a medieval chantefable. The colorful backgrounds highlight Reiniger's beautiful, detailed black silhouettes. Intertitles and narration allow the viewers to understand the story of these two protagonists in love, who are from different social classes and whose families reject the union. The film is quite long for an NFB short (fifteen minutes) and their incredible epic is reminiscent of the impossible love story of Romeo and Juliet.

Another creator marginalized by historical documentation, but that must be mentioned, is Alice Guy-Blaché (1873–1968), arguably the first woman director in the history of live action cinema. Guy-Blaché began her career as secretary to Léon Gaumont, who later became president of the Gaumont Film Company. While working as a secretary, she met the Lumière brothers and discovered their invention: moving images projected onto a sheet. She worked with them to film street scenes. Interested in literature and theatre, she approached Gaumont to produce cinema scenes. Thus, she wrote, directed and produced *La fée aux choux* [FR] (Guy-Blaché, 1896). To my knowledge, this production is the first film directed by a woman in the history of cinema.

FIGURE 3.3 *Aucassin and Nicolette.*

Source: Reniger, 1976, © NFB, all rights reserved.

After the success of her first film, Alice Guy-Blaché was promoted to director of film production at Gaumont, although her official job title remained that of secretary, which saved her employer from having to pay her a second salary. Between 1900 and 1907, she directed more than a hundred short films. Her greatest success (in France) was a film entitled *La vie du Christ* [FR] (Guy-Blaché, 1906). An ambitious project for its time, both in its duration (thirty-five minutes) and in its scale (a hundred extras, sumptuous sets and original staging), its realization is wrongly attributed in the credits to her assistant. For a long time, Guy-Blaché remained unknown to most scholars interested in the origins of cinema, because the production of several of her films had been attributed to men.

She moved to America in 1907 and founded her production studio: Solax Film. "Guy's exile coincides with the expansion of a profitable film industry in France" (Rollet, 2017, p. 10, our translation). Her films produced in the United States are very successful. She made the headlines because she was a woman running a lucrative film company grossing over twenty-five thousand dollars a year. In 1912, she was famous and considered a reference within the American film industry. Without consulting her, her husband sold for a pittance the rights to *The Lure* (Guy-Blaché, 1914). This film became one of the biggest successes of that time. Her spouse left her for her main actress, and she had a hard time getting over it. Her production studio was sold at auction. She returned to France in 1922 with her two children. Penniless, she moved in with her sister. At age 49, she was unable to reintegrate the world of French cinema; she had been forgotten. She earned a living by writing children's stories for magazines, signing her texts under male pseudonyms.

Several women were active in early cinema. "Women producers are ... numerous. These positions, involving money and decisions, are rarely occupied by women today, with a few exceptions such as Kathleen Kennedy or Bonnie Curtis. Sherry Lansing directed Paramount from 1992 to 2004. The only woman in history to hold such a position, she is also seen as one of the most powerful—and modest—women in the United States" (Rollet, 2017, p. 13, our translation). There are many who worked in early cinema whose stories deserve to be told, but due to space limitations, I will only mention a few names here: Judith Crawley (director), Lois Weber (screenwriter), Anita Loos (screenwriter), June Mathis (screenwriter), Frances Marion (screenwriter), Margaret Booth (editor), Barbara McLean (editor),

Musidora (actress and producer), Germaine Dulac (director and producer), etc. (Rollet, 2017).

Considering the multiple examples of women's marginalization in cinematographic production, it is not surprising that they demanded better access to the discipline. The next chapter focuses on this phenomenon, specifically on the NFB's particular situation, with the implementation of various positive discrimination programs to promote women's access to directing.

NOTES

1. The Bureau of Censorship had the freedom to ban films it deemed inappropriate and it had the freedom to cut clips from feature films as it saw fit.
2. About an archive sequence shot in China that had a great impact on her, Denault wrote: "The nuns play with the children in the courtyard of the orphanage, then everyone stops, the camera turns to an old gentleman pulling a cart. The camera moves towards the cart and slowly reveals its contents: little swaddled babies, stuck against one another" (Denault, 1996, p. 93, our translation).
3. " 'Undress your neighbour' would become the mantra of Québec cinema in the late 1960s and early 1970s" (Ravary-Pilon, 2018, p. 62, our translation).
4. Translator's footnote: "Fesses" is a euphemism in Québec culture to talk about sexuality. "Films de fesses" is an expression meaning pornographic films.
5. *La vie rêvée* [FR] (Dansereau, 1972) is the first feminist fiction feature film directed by a woman. *Mother-To-Be* (Poirier, 1968) is the first feminist documentary feature film directed by a woman.
6. The author cites *Mon enfance à Montréal* [FR] (Chabot, 1970), *Ty-Peupe* [FR] (Bélanger, 1971) and *Ainsi soient-ils* [FR] (Patry, 1970).
7. Translator's footnote: "Les fées ont soif" [FR] (The Fairies Are Thirsty) is a play written by Denise Boucher. The play is an exploration of the role of women through time. The three protagonists—a housewife, a whore and the Virgin Mary—fight to break out of the stereotyped roles in which they have been imprisoned.
8. As such, there are many examples of feminist films directed by men: *Offside* (Panahi, 2006), *Julia* (Zinnemann, 1977), *Story of Women* (Chabrol, 1988), *Impromptu* (Lapine, 1990), *Thelma & Louise* (Scott, 1991), *G.I. Jane* (Scott, 1997), *The Circle* (Panahi, 2001), *Le procès de Bobigny* [FR] (Luciani, 2006), *4 Months, 3 Weeks and 2 Days* (Mungiu, 2007) and *Polytechnique* [FR] (Villeneuve, 2009). Within the NFB, men directors addressed feminist notions in their films as early as the 1960s, notably with the *La femme hors du foyer* [FR] series. Among the works created in this series are: *Il y eut un soir, il y eut un matin* [FR] (Patry, 1964), *Solange dans nos campagnes* [FR] (Carle, 1964) and *Caroline* [FR] (Dufaux et Perron, 1964).

9. Besides, what is a "masculine" film?
10. Among the books identified by Vivian K. Taylor (author of a dissertation on Reiniger) that claim Disney made the first animated feature film are: *The Art of Walt Disney* (Field, 1942), *The Art of Walt Disney: From Mickey Mouse to the Magic Kingdom* (Finch, 1973), *The Disney Films* (Maltin, 1973), *The Film 100: A ranking of the most influential people in the history of the movies* (Smith, 1998) and *Disney, Pixar, and the Hidden Messages of Children's Films* (Booker, 2010).

CHAPTER 4

Feminist Uprisings in Cinematographic Creation at the NFB

F EMINIST ART IS POLITICALLY engaged, it reiterates the socioeconomic and cultural claims of women. In the feminist artistic practice, women speak up to express their own reality as well as the reality of other women. They portray their oppression and promote their rights while raising public awareness for their various conditions, thereby disseminating information on the changes demanded by feminist movements. With women gaining access to director positions at the NFB and the creation of pioneering works in fiction, documentary and animation, it is possible to witness the representation of women by women, as well as their professionalization within a government institution. The actuation of a double political representation of women (in front of and behind the camera) is therefore taking place at the NFB. What is at work here is feminism infiltrating a governmental body and creating cinematographic representations within the confines of a liberal egalitarian State feminism.[1]

THE SOCIO-PROFESSIONAL SITUATION OF WOMEN AT THE NFB

The late 1960s and early 1970s were a pivotal time for women's condition in Canada. The "second wave" of feminism focused on obtaining recognition that the problems experienced by women in the private sphere concern

DOI: 10.1201/9781032694382-6

society as a whole. Feminists were bringing new causes into the public sphere. For example, with the rise in divorce rates, single-parent families were increasing, resulting in a fundamental change in family structure. Inevitably, more women must work. As society changes, so does the role of women. Under these conditions, some thirty feminist groups were coming together to demand that the federal government establish a commission of inquiry on the condition and equality of opportunity for women in the country. The *Report of the Royal Commission on the Status of Women in Canada* (RCSW) (1970) addresses the place of women in Canadian society. During this period, characterized by a massive return of women to the workforce, a question that preoccupied mothers was: should I stay at home to take care of my children or should I work?

The president of the Commission, Florence Bird, a Toronto-based bilingual journalist, did not identify as a feminist.[2] Composed of five women[3] and two men[4] (sociologists, demographers and jurists), the Commission's objective was to paint a portrait of the situation of Canadian women. The hearings lasted for six months in 1968 and were held across Canada. To ensure that as many women as possible were reached, the debates were held in places they felt comfortable coming to (shopping malls, libraries, the YWCA, etc.). These hearings were also televised. The Commission heard over 900 people, received over 1000 letters and 468 briefs. The Commission casted a very wide net and was interested in the condition of women from a social perspective. It was no longer an individual matter: society as a whole was responsible for the improvement or deterioration of the condition of women.

The Commission's conclusion was very clear: the status of women in Canada must be improved to ensure that they have equal opportunities with men in all spheres of society. This observation is in accordance with egalitarian liberal feminism. Among other things, it is by educating the population about the persistent and unfavorable prejudices towards women that it will be possible to eradicate discrimination. The Commission emphasized the importance of recognizing the value of housework and noted that women had very little to no money in their bank accounts. In the labor market, they were paid less than men. It was also noted that the education of young girls did not meet the expectations of the labor market.

The report contained 167 recommendations and more than two thirds of them have been implemented. Recommendations include pay equity, protection for women in the event of divorce, non-sexist education, taking into account the condition of housewives and indigenous women (such as abolishing the loss of indigenous status for those who marry non-indigenous men). Federal and provincial government agencies were created, including the Council on the Status of Women (in all provinces). Undoubtedly, the RCSW marks an important turning point in Canada. It demonstrated that discrimination against women in the labor market and in the education system reproduced societal values and that stereotypes about their qualities and abilities diminished their opportunities to reach their goals. It is not surprising that feminist movements are becoming increasingly radical in their critique of androcentric society. Radical feminists want to subvert the hierarchical framework of society. They want to achieve equality by overthrowing, or even destroying, the system. In the field of cinema, whether in animation, documentary or fiction, the emergence of feminist practices in the film industry was marked by the influence of these radical claims. The "second wave" of feminism in Québec and in Canada is part of major transformations in society.

According to my research, the first feminist film produced by a woman[5] at the NFB is *La beauté même* [FR] (Fortier, 1964; Figure 4.1).[6] About her

FIGURE 4.1 *La beauté même* [FR].

Source: Fortier, 1964, © NFB, all rights reserved.

film, Fortier said, "I made a little film about the beauty of women. I was not a feminist, but these were things that concerned me, because I thought from my own body" (quoted in Daudelin, 1980, p. 15, our translation). This nine-minute film meditates on the stereotypes of female beauty and the factors that contribute to its promotion. By illustrating the inner monologue of a woman, played by Monique Miller, the protagonist reflects on beauty. At first, she defines it from the perspective of others "I see myself unceasingly through the eyes of others, I see myself sometimes as a flower, a child, an idol, sometimes as a mother, a servant, an enchantress, a witch" (Fortier, 1964, our translation).

The film then addresses how popular culture appropriates women's bodies and fetishizes them to please the heterosexual male gaze: "I have often wondered what beauty is. I see it appear and disappear in me as the hours pass by. I would like to seize it, to keep it all day long. Where is my beauty? Who am I when I am far from the gaze of men? I have tried to please since childhood. I must please. Beauty contests daily, beauty classes in Atlantic City" (Fortier, 1964, our translation). This cautionary film denounces the Miss America beauty contest where young women parade in evening gowns and in bikinis: "A few wrinkles tomorrow and the game will be lost. . . . Beauty in pieces. Dangers of the eyes on me. They trap me. . . . I want to run the risk of beauty" (Fortier, 1964, our translation).

Fortier's avant-garde film criticized beauty pageants four years before they were denounced by radical American activists in 1968, a pivotal year for protest movements. In the United States, radical feminists strongly denounced the representation of women in popular culture and mass media. They also condemned the commodification of bodies and the consumerist discourses that imprison women to beauty standards. These feminists attacked the symbolism of the Miss America pageant. One of the brains of the operation was Carol Hanisch whose slogan "The personal is political" became famous. Shulamith Firestone[7] also advocated with radical feminists denouncing the fact that black women could not participate in Miss America because they would not fit its beauty criteria. Yet, "Black is beautiful! "[8] The activists then created the *Freedom Trash Can* in which they discarded magazines (notably *Playboy*), girdles, curlers, bras and other instruments of torture in the name of beauty. They criticized the capitalist system and crowned a sheep to highlight by derision the resemblance of the Miss America contest with those of the agricultural fairs. Can makeup hide the scars of women's oppression? In Fortier's film, mannequins in downtown window displays and on magazine covers echo the discourses that bombarded women with stereotypical images to which they should conform. By questioning her relationship to beauty, Fortier concludes that it can only come from within, from self-love. By reversing the male gaze that fetishizes women, she invites the female gaze to recognize its own value.

To my knowledge, Anne Claire Poirier is the first woman to direct a feminist feature documentary in Québec: *Mother-To-Be* (Poirier, 1968). Moving back and forth between genres (documentary, autobiography and fiction), Poirier explores pregnancy, childbirth and motherhood. She illustrates the inner monologue of a woman who is expecting her second child and reveals her concerns, her worries and fears. The narration is inspired by the director's personal diary and it is her voice that can be heard. Borrowing, at times, from the live camera aesthetic, Poirier sneaked into a delivery room documenting a real birth. These shocking images present to the cinema a feminine reality that was hidden from the public. Indeed, men were generally excluded from the delivery room in the 1960s and cameras were certainly not allowed.

The film illustrates postpartum feminist issues. The protagonist struggles to reconcile her family life and her professional life. Exhausted by routine, she neglects herself to take care of others. She feels trapped, crushed under the responsibilities and mental burden that she carries alone. She is unhappy and torn between the guilt of leaving her children at daycare and her desire to enter the labor market. She questions her relationship with her partner, which has changed since they had children, and her partner's desire for her body, which has also altered after two pregnancies. By presenting the reality of one woman, Poirier's film echoes the real lives of other Quebeckers and Canadian women. She shows the real oppression of women in their maternal role. About her work, the director said:

> Of course, I am a feminist, in the sense that I want the well-being of women. My cinema is political, committed to the most important liberation movement of our time. But whatever subjects I tackle whether it is aging, love or war, my cinema will always be feminine. It is like that, it is neither better nor lesser, I am a woman.
>
> (Poirier, 1980, p. 18, our translation)

As for the English-language productions at the NFB, *The Things I Cannot Change* (Ballantyne, 1967) is a feature-length documentary that paints a moving portrait of a very poor family in Montréal. Amid the father's unemployment and his troubles with the police, the director documents the family's struggles to offer food as well as their miserable living conditions. The parents will soon welcome their tenth child and their lack of concern for the poverty in which they are raising their family is shocking. The father says: "I think children are nice if you can afford them. I don't think I can but I still want them. . . . They are not hungry. They have a roof over their heads and I try hard to give them . . . clothes. Lots of hand-me-downs. I am not proud" (Ballantyne, 1967). When the director asks the mother why she has so many children, she replies: "We've got nine children. And another one coming, that's the worst. . . . Well I don't know. That's nature so you have to ask that. . . . I heard so much about birth control pills. But I've heard they do this and they do that" (Ballantyne, 1967). The film was a wakeup call for institutional authorities: it crudely demonstrates sociocultural problems such as the lack of education, poverty, parental neglect and violence.

According to feminist historian Nicole Van Enis (2012), 1968 marks the beginning of the "second wave" of feminism. This period was characterized by numerous uprisings around the world. Among the major events of 1968 were "May 68" in France, the "Prague Spring" in Czechoslovakia, the "Tlatelolco Massacre" in Mexico, the murder of Martin Luther King as well as many student revolts. These events had many repercussions, including in women's creations.

In 1967, the NFB set up the Challenge for Change program with the threefold objective of giving marginalized people a chance to express themselves through cinema. Firstly, this initiative aspired to allow the expression of minority cultures through the seventh art. Secondly, the program aimed to disseminate knowledge about minority communities to the public and to decision-making bodies. Thirdly, the goal of these films was to gather valuable information from minorities to better understand their realities, visions and challenges.

The program was based on the belief that people were able to identify their problems and find solutions. The NFB's audiovisual resources were available to Canadian populations from minority cultures. The government encouraged the artistic expression of minorities to counterbalance the traditional representations in national cinema. "Challenge for Change became one of the few cinematographic projects in the world to openly and officially support social change" (Carrière, 1984b, p. 24, our translation). Poverty in

Canada is one of the major issues presented by the program. In turn, this initiative promoted the emergence of women filmmakers and feminist filmmaking practices: the vision of women is also in the minority. In the English department, women creators worked with Studio D. In the French department, it all began with the *"En tant que femmes"* [FR] program.[9]

POSITIVE DISCRIMINATION MEASURES

The *"En tant que femmes"* [FR] program was an initiative that only affected live action films. Many women workers within the NFB felt doubly aggrieved: they had no access to filmmaking and the jobs they were given were alienating. They wished to disrupt the policies and institutional structures governing access to filmmaking and the allocation of positions. In her research published in Carrière's book, Blais noted two problems within the NFB: women's assistantship positions and, proportionally, their greater number in certain functions. She wrote:

> women represent 40% of the overall population [at the NFB], yet they are over-represented in three categories (administrative services, secretaries and clerks) which offer the lowest salaries and the fewest opportunities for advancement. They are under-represented in a good number of categories (among other positions: film agents, technicians, camerapeople and film production) where they are found on the lowest salary scale, whereas men are distributed throughout to the various levels on the salary scale.
>
> (Blais, 1983, p. 204, our translation)

A similar observation is made in the internally published article entitled *"Qui sont les femmes qui travaillent à l'ONF?"* [*Who are the women working at the NFB?*] (*Médium Média*, 1973, p. 11). It criticizes the place of women at the NFB and the work they are given within the institution: "In the French department, there are two women directors out of 21, two women in the editing department, no women cameraperson, three women out of ten in the animation department . . . and many secretaries and receptionists" (*Médium Média*, 1973, p. 11, our translation).

In the spring of 1972, director Kathleen Shannon (founder of Studio D) conducted a survey to learn more about women workers at the NFB. The preliminary compilation of Shannon's questionnaire provided very revealing statistics: 76% of women worked at the NFB for financial reasons, 66%

of respondents felt that they were underpaid, 26% felt that a man doing the same job would be better paid, 25% did not like the work they were doing, 50% reported that they had had difficulty getting hired or promoted because they were women, and 38% felt that they had been discriminated against because of their gender.

Under these circumstances, the introduction of the Challenge for Change program offered them an opportunity. "A minority in terms of the power they hold—or do not hold—, women as a community are a prime subject for a program like Challenge for Change" (*Médium Média*, 1973, p. 3, our translation). The NFB did not have a specific mandate to produce feminist films. However, it had to open up to the plurality of minority viewpoints in Canada. Visibly disadvantaged in terms of the number of films produced at the NFB, the women's perspective is one of these minority viewpoints.

Even if the possibility of producing subversive films seemed contradictory within the limits of institutional production, feminist directors invested this place of power—the NFB—to make claims. On March-21st 1971, Jeanne Morazain, Monique Larocque and Anne Claire Poirier (all employees at the NFB) suggested the creation of the "*En tant que femmes*" [FR] program. Their goal was to produce a series of films about women's experiences, directed by women and, where possible, with an all-women crew. Morazain, Larocque and Poirier collectively wrote the voluminous research report "*En tant que femmes*" [FR] (1971), which they submitted to the federal government. In this report, they described their various oppressions:

> Enough data and facts have been uncovered and widely disseminated in the last decade to make us believe that discrimination against women is no longer denied, and that the Freudian portrait of the essentially "passive, narcissistic and masochistic" woman is a thing of the past. Discrimination is not yet ancient history. . . . The solution does not lie in a single reform of the existing social order; it will come from a new society, from a profound revolution of attitudes and mentalities, from the overthrow of the sexist regime like all the other regimes that rely on violence and domination.
>
> (Morazain *et al.*, 1971, p. 1, our translation)

One of the main concerns of this cinematographic proposal was the denunciation of the stereotypes that women face. The women authors challenged the institutional rigidity of the sexist education instilled in children that perpetuates traditional social representations and the domination of women by men. They bring to the forefront the construction of gendered roles and the division of tasks according to gender, which are social constructs acquired since childhood. Women authors wanted to create films to revalue the depictions of real women, anchored in the daily life and context of the 1970s:

> The portrayal of a woman transmitted by the cinema, literature, humor, publicity . . . (all controlled by men) makes her a neurotic, a shrew, a nuisance, a stay-at-home. . . . The desired, upheld and extolled female emotionality was utilized as a pretext to exclude women from centers of decision-making and politics because women were said to be incapable of logic and command, and because the "hysterical" manifestations of that same emotionality was feared. Obedience and submission were ensured by maintaining their sense of inferiority through social, religious and moral laws.
>
> (Morazain et al., 1971, p. 2, our translation)

Creating films to stop the discrimination of which they are victims, offering a women's gaze on society and denouncing stereotypes and taboos were the objectives pursued by Morazain, Larocque and Poirier. They wanted to tell a different story, by talking about "women who have distinguished themselves in our history in roles other than that of mothers, teachers or nurses" (Médium Média, 1973, p. 3, our translation). They were influenced by the leading authors Betty Friedan, Germaine Greer and Kate Millett (quoted extensively in the research report). For the ideation of their feature films, filmmakers value group work and collaboration between participants: "rather than trying once again to explain ourselves to others, we are going to try to find out who we are, who women are, what women's needs are, by talking to each other, as honestly as possible, without worrying about what others will think" (Médium Média, 1973, p. 2, our translation). Morazain, Larocque and Poirier rely on the research report of the RCSW and its recommendations: "'En tant que femmes' [FR] is an experience that is probably unique in the world . . . its acceptance by the NFB is the story of a struggle. These films were therefore not a dissertation on women, but a collective undertaking by a group of women speaking in their own way about what concerns them and other women" (*Médium Média*, 1973, p. 1, our translation).

Getting the "*En tant que femmes*" [FR] project accepted proved to be difficult as the decision-making hierarchy was almost exclusively composed of men: "The men who made up most of the program committee were already tired of hearing their wives complain about 'nothing'— as they put it—without having all women do the same in NFB films!" (Dansereau, quoted by Ouvrard, *Le Nouvelliste*, 1974, n. p., our translation). The project also needed a double approval. In addition to being reviewed by the institution's programming committee, the federal government also needed to give its approval. Morazain, Larocque and Poirier needed the go-ahead from a special interdepartmental committee. Nevertheless, the creation of the series was sanctioned in September 1971. For three years, the films made by the women in the French department illustrate a social reality denounced by the feminists of the "second wave" such as marriage, abortion and the historical invisibilization of women. By working with women from all over Québec coming from various social backgrounds, Morazain, Larocque and Poirier aimed at representing their female characters under a new light. They conceived protagonists who go about their daily lives while questioning their realities and common oppression. They are "ordinary" women for whom the directors neither promote their physical appearance nor glorify their existence. These films are anti-sexist, non-radical and revalue the specific contribution of women to Québec society by also offering a positive image of traditional roles and daily life. "Questioning, redefining, no longer accepting are frequent terms in the films' synopsis" (Carrière, 1983a, p. 196, our translation). This is how Morazain, Larocque and Poirier illustrate the contribution of women to society through their minority viewpoint, while creating female cultural content within films with a free style, both in terms of form and content.

"*En tant que femmes*" [FR] was an important moment for NFB employees, as it was the first time women came together to speak out within the institution. These productions questioned the social dictates in which they evolved. The redefinition of women's identity occurs at both the individual and collective levels:

> The films show that, despite their differences, women have the same condition: they are all housewives, victims of history and sexist

education. . . . The alienating housework is explicitly denounced, as is the harassing responsibility for women to raise children alone.

(Carrière, 1983a, p. 201, our translation)

During the program's three years, six productions (all live action) focusing on various feminist themes were produced. *Souris, tu m'inquiètes* [FR] (Danis, 1973) explores the loss of identity in marriage and motherhood. *À qui appartient ce gage?* [FR] (Blackburn *et al.*, 1973) questions daycares and the desire to nationalize them. *J'me marie, j'me marie pas* [FR] (Dansereau, 1973) examines the complex relationships that women have with men. *They Called Us "Les Filles du Roy"* (Poirier, 1974; Figure 4.2) analyzes women's identity and their place in the labor market. *Les filles, c'est pas pareil* [FR] (Girard, 1974) investigates female adolescence and *Le temps de l'avant* [FR] (Poirier, 1975) discusses contraception and abortion.

At the time, this series was unsettling and the subjects were shocking. The filmmakers entered homes and turned their cameras on intimacy. They dared to present the private in public. As previously mentioned, the screening of films outside of cinemas was an essential activity for the NFB,

FIGURE 4.2 *They Called Us "Les Filles du Roy."*

and the promotion of the works in the series used this strategy to reach out to women by encouraging them to get out of the house to discuss their common problems. On television, the series gained great visibility with its broadcast on Radio-Canada.[10],[11] Hotlines were set up after the broadcasts, where more than 350 calls from the public were recorded (19% of them were made by men). The institution also received 1800 written responses. The series was broadcast in the regions (via the Ciné Vidéo-Bus), in schools, in community centers, in church halls and in French-speaking networks outside Québec.

Lively debates ensued after the screenings of the films in the "*En tant que femmes*" series. The feature films were unifying and stimulated discussions. The initial objective of breaking the isolation of women to create a sense of solidarity was achieved. Women were also sometimes given the opportunity to learn about filmmaking after the screenings by experimenting with the technique. During the circulation of the series' films, short films and animations are also programmed.[12]

In her MA thesis on the Challenge for Change program, historian Louise Carrière points out the downsides of the "*En tant que femmes*" project by criticizing the aesthetics of the films, which she deemed not very innovative. She also notes that the theme of women's poverty, which was one of the founding principles of the Challenge for Change program, is completely ignored. The specificity of the point of view is also denounced by Carrière: "This subjective view will be that of highly educated, professional women, most of whom come from fairly privileged backgrounds" (Carrière, 1983b, p. 180, our translation). Thus, minority views of women are not portrayed in the series.

The films from the "*En tant que femmes*" series take root in a white egalitarian feminism as they mostly reflect the issues of the more affluent social classes:

> Seeking a series that faithfully mirrors the concerns of the women of that time, of all women, would be a mistake. . . . It is from this reality of privileged women that they address the problems of their sisters . . . which explains in part its limitations.
>
> (Carrière, 1983b, p. 181, our translation)

The corpus of "*En tant que femmes*" [FR] is a unique cinematographic legacy because it presents a specific cultural content of the "second wave" of feminism. "Filmmakers are not using identification with the women portrayed in the movies, but rather with the identified problems" (Carrière, 1983b, p. 199, our translation). The filmmakers highlight the invisible work of women, their experiences and their vision. They use cinema to promote their claims. By showing Québec and Canadian women their conditions of subjugation and by proposing avenues for change, women directors work to raise awareness in the private sphere.

> The "*En tant que femmes*" [FR] series is extremely important for women filmmakers in Québec, because it constitutes a first opening in terms of filmmaking. Obviously, it is limited to the NFB, but it is nonetheless a first open door to filmmaking.
>
> (Carrière, 1981, p. 47, our translation)

If the "*En tant que femmes*" [FR] program changed the production process by granting filmmaking to a minority perspective, that of women, it also had a long-term effect on gendered power relations within the institution. The NFB replicated the behavior of other federal institutions that gave women a more equitable place in the labor market, thus encouraging their professionalization. As for the English department, women gained access to filmmaking through the establishment of a more permanent initiative: Studio D.

Studio D was founded in 1974 under the initiative of Kathleen Shannon. This feminist production unit was active for twenty-two years, until 1996. Very few animated films were created, the production consisted of mostly live action films with a focus on documentaries. Studio D was unique in the world: to my knowledge, it is the only feminist film creation unit financed by a State institution.[13] The program "addresses the specific information needs of female audiences and provides women with the opportunity to express and develop their creative potential through film, ... a place where they can work together in a collective atmosphere of mutual support" (Burnett, 1980, p. 33, our translation[14]). Studio D's mission was to produce films by, for and about women so that they could generate their own media representations.

Several films left their mark on Studio D, particularly the *Working Mothers* series (1974–1975), funded by Challenge for Change. This series of short films placed the challenges of working women at the center of Canada's cultural production in order to raise awareness of their employment conditions. It was in fact a critique of the economic conditions of Canadian women. Eleven films were produced in this series: *The Spring and Fall of Nina Polanski* (Hutton et Roy, 1974), *Would I Ever Like to Work* (Shannon, 1974h), *Luckily I Need Little Sleep* (Shannon, 1974d), *Mothers Are People* (Shannon, 1974e), *Tiger on a Tight Leash* (Shannon, 1974g), *It's Not Enough* (Shannon, 1974b), *Extensions of the Family* (Shannon, 1974a), *They Appreciate You More* (Shannon, 1974f), *Like the Trees* (Shannon, 1974c), *Our Dear Sisters* (Shannon, 1975) and *They Lived Happily Ever After* (Angelico et Henderson, 1975). The films in the *Working Mothers* series were broadcast twice during a pan-Canadian tour in 1975. This broadcasting method is similar to that of the "*En tant que femmes*" [FR] series because the members of the distribution team "became determined to hear people's thoughts and feelings. Numerous 'kitchen screenings' gave women a space to conduct intimate discussions and to express opinions about their lives" (Ryohashi, 1995, p. 30). Women viewers recognized themselves in the documentaries which helped women become aware of the unequal treatment they received. Many films produced at Studio D had a profound impact on Canadian cinematography. It would take too long to list them all, but two productions related to my research interests caught my attention: *Some American Feminists* (Brossard *et al.*, 1978) and *Not a Love Story: A Film about Pornography* (Sherr-Klein, 1981).[15]

In 1975 and 1976, three women directors (Nicole Brossard, Luce Guilbeault and Margaret Westcott) went to New York to film *Some American Feminists* (Brossard *et al.*, 1978; Figure 4.3). They recorded interviews with radical feminists such as Betty Friedan, Kate Millett and Rita Mae Brown. The documentary seeks, among other things, to grasp the reasons for the identity crisis within the feminist movement[16] by revealing its internal divisions, particularly on the issue of race and lesbianism. Several perspectives clashed during the "second wave": homosexual feminists no longer recognized themselves in the feminism defended by heterosexual women, black feminists did not adhere to the preoccupations of white women, and American and French feminists were lost in the translation of transatlantic discourses. "Women's experiences multiply, transform, and seemingly distance them from the common conditions of oppression that had initially allowed them to come together" (Descarries et Corbeil, 1991, p. 354, our translation). The internationalization of the movement led to the multiplicity of perspectives, paving the way for the transformation and

FIGURE 4.3 *Some American Feminists.*

Source: **Brossard *et al.*, 1978, © NFB, all rights reserved.**

democratization of feminist movements. The theories of black feminism and lesbian feminism stemmed from these intersectional questionings:

> issues of racial or national identity compartmentalize the move-
> ment, and the common solidarity of women everywhere is quickly
> undermined by the suspicion of ignorance of the problems specific
> to each identity group, by the fear of seeing the creation of new
> forms of domination between homosexuals and heterosexuals,
> between bourgeois and proletarians, between mothers and non-
> mothers, between white women and black women.
>
> (Hirata *et al.*, 2004, p. 141, our translation)

Black Feminism emerged in the late 1960s. Domination was not only the product of gender, but also the result of class and race. Black femi-nists wanted to undo the stereotypes associated with black women. Part of Black Feminism also attacked White Feminism, which they deemed racist. Feminist groups evolved in parallel and, in the southern United States, some groups did not even mix racially. Southern feminists rejected the style of Northern lesbian feminists. By presenting a series of interviews with radical feminists, *Some American Feminists* provided "an insight into those activists who influenced the women's movement" (Carrière, 1981, p. 50, our translation).

Not a Love Story: A Film about Pornography (Sherr-Klein, 1981; Figure 4.4) must be mentioned as it is one of Studio D's most influential productions. This progressive documentary takes a look at pornography by portraying stripper Lindalee Tracy.

Because the film includes sexually explicit clips from hard-core pornographic films and magazines, the Saskatchewan Censor Board as well as the Ontario Censor Board banned it from public screening. However, there were about 300 private screenings in Ontario alone. In Montreal, the film became the largest grossing film in Film Board history as a result of a nine-month commercial run in theatres (Ryohashi, 1995, p. 34).

This film explores the representation of women's naked bodies in magazines, pornographic films and strip clubs. The director, Bonnie

FIGURE 4.4   *Not a Love Story: A Film about Pornography.*

Sherr-Klein, seeks to understand the reasons for the commodification of pornography. Lindalee Tracy, the protagonist who works as a stripper, does not believe she is a victim. She sees herself as a performer whose profession has taught her a lot about relationships between men and women. She does not expect arrogance or pity for her chosen profession.

The film shows that the democratization of access to pornography has enabled the industry to flourish. As a result, pornographic representations have become more and more daring and explicit. In an interview, Kate Millett stated that pornography does not end sexual repression, but rather encourages it. As competition increased and because editors wanted to stand out, the standards of what can be presented changed: the sexual depiction of women became increasingly violent and subjugating. In an interview, a pornographic magazine editor said that he believes that the women's revolution is to blame for the most popular male fantasy: having a woman on her knees performing oral sex. In this position, she is gentle and submissive. The images produced by this industry encourage the degradation of women while maintaining violent fantasies. There is no love; only raw sexuality, and a couple's intimacy and imagination can be polluted by it.

However, not all films are as radical, as the mandate of the program was to portray the various issues that women face. Studio D was therefore, in a way, caught between the feminist movement and cultural ghettoization: "Celebrated as a 'national treasure' and the only state-sponsored feminist film studio in the world, Studio D has been criticized for embracing the politics of 'liberal feminism', for producing rigid and reductive filmic representations of women" (Vanstone, 2003, p. iv). Since women directors created within a state-funded institution, this inevitably led to compromises:

> The institutional view is fundamentally the result of a State philosophy to formalize and channel the existence of lobbies. . . . The major characteristic of this view is that it draws its legitimacy and its means of intervention from its relationship with the State and that it acts as a mediator between the State apparatus and the women's revolt.
>
> (Lamoureux, 1986, p. 40, our translation)

As with the "*En tant que femmes*" [FR] series, Studio D productions were criticized for their representations of a bourgeois feminism, producing partial, limited and homogenous representations of Canadian women (white, heterosexual, educated and privileged middle class). Paradoxically, the representational limits of such feminism would essentially lie in the inability to reconcile radical feminism with the parameters of the State institution that produced the films, since the latter wanted to destroy the frameworks of society and sought to evolve outside the existing power structures. These productions therefore proposed an institutional feminism in which women producers and directors could create works only by complying with the ideological vision of the NFB. This is false. Some women creators enjoyed a great deal of freedom, but it was not without its challenges.

Films such as *Like the Trees* (Shannon, 1974c) and *Our Dear Sisters* (Shannon, 1975), both from the *Working Mothers* series, highlight the challenges that non-white women from non-privileged backgrounds face. *Our Dear Sisters* portrays Alanis Obomsawin, an Abenaki singer, filmmaker and single mother who never married. *Like the Trees* (Shannon, 1974c) is a short film made in Alberta that portrays Rose who discusses the stereotypes she faces as a Métis woman who wants to work in the city. To meet expectations, she would be required to have a specific haircut, wear high-heeled shoes, don a particular style of clothing, and speak English flawlessly.

Despite all of its productions, including the Oscar-winning film *If You Love This Planet* (Nash, 1982), the dissolution of Studio D was sanctioned in 1994 due to cuts made to the NFB by the federal government. The abolition of Studio D was a loss for all Canadians as the unit produced unique films about women's oppression from their perspective.

Regarding film animation, as I mentioned previously, Evelyn Lambart worked at the NFB from 1942 to 1974, collaborating with Norman McLaren before devoting herself solely to her own films. Before the NFB moved from Ottawa to Montréal, Alma Duncan and Audrey McLaren produced the animated film *Folksong Fantasy* (Duncan and McLaren, 1951; Figure 4.5). Denault wrote:

> [This film] was not released until 1951 and bears only Alma Duncan's name as animator. No one was named as director. . . . Other [women animators] were just passing through: Gretta Ekman and Helen MacKay, whom we have only come across by chance. Research tools in this field are so non-existent that we do not know whether chance will not allow us to discover others one day.
>
> (Denault, 1996, p. 75, our translation)

FIGURE 4.5   *Folksong Fantasy.*

Source: **Duncan et McLaren, 1951, © NFB, all rights reserved.**

In Montréal, Denault also discovered Alice Lemire who was hired in the animation department in 1958. She did animation on films but never acted as a director:

> Most of the women we traced remained in the shadows because they performed a variety of tasks, including animation, but without the official title of animator.... Without the title or the recognition in the credits, how could they and their work be identified?
> (Denault, 1996, p. 77, our translation)

While women employees at the NFB came together to create feminist production units through *"En tant que femmes"* [FR] and Studio D, no similar grouping occurred in the French and English animation departments. In animation, protests or demands for access to filmmaking were not made because, from the end of the 1960s—under the aegis of René Jodoin—, three women gained access to filmmaking.[17] In the early 1970s, several other women animators became directors of short films.

Most of these women were initially trained as interns or assistants on other people's productions, as it was impossible at the time to formally study animation. The first women directors to be assigned to an animation project usually began with educational films. Evelyn Lambart questionned mapmaking with *The Impossible Map* (Lambart, 1947). Clorinda Warny worked on mathematics with *Multiplication 1* (Warny, 1 (1971a) 1972), *Multiplication 2* (Warny, 2 (1971b) 1972) and *Multiplication 3* (Warny, 3 (1971c) 1971). Francine Desbiens was assigned to the chromatic range of colors in *The Little Men of Chromagnon* (Desbiens, 1971). Anastasia Michailidis directed *We* (Michailidis, 1974), a film about the importance of social acceptance. Joyce Borenstein also directed *Five Billon Years* (Borenstein, 1981) which focuses on the scientific aspect of the creation of the Earth.

As far as women's assistantship, it was a phenomenon that, for some, lasted for several years. Lambart devoted herself for more than twenty years to McLaren's career, Francine Desbiens assisted Bretislav Pojar in directing *Balablok* (Pojar, 1972) and *E* (Pojar, 1981), and Suzanne Gervais assisted Co Hoedeman on *Tchou-Tchou* (Hoedeman, 1972). However, it would be wrong to think that the phenomenon of assistantship is unidirectionally a men-women dynamic as several women animators were supported by other women animators. Notably Clorinda Warny who was assisted by Lina Gagnon and Suzanne Gervais for *Beginnings* (Warny, 1980). Suzanne Gervais began her career as an assistant to Clorinda Warny. Therefore, it cannot be said that assistantship at the NFB was a matter of women serving men. However, I did not find the opposite phenomenon, that is, men assisting women animators.

I have also noted that the vast majority of women animators were recruited for low-cost productions, including the *Poets on Films* series, which gave several of them their first opportunity. This series was a co-production that represented poems by Canadian authors. The recruits Bozenna Heczko, Elisabeth Lewis, Janet Perlman and Gayle Thomas worked on *Poets on Film No. 1* (Heczko *et al.*, 1977), Joyce Borenstein, Janet Perlman and Veronika Soul worked on *Poets on Film No. 2* (Borenstein *et al.*, 1977), and Francoise Hartmann worked on *Poets on Film No. 3* (Doucet et Hartmann, 1977). What should be pointed out is that, out of the ten animation filmmakers working on this very low production cost series, eight were women and two were men (Sheldon Cohen and Robert Doucet).

The "modernization" process of the status of women depended largely on the State, which "must set an example and be at the forefront of the change in social practices" (Lamoureux, 1986, p. 82, our translation). The next chapter focuses on the joint actions of the federal government and the NFB to highlight the International Women's Year in 1975.

NOTES

1. Concisely, egalitarian liberalism is a philosophy of equal opportunity. By applying egalitarian liberalism, the state creates a society that aspires to justice, freedom and equality (economic, social and political) of all its citizens. The fair distribution of resources, the recognition of human rights, and equitable access to services and jobs are fundamental pillars of the values promoted by egalitarian liberalism.
2. Florence Bird, for example, wanted to be called by her husband's first and last name: Mrs. John Bird.
3. Florence Bird, Elsie MacGill, Lola M. Lange, Jeanne Lapointe and Doris Ogilvie.
4. Jacques Henripin and John Humphrey.
5. Her first film was À l'heure de la décolonisation [FR] (Fortier, 1964), produced by Hubert Aquin.
6. Fortier did not direct any other films but devoted her career to editing. She worked with Anne Claire Poirier, Pierre Perrault and also with Denis Arcand on his film Le déclin de l'empire américain [FR] (Arcand, 1986).
7. Shulamith Firestone was a radical feminist, co-founder of the New York group Redstockings, and author of the acclaimed The Dialectic of Sex: The Case for Feminist Revolution (Firestone, 1970). Firestone wanted to deconstruct society to better rebuild it: she advocated the destruction of social organization. She believes that the sexual class system (Firestone, 1970) is the most important social and economic division and constitutes the epicenter of women's oppression. For her, pregnancy is barbaric, giving birth is like shitting a pumpkin (Firestone, 1970) and infancy is the supervision of a nightmare. Simone de Beauvoir said of Firestone's book that she is proposing something new because she links the liberation of women with the liberation of children (Faludi, 2013, our translation).
8. Behind the Miss America show, there are also commercial aims that promote and sell a seaside resort.
9. As we have seen, the division of production studios into two distinct administrative entities (French and English) in the early 1960s favored independent management of their employees' creative conditions. Thus, the feminist demands of both the French and English sides, although similar, were made in parallel and gave rise to two distinct initiatives: "En tant que femmes" for the French-speaking Canadians and Studio D for the English-speaking Canadians.
10. Translator's footnote: Radio-Canada is a state-owned TV channel. It is the French equivalent of CBC.

11. Four films were broadcasted without commercial breaks on Radio-Canada: *J'me marie, j'me marie pas* [FR] (January 9th 1974), *Souris, tu m'inquiètes* [FR] (January 16th 1974), *À qui appartient ce gage?* [FR] (February 27th 1974) and *They Called Us 'Les Filles du Roy'* [FR] (March 13th 1974).

12. Among others: *La beauté même* [FR] (Fortier, 1964), *Women on the March* (Tunstell, 1958) and *Our Sports Car Days* (Elnécavé, 1969).

13. Not too far, at the same time, there were the Vidéographe centre, the Groupe Intervention Vidéo and Vidéo Femmes (formerly named La femme et le film and founded in 1973 by Helen Doyle, Nicole Giguère and Hélène Roy). Vidéo Femmes is "a centre for the production and distribution, and animation of videos made by and for women. . . . It is a 'feminist collective of video intervention.' . . . Our choice of video as a means of expression and communication was made clearly and definitely at the official founding of our centre" (Giguère et Pérusse, 1980, p. 35, our translation). Indeed, video, being a more flexible and less expensive medium than film, becomes a favored and more accessible tool, particularly for women who "saw it as a preferred tool for social intervention" (Giguère et Pérusse, 1980, p. 35, our translation).

14. Translator's footnote: The original quote was taken from a text that was translated from English to French, however, since we were unable to find the original text, we have translated this quote back into English for the benefit of the reader.

15. Other films produced by Studio D explored taboo themes on childbirth such as *An Unremarkable Birth* (Beaudry, 1978), *Abortion: Stories from North and South* (Singer, 1984) and *A Mother and Daughter on Abortion* (Signer, 1987).

16. The beginning of an ideological split in the feminist movements was evident in the "first wave" as women questioned their fundamental role in modern society. Some also questioned the cultural expression of sex and the fabrication of gender and believed that attitudes and behaviors were standardized by normative heterosexuality.

17. In 1969, Viviane Elnécavé signed *Our Sports Car Days* (Elnécavé, 1969), then Francine Desbiens and Michèle Pauzé joined Pierre Hébert and Yves Leduc to co-direct *Le corbeau et le renard* [FR] (Desbiens *et al.*, 1969).

CHAPTER 5

A Film to Highlight the International Women's Year

IN CANADA, IN THE wake of the recommendations of the *Royal Commission on the Status of Women in Canada*, the 1970s saw the implementation of several pro-women initiatives. The Parliament of Canada passed the Divorce Act (1968); abortions became legal in hospitals (1969); Dr. Morgentaler opened his first abortion clinic in Montréal (1969); the Front de libération des femmes du Québec was founded (1969); women could be jurors (1971); in Québec women were elected to the House of Commons (1972); the Conseil du statut de la femme du Québec (1973) and the Canadian Advisory Council on the Status of Women (1973) were established; the Charter of human rights and freedoms formally prohibits discrimination on the basis of sex (1975); the recommendations of the Conseil du statut de la femme du Québec were published in *Pour les Québécoises. Égalité et indépendance* (1978), etc. These various initiatives show the feminist movements' ability to infiltrate political institutions.

The United Nations declared 1975 as the International Women's Year in order to promote women's rights throughout the world. The Canadian government followed suit and, in order to raise public awareness on the status of women and their socio-professional situation, commissioned the production of an animated film entitled *A Token Gesture* (Lanctôt, 1975).

DOI: 10.1201/9781032694382-7

This eight-minute color film was produced jointly by the federal government's Women's Program Department of the Secretary of State (Julie McGregor) and the NFB (Don Arioli and Wolf Koenig). From the start of the short film, the government wanted to work with Don Arioli to script the project, since he had written *Propaganda Message* (Nelson, 1974).

Propaganda Message is a short film highlighting preconceived ideas about Canadian identities (French and English-speaking, Black, Italian, Jewish, First Nations, etc.) and which uses a certain type of humor to, for example, challenge the prejudices that French-speaking and English-speaking Canadians have towards each other. Here is an excerpt from the film's narration:

> Le Canada est divisé par un conflit racial. Basically, the French are nice people but they are dominated by the church. Their families are too big. They are all anarchists trained in Algeria. They haven't got the brain to hold executive jobs. Anyways, they are all separatists. I must say, though, they have lots of rhythm . . . Les Anglais sont toutes pareils. Ils contrôlent tout. La haute finance, les grosses compagnies . . . Sont insensibles, froids, frigides même ! C'est toutes des monarchistes. Il faut admettre qu'ils sont plus doués pour les affaires. Mais ils ne savent pas jouir de la vie.
>
> (Nelson, 1974)

For the Women's Program, it was essential to use humor to convey the message on the status of women. The federal government therefore preferred using film animation as opposed to live-action films, since:

> many viewers may feel hostile or threatened by women's issues. The film attempts to make the viewer laugh at his/her own foibles while understanding the discriminatory attitudes which they reflect. Audiences expect to laugh at animation and such film can present ideas humorously which in a live action would be ponderous and threatening to the audience.
>
> (NFB Archives, s. d.)

The production wanted to illustrate how sexist attitudes prevented women from fully participating in all spheres of society; demonstrate how preconceived notions hinder women's access to equality; exemplify stereotypical representations in dominant discourses and foster the understanding of sexist behaviors while promoting a positive attitude towards the changing role of women in society.

Early internal communications between the NFB and the Women's Program indicated a desire to create an animated production to be overseen by Kathleen Shannon and Wolf Koenig. Strangely, at the end of the production process, Kathleen Shannon is absent from the credits. As the executive producer of Studio D, she had significant expertise on the situation of women in Canada. By looking at the film's content it can easily be understood why Shannon preferred to withdraw from the creation process.

A TOKEN GESTURE (LANCTÔT, 1975)

The film begins with a wide shot of a city. In a bedroom, awakened by the crying of a baby, a man, snug under the covers, says: "Honey, the baby is awake. While you are up, could you get breakfast? I'm starved. Honey? Honey? Sweetheart? Woo-hoo! Stella? Where are you?" (Lanctôt, 1975). Wide shot of the city. Several male voices intermingle and whine: "Where is my breakfast? Sylvia? Fiona? My sock has a hole in it! I'd like my coffee! Just get the phone . . . Where is my sponge?"

A plane passes through the sky: "This is your pilot speaking, I'll be serving drinks momentarily." It cuts to a shot where several men's faces are crying like babies: "They have left us!"

The faces of crying men are now on the first page of a book. A stocky man with a moustache sits at his desk, closes the book and throws it in the trash. He says: "This computer projection is ridiculous. It certainly can't happen here." He turns to his secretary, a slender, young blonde woman. He tells her: "Isn't that right Miss Nomer?[1]" She replies: "Yes sir!" The boss says: "I'd like my coffee now please." Miss Nomer automatically replies: "Yes sir!" If the character of the secretary is stereotyped (tall, thin, young and blonde), the boss is the opposite of the ideals of male beauty: small and fat. As he is represented in a caricatured way, he is not very credible (see Figure 5.1). When comparing the protagonists, there is a reversal in the physical stereotypes between men and women, as the secretary is taller than the boss. In a heteronormative world dominated by men, their deviations from the body norms are quite easily forgiven; however, those deviations are still denied to women. In the animation, being a short, paunchy and bald boss is still acceptable.

FIGURE 5.1   *A Token Gesture.*

The boss addresses the audience: "Hello . . . I'm the spokesman . . . Uh . . . The spokesperson. Hehe . . . for the Department of Needs and Responses. It's been brought to our attention that women appear to be victims of unfair treatment." The secretary moves slowly towards the office, a whip cracks above her head. A ball and chain are attached to her left arm making her movements difficult. This sequence shows the secretary must submit to her employer. The boss orders her: "Make that a black coffee!" Without flinching, Miss Nomer robotically goes back for a black coffee.

Sitting at his desk, the boss resumes: "In any case . . . We feel it is our duty to evaluate the issue from all angles." As Miss Nomer returns, the boss adds: "And curves!" He laughs loudly at his dirty joke, and Miss Nomer's cheeks redden. Furious, but remaining silent, she leaves. This film, in a way, denounces certain forms of sexual harassment that women are sometimes victims of at work. Later in the animation, the boss will even go so far as to pinch the secretary's cheek, which reddens under the strength of his hold. The boss thus allows himself a sexist comment by alluding to her curves and a second form of violence—physical—by granting himself permission to touch her face to pinch it.

The boss continues: "Ouh . . . Thank you, dear! It's quite possible we have ignored the demands of women. So the least we can do is make a TOKEN GESTURE.²" It then cuts to the title of the film, then to its opening credits. It is worth highlighting that the film credits are at the beginning of the short film rather than at the end. This is atypical for the NFB because, in the vast majority of films—not to say all of them—the credits are at the end. This may be a demonstration of the desire to emphasize that 22 women worked on a film dedicated to the International Women's Year, and only 16 men.

Sitting at his desk, the boss goes on: "Now then . . . First let's look at the facts." The background takes the appearance of graph paper. A woman changes position in order to translate the boss's words into images. "It has been established that women have a tendency to be smaller, weaker, gentler, more affectionate, cute, loyal and submissive." Here, the representation of "the" woman could not be more reductive: she is dressed in a pink bikini, high-heeled shoes and has long brown hair. As she is described, she dances, puts her hand to her forehead and pretends to faint to illustrate her weakness. This misogynistic description of feminine qualities culminates in the transformation of the woman into a pink dog who then transforms into the secretary bringing the boss a packet of mints. He tells her: "Isn't that so Miss Nomer? Did you get my mints, hum?" Without answering, the secretary places the box on the desk and leaves.

A second scene follows and a man changes his position to represent the boss's words. Still addressing the audience, the boss says: "On the other hand, men are taller, stronger, more competitive, aggressive and domineering." The woman has turned into a pet dog while the man turned into a big beast, resembling the Yeti. The man is compared to the woman, but his value is always reasserted in a better light, which reinforces the stereotypes of gender division and male superiority. The boss asks: "Right Miss Nomer?" Miss Nomer says: "Well. . . ," and without giving her time to answer, the boss rises from his chair and continues: "We do share some characteristics. For example, I happen to like pink. I can type. I hate washing dishes too." He then pinches Miss Nomer's cheek, which reddens under the strength of his hold. The secretary is angry. The boss says: "And I am not a very good driver." He returns to his desk and says: "I know, I know, we can't have babies. But you can't grow beards! Hahaha!" Sitting behind her typewriter, Miss Nomer seems bored. The man continues: "Now I am not saying that men are superior. But you cannot deny the evidence that history gives of man's inventive genius."

The next part casts a more positive look on the influence of women on society as it demonstrates their place in history. This third scene occurs in prehistoric times and showcases a man and a woman hitting rocks against another. Together, they start a fire. In the same frame, right next to them, a man writes the unfolding events on a slate. This historian writes: "And today, fire was discovered by a man and a wo . . . Hum . . . I am running out of space here . . . Man! That is good enough. They will get the idea." Due to a lack of space, the historian gave credit for this discovery to the "universal" man. This sequence efficiently illustrates how women were alienated from historical discourses despite their contribution to these events.

The next scene touches on the invention of the wheel which is presented as a collaboration between both sexes rather than an invention exclusively made by men. In the Egyptian empire, a man runs to the edge of a cliff holding a round stone and jumps down screaming: "Honey, I have just discovered the parachute!" At the bottom of the cliff, the woman picks the man up by his feet. The man, tied to his "parachute," is carried by the woman like a wheelbarrow. This represents the common invention of the wheel. The historian writes: "Once again, man surprises us with his genius. The invention of the wheel will undoubtedly open up new avenues for mankind."

Back in the office, the boss says: "And another thing you cannot deny are the biological facts. Boys are boys and girls are girls. And we are born that way." A long scene on biological stereotypes follows. The background consists in a graph paper divided in two: a blue left side and a pink right side. Two naked babies are sitting next to each other. Man narrator: "Hey it's a boy! Have a cigar!" Woman narrator: "Ho . . . It's a girl. Have some candy and flowers!" The baby on the left now has a blue outfit and the baby on the right, a pink one. Man narrator: "Hi Son . . . look at those muscles, wow!" Woman narrator: "Isn't she cute? Isn't she dainty? Hello sweetheart!" A brown teddy bear appears on the lap of the baby dressed in blue. Man narrator: "Gee, I hope he does not rip it apart!" The same teddy bear appears on the lap of the baby attired in pink. Woman narrator: "I hope it is not too heavy for her!" The baby boy stands up, his legs are shaking. Man narrator: "He stood up! He is strong as an ox!" The baby girl stands up, her legs are shaking. Woman narrator: "She is standing, what a little baby girl." The little boy is now wearing shorts and a t-shirt whereas the girl is wearing a pink dress. The boy tries to look under the girl's dress and she pulls his shorts down. Together, the man and the woman narrators intervene: "You mustn't play with those. No! No! No! Play with these." A little red truck appears in the boy's hands and a doll appears in the girl's. Man narrator: "That's a boy! Hahahaha!"

The little girl is now dressed in a tutu. Woman narrator: "Isn't she cute? Ho, you will make a wonderful dancer." The little boy is dressed as a boxer. Man narrator: "Come on, toughy! Put on those gloves and don't be a sissy." Woman narrator: "Come on now, show us how you can dance. Oh, no, no . . . You are as clumsy as a boy." The boy accidentally hits the little girl. Man narrator: "Not so rough, she is only a girl!"

In front of the grey graph paper serving as a background, the boy turns into a teen. In the public sphere, he replicates the actions stated by the masculine voice. Man narrator: "Be a man and pass the test. Smoke and swagger like the rest. Drink a beer and crush the can. Don't let on you hurt your hand. Show them real and act real though. Don't be like a powder puff. And when the girls come out to play, rig them in on manly way."

The little girl also transformed into a young woman. She is in a house and replicates the actions uttered by the feminine voice. Woman narrator: "Now when you are walking down the street, this is how to move your feet. Make sure you are not too fat or strong, you don't want the boys to take you wrong! Pluck your eyebrows and dye your hair, act shy, helpless when he is there. And don't be clever or too smart. That is no way to win his heart." The man and the woman get married, and kiss with stars in their eyes. This segment highlights gender stereotypes, individual worth as well as the inequalities in how the little boy and the little girl are treated by their parents. The woman's power lies in her beauty, her seduction. Her social success is based on marriage in which the husband provides her with respectability and stability. In this universe, singleness is seen as a failure.

At work, the boss considers an alternative thought: "And if that won't make them happy, we'll pass a law making everyone the same. That would be something, wouldn't it? I can see it now . . ." A baby cries. The man and the woman get out of bed at the same time and say, one after the other: "I'll get up. I'll get up." They run in their bedroom and into each other. The parents say: "I'll get the baby. I'll get the baby." The mother holds the baby in her arms and the father tries to take it away from her. They say: "I'll burp the baby. I'll burp the baby." The parents are in the kitchen and sweep the floor. "I'll clean and sweep. No, no, I'll clean and sweep." The man and the woman try to get out of the house at the same time, but they get stuck in the doorframe that is too small for the two of them: "I'll go to work. I'll go to work." At the restaurant, the spouses fight for the bill: "I'll pay. No, no, I'll pay." On a construction site, the woman tries to take the jackhammer from the man: "I'll dig the hole. I'll dig the hole." Both are dressed as goal-keepers and try to stop the pucks that are thrown at them: "I got it. I got it." The man and the woman are astronauts in space and are linked to their rocket ship by a tube: "I'll close the airlock. I'll close the airlock." Both are in bed: "I'll get on top. No, I'll get on top. Let me get on top. It's OK, I'll get on top. Come on! Then we both get on top." The two characters try to do the exact same things at the exact same time which is counterproductive. This slightly foul humour highlights men's deep incomprehension and the inef-fectiveness of official or "common sense" solutions. Equality does not con-sist in two people doing the same things at the same time. In his office, the boss concludes: "This may be a utopian ideal but we are striving to make it a reality. This file is under . . . Under . . . Equality. Miss Nomer? Miss Nomer? Miss Nomer! " A large shot of the city where multiple voices of whimpering men arise. "They have left us!" This marks the end of the film.

REVEALING ARCHIVES ON THE ORIGIN OF THE INSTITUTIONAL DISCOURSE

Three references to *A Token Gesture* appear in the NFB's archived pro-gramming committee reports: two in 1975 (see Figure 5.2) and one in 1976. The first occurred in the meeting of February 13, 1975, at which

```
4.  Token Gesture - Executive Producer:  Wolf Koenig
                     Producer:            Julie McGregor
                     Director:            Don Arioli
                     Length:              8-10 minutes
                     Audience:            General
                     Cost:                $111,240  ($29,505 outside)
                     Co-sponsor's (Secretary of State's) share:  $77,000

    An animated film about the need for changed attitudes towards women in our
    society.
```

FIGURE 5.2 Excerpt of the English programming committee's report from February 13, 1975.

Source: © NFB, all rights reserved.

12 women and 11 men were present. Nevertheless, only two women and six men[3] had the right to vote on the film's production launch.

At that time, employees were discussing the scenario rather than the finished film. It should be noted that Micheline Lanctôt, the director of the film, was absent from the meeting. Furthermore, her hiring letter as director dates from April 3, 1975, two months after that meeting. On February 13, official documentation on the presentation of the project's scenario to the programming committee did not mention Micheline Lanctôt as its director, but rather Don Arioli.

During that presentation of the scenario, Julie McGregor who worked for the Women's Program explained that the short film was initially made for a general public although the storyboard presented to the committee for approval was primarily geared towards men.

Irene Angelico, an observing director at the meeting, criticized the storyboard and qualified the end of the film as confusing with this version showing the women leaving when they were offered to work collaboratively with the men. This could have been given the impression that women left the labor market because they did not wish to share the burden of professional work which completely went against the pursued goal. Don Arioli agreed with the fact that the end of the film could be misinterpreted and mentioned how the storyboard submitted to the committee consisted in a first draft to which multiple changes would be brought during production.

Other people expressed similar criticism. Gloria Demers opposed to the production of the film. With the storyboard subject to so many changes, she asked that the storyboard be resubmitted to the programming committee who no longer knew exactly what it was voting on. "However, members of the Committee seemed reassured by the fact that the content was to be supervised by a woman who, in her official position, was hardly likely to let anything pass which might prove objectionable to women" (NFB Archives, February 13, 1975).

The programming committee concluded that one woman's opinion (Julie McGregor's), corresponded to all women's opinion. If Julie McGregor did not feel insulted by the film's message, all women would agree. In other words, the storyboard did not really receive a final approval. Out of the eight people entitled to vote (six men and two women), seven people were in favor of the approval whereas the other refrained from voting. It seems that the voting members did not consider the objections of the "observing" women who were against the storyboard's content. This version of the storyboard to which unknown changes would be applied was approved as "definitive." During the next meeting, reproof was administered to the programming committee:

> As for *A Token Gesture*, the Chairman had been criticized after the meeting by a couple of the women who were present for not asking for a resubmission. So much was going to be changed in the storyboard that they felt that the committee did not actually know what it was voting on. His own feeling had been that the woman producer from the Secretary of State's office was a sufficient insurance—she was not likely, and could not afford, to make a film that would offend women. As well, there had been enough women at the meeting to object if they found the situation really objectionable. It had been suggested that he should have encouraged them to speak up, which he felt would have been condescending. He suggested that if the women on the committee had asked for it to be resubmitted, he would have put that to the vote.
>
> (NFB Archives, February 20, 1975)

There was the display of a deep internal discomfort regarding the project meant to highlight the International Women's Year. The women who attended the meeting as "observants" (who were also numerically dominant which might have been a first in that type of meeting) expressed how they were not listened to. Even though, some of them truly communicated their discontent during the meeting of February 13, 1975. Were the quiet others reluctant to express their opinion for fear of being ridiculed?

This situation is worrisome considering how the film's theme touched on the revaluation of the equal status between men and women in the labor market. The assembly's president, Arthur Hammond, responded by putting the blame on the women: if they were unsatisfied, they should have expressed their opinion and he would have called for another submission. However, the women who spoke up did not hold the right to vote. This meeting of February 20, 1975 continued and the president made no efforts to respond to the women's discontent. This lack of intervention confirms that the women's opinions did not hold the same value as the men's. However, the final report of the film's production says: "The storyboard was presented and approved by the NFB/ONF Program Committee on February 13, 1975" (NFB Archives, n. d.). The storyboard's content was never brought up again, despite the worker's denunciations. Official documentation on the production report makes no mention of the women's discontent nor the dividedness on the content. Ironically, the NFB's decision process reproduced what it had aimed to denounce.

However, the Women's Program was very clear on the procedure to create the film: "No changes can be made after final storyboard approval as each frame must be coordinated exactly to sound and script" (NFB Archives, September 16, 1974). The storyboard was brought into the production stage without being definite. In internal documentation, Arthur Hammond wrote a memorandum to Wolf Koenig, Julie McGregor and Don Arioli:

> After the program meeting on February 13, I was fairly heavily criticized by a couple of people for not having asked that the storyboard of *Token Gesture* be resubmitted when it had been revised. . . . My own feeling was that Julie McGregor's connection with the film was a guarantee that nothing would emerge that was going to offend women. I also felt that there were enough women at the meeting to object if they felt something was objectionable. However, I have been told that some of those present were still somewhat hesitant to speak up in the committee and that their silence did not indicate total peace of mind about the project. However, at the following meeting, when this was discussed, I said that I would write you this note to say that there are a number of women who would like the opportunity of seeing the revised storyboard . . . and I'm sure you won't object to their looking at it and discussing it with you, if they feel inclined to.
>
> (NFB Archives, March 12, 1975)

In her response to this note, Julie McGregor also confirmed her intention to pursue the making of the film despite the disregarded women's discomfort. In this memorandum, she answered:

> I am a strong believer in the "speak now or forever hold your peace maxim." While recognizing that women in our society have never been taught to be assertive and outspoken, I felt there was ample opportunity for women to contribute at that meeting and afterwards. . . . I felt totally at ease and free to talk at the program

committee meeting. . . . Women, as well as men, must learn to speak their feelings in spite of their socialization. If they do not have 'total peace of mind' about a project, they must be prepared to verbalize those feelings even in intimidating circumstances. . . . To me, to keep silent at that point is to forfeit the right to be critical later. . . . I am satisfied with the storyboard and my concern now is that production be hurried along so that we may release the film on time.

(NFB Archives, March 21, 1975)

There was no further follow-up on the controversy around the content of the storyboard after Julie McGregor's memorandum. When researching for this book, a storyboard of the film, most probably the programming committee's "approved" version, was found. The beginning of the screenwriting project and the actual film are mostly alike: a man wakes up and, in his bed, searches for his wife to fill his and the baby's needs. Then, throughout the city, men call for women's services.

However, it is surprising that certain excerpts of the storyboard were left as is in the short film. The decision to keep the correlation between the submission of women and dog obedience is rather questionable (see Figure 5.3).

Some scenes were cut. In the second excerpt, the boss is thinking of the best term to refer to women: "It's about time we recognize whatever you wish to call them, the better half, the weaker sex, the female of the species, after all, they do make up to 52% of the vote er . . . public!" (Arioli, n.d.; see Figure 5.4). This is a pejorative way of describing women. The boss implies that he only acknowledges women because of the political weight granted to them by their right vote.

FIGURE 5.3   Excerpt of the storyboard (1) of *A Token Gesture*.

Source: Arioli, n. d., © NFB, all rights reserved.

The third excerpt, which was also cut, shows the boss embracing his secretary in a way that, in terms of current norms, showcases a typical demonstration of unwanted sexual contact which is also a form of sexual harassment: he presses his head on her breasts. He maintains gender stereotypes by believing that flower-patterned clothes are the opposite of masculinity which is, in this case, symbolized by his chest hair (Figure 5.5). Some of these ideas remained in the final cut after having been slightly modified, such as the part on social representations of women and the professional stereotypes to which they are confronted.

FIGURE 5.4   Excerpt of the storyboard (2) of *A Token Gesture*.

Source: **Arioli, n. d., © NFB, all rights reserved.**

FIGURE 5.5   Excerpt of the storyboard (3) of *A Token Gesture*.

Source: **Arioli, n. d., © NFB, all rights reserved.**

"Typist, teacher, secretary, nurse. . . . These are jobs to look for first" (Arioli, n. d.; Figure 5.6). The final film does not show prestigious careers for women either. Feminine careers have long been limited. Women work in factory, retail, office and care (social workers, maids, nurses and teachers). These low prestige jobs are usually paid less than those held by men. "Housewife, Mother—learn those too. . . . That might be the life for you. Also learn to cook and sew—and meet a guy with dough" (Arioli, n. d.). There was the precise sexism denounced by women of that time: the idea that women produced a "capital" (kids). They gave their existence meaning with housework and remained financially dependent. The message was that if a woman was trained as queen of the house, she could meet a rich man that would support her needs. That is where her happiness resided. This message which was not necessarily meant to be taken at face value was very conservative and although not radical, still slightly allowed for the questioning of stereotypes. Fortunately, this part did not appear in the film either.

Apart from its content, an essential part of the analysis of *A Token Gesture* regards women's participation in its creation and production (see Figure 5.7). Julie McGregor was granted the title of producer. On

FIGURE 5.6 Excerpt of the storyboard (4) of *A Token Gesture*.

Source: **Arioli, n. d., © NFB, all rights reserved.**

FIGURE 5.7 Excerpt of the storyboard (5) of *A Token Gesture*.

Source: **Arioli, n. d., © NFB, all rights reserved.**

February 13, 1975, during a meeting of the programming committee, the president asked McGregor whether she had worked in production to which she had replied "no."

She added that she felt uneasy with being named producer of the film. It did not feel right since her work rather consisted in focusing on content. The attribution of the producer title to Julie McGregor was contested internally. In the film's files, an anonymous note mentions: "It should be noted that Wolf Koenig named Julie executive producer knowing that she had no knowledge of film production. The only valuable reason is that a film produced for the International Women's Year had to have a woman appear in its credits. Nice, rigged story and another chapter on the team director's stumbles" (NFB Archives, August 12, 1975, our translation).

In the fall of 1975, before the film was completed, Julie McGregor was internally reassigned to state secretary relationships. Her superior was therefore required to continue production supervision. It is rather rare for a producer to pull from the ongoing production of a film. In the archives, another document mentions the staff that was to be assigned to the film:

> One of the first requirements of the production was that it employs women wherever possible in the production. Micheline Lanctôt, a gifted animator and a talented actor, was chosen to animate and direct the film. Women were drawn from all parts of NFB/ONF to contribute their skills. Because the Women's Program felt that all the women who were involved in the production should be given credit, the list of credits is slightly longer than usual.
>
> (NFB Archives, n. d.)

Considering this excerpt, multiple questions arise. If the credits are longer than usual, does it imply that it is common for women working in film production not be included in the credits? What about Micheline Lanctôt who was catapulted, in April of 1975, to the ongoing production of the film while seemingly having no control over its content? Should it be concluded that she was given the position in replacement of Don Arioli, as a figurehead, to promote how the film had been directed by a woman? What were Micheline Lanctôt's true status and role? Did she have an influence over the work and its content? Who is speaking in this film? To whom? By whom? Whose voice is heard?

In April 1976, the film was selected by Columbia for theatrical distribution.

> A *Token Gesture* was screened for a total of 267 days between July 1976 and the end of March 1977, multiplied by the number of daily screenings determined by the theatres themselves. A *Token Gesture* seems to have been particularly popular in Toronto and Vancouver.
>
> (Dennie, April 22, 1976, our translation)

However, this distribution only reached an English-speaking audience. The French version of the film was never made due to a funding issue: which of the two organizations should have provided the necessary funds to direct the French version? Women's Program believed that the necessary $12,000 to pay for the French version should have come from the NFB and the NFB believed the Woman's Program should have provided the funds. Multiple official documents report the back and forth between different actors on the necessity of producing a French version. Beyond the issues related to funding, including the idea of equally sharing the fees, the impossibility of the French version's production was clear: "its humor (!!!) cannot be rendered in French. . . . A French version of the film would lead to ridiculing reactions to which the secretariat, and us, would fall victim" (Charette, January 26, 1977, our translation). In another memorandum, Jean-Paul Vanasse wrote:

> As the president, though unwillingly, of the Versions committee, I'm forced to tell you unpleasant news that you will know how to make the sponsor swallow. The committee unanimously disagreed with a French version of *A Token Gesture*, not for its corniness, but for its type of humor that finds no equivalent in French, making it ineligible for another version or a translation. We believe that it's enough to be "idiots" in only one language.
>
> (Vanasse, March 4, 1977, our translation)

As specified by Lucile Bishop in a memorandum, this impossibility to translate the film put a stop to its distribution, since "the ministry is required to release everything in the two official languages: brochures, books, films, and that, simultaneously. The original version was therefore shelved except for the 35 mm version distributed by Columbia" (Bishop, April 22, 1976, our translation). In *A Token Gesture*, the main character is a man, and his secretary stays silent. However, in a memorandum, Julie McGregor wrote of the intended film she wished to make with the NFB:

> Now I don't mean that the film should be anti-male because that would defeat the whole purpose but I am concerned that it not to be a film about a man's reaction to the women's movement. It would be very wrong to make the man the central character of the thing even if he is portrayed as a bombing or befuddled.
>
> (NFB Archives, October 31, 1974)

McGregor spoke of a feminine character that would ponder over the representation of women in the media and the way these representations diverged with those women aspire to. McGregor also wrote:

> What I think you could stress here is the unrealistic fears that men have about what that restructured society will be like—is this really an end to Mom and Apple Pie, will hordes of bra-burning women swoop down and take away his job, chain him to the kitchen sink and they retire in the library for brandy and cigars. I really think that most men are not afraid of thinking, breathing, independent women but rather of some obscure "liberated women" image that is tucked away in some dark corner of the jock strap.
>
> (NFB Archives, October 31, 1974)

McGregor spoke of a woman protagonist that would be a pilot or a CEO. A woman character that would be no superwoman, nor a radical feminist opposed to motherhood, but that would react to the discrimination of which she was a victim. McGregor asked that the film touched on the true oppression of women, such as the lack of access to daycare and the loss of freedoms in marriage. "Many women now find that going to work has merely meant they are doing twice as much work as before rather than changing the marriage and domestic arrangements" (NFB Archives, October 31, 1974). Considering the finished version of the film, some may wonder whether Don Arioli actually read Julie McGregor's note. Her suggestions were very relevant. What was the balance of power between

McGregor, Arioli and Koenig? McGregor ends her description of the project which she sent to Arioli and Koenig:

> Sorry if these ideas don't seem too clear (but women are so illogical) or if they conflict with discussions we have had before (it's a woman's right to change her mind). Of course, you couldn't have guessed what we wanted (women, on the other hand, are so intuitive). Just writing this has made me so excited about doing the film (women are so emotional), and I'm really looking forward to meeting with you on Thursday (I hope the moons are right, women are influenced by them, you know). I enjoy working with you both so much—but then you men are so masterful.
>
> (NFB Archives, October 31, 1974)

McGregor hereby made statements filled with sarcasm and irony to her masculine peers. However, like Micheline Lanctôt, she did not oppose herself to their vision. This hints that she might have given Arioli and Koenig *carte blanche* for the film's content. She failed to act on the power she possessed with the role of producer that had been given to her. At last, *A Token Gesture* did not participate in changing gender representations: this film is neither radical, nor does it make claims for change. The woman protagonist is a submissive secretary unable to stand up and express her discontent. McGregor wanted a woman protagonist that had the power to act, but that was not shown in the film. It should also be highlighted that *A Token Gesture* touches on the exploitation of a white, skinny, blonde, woman. Women were exploited and affected differently based on the sexist measures of the labor market. There were yet no allusions to the systematic discrimination based on age, race or appearance. The representation of the secretary reinforced the domination stereotypes found in professional hierarchies. Miss Nomer served the man and failed to express her opinion on her situation. She did not stand up for herself, nor did she express herself. The audience never gets to hear her. Should a link be made between the secretary's situation and the NFB's workers who wished for the storyboard to be changed before being moved to production? The secretary never took back ownership of her voice, nor expressed her thoughts on her professional, social, economic and political domination. Wouldn't a discussion with the man have allowed her to assert her point of view?

This film did not touch on essential issues, such as women's true battles against rape, exploitation, violence, daycare, free access to abortion, sexual liberation, etc. Some may want to blame feminist animated films directed at the NFB in the 1970s for having failed to talk about domestic violence and rape, but was it even possible? There might have been censorship and a will, on the NFB's part, to avoid talking about these matters. *A Token Gesture* does not either talk about the basis of intersexual relations, the exclusion of a sex by another.

A Token Gesture did not fulfil its potential to put forth a feminist experience and subjectivity despite the many topics that could have been explored. There were no signs of resistance in what was shown and no difference in gender representations. Produced within the limits of an institutional feminism, it did not represent strong emancipated women that challenged the system and social order. Where was the female gaze in that story? It could only have been found with a production willing to accept the subjectivity of a personal and solidary point of view.

The first part of this book allowed to establish women's socioprofessional conditions in Canada along with the infiltration of feminist claims in the cinematographic device of the State. The second part will focus on the analysis of women animators' personal works in the 1970s and 1980s. The selected films eloquently illustrate the professional situation of women artists at the NFB based on the very fact that they are women.

NOTES

1. A *misnomer* is the inaccurate use of a term to refer to something that has a moral or political value. In English grammar, it is emphasized that the misnomer is often a product of the language's history, in the same way as metaphors or anachronisms. This pun could represent the boss' misuse of his secretary as a servant without considering her opinion. In no case does he address her as his equal. When he asks for her opinion, he does not expect her to answer.
2. Here, a *token* could be interpreted as a symbol. In the film, the boss, acting as a spokesperson, tries to help improve the condition of women. However, behind his façade, he is condescending and not very credible. In the title of the film, *token* is used as an adjective to qualify the symbolic gesture of the State and its willingness to educate the population on the importance of achieving equality between men and women. With this film, the NFB and the federal government are making a token gesture.
3. Arthur Hammond (programming director), Bob Verrall (production manager), John Boundy and Barbara Janes (distribution representatives),

and cineasts John Spotton, Mike McKennirey, Bill Pettigrew, and Ginny Sikeman attended the meeting. Mike Rubbo, Leonard Goodman, Wolf Koenig, Don Arioli, Dorothy Courtois, Gloria Demers, Doug MacDonald, Maureen Mosseau, Julie McGregor, Louise Spence, Janet Preston, Carmel Kelly, Irene Angelico, Beverly Schaeffer, and Anne Gally also attended the meeting as observants which meant that they did not hold the right to vote but were allowed to express their opinions.

2

Animated Films Under the Feminist Lens

CHAPTER 6

Motherhood, Mental Load and Mystification

S IMONE DE BEAUVOIR, FROM THE end of the 1940s, sheds light on the differential power between the social construct that is gender (which mandates feminine or masculine behavior) and biological sex in her writings and denounces the secondary position in which women are confined in society.[1] Beauvoir being the first to declare that society is responsible for making up the "female" gender thus foresees the theory of social constructivism and the imposition of specific roles according to sex. She suggests a project for the liberation of women:

> One is not born, but rather becomes, woman. No biological, psychic, or economic destiny defines the figure that the human female takes on in society; it is civilization as a whole that develops this intermediary product between the male and the eunuch that is called feminine.
>
> (Beauvoir, 1953a, p. 273)

She proposes a phenomenology of women's experience in the androcentric society in which she reports their submission. Beauvoir argues this domination either exerted by force or suggested by conditioning, results from a set of rules, symbols, roles and attitudes imposed by the male privileged group. In stating the mechanisms of social constructivism, she presents a new perspective on the marginalization of women and the attitudes they

DOI: 10.1201/9781032694382-9

have to adopt to avoid exclusion. Her political writings advocating for the progress and the emancipation of women allowed for a certain institutionalization of the feminist discourse. Simone de Beauvoir criticizes representations with the will to change them: she offers a social analysis of the subordinate role assigned to women in the institutions that are marriage, motherhood, and the labor market. She notices that the androcentric society model confines women to dependency and subjugation to men. Dividing the sexes and establishing a hierarchy allow for the exploitation of women's labor while claiming that their work is worth for less than the work of their male counterparts.

To shed light on the social construct of motherhood, this part will focus on a colored animated short film titled *Happiness Is*. The film of seven minutes was directed in 1972 by Clorinda Warny and produced by Gaston Sarault. It tells the story of a young mother pushing her inconsolable baby around in a stroller. In vain, she tries to calm her baby down by all possible means. She starts feeling anger, helplessness and disarray. Then, childcare professionals, all men, come to offer advice. The toy retailer believes she should encourage her child's development through play, the psychoanalyst looks for the solution in the child's repression of his unconscious whereas the military trains the baby to be submitted to orders. The men fight to determine which one of them offers the best solution.

HAPPINESS IS (WARNY, 1972)

Similar to Evelyn Lambart, Clorinda Warny started directing animated films at the NFB, with three animated educational films[2] pertaining to Zoltan Dienes' mathematical theories. The objective of these films is to offer a visual demonstration of the concept of multiplications to facilitate children's comprehension. *The Egg* (1971) was Warny's first personal film directed at the NFB: it is an impressionist exploration of the cycle of life in different cultures and civilizations, such as Egypt, India, and Greece. *Happiness Is* is her fifth solo project at the NFB.

At the beginning of *Happiness Is* (Figure 6.1),[3] the mother proudly walks around with her baby in a stroller. She is happy and her smile is bright. She is pretty and well dressed, visibly put together for her outing: hair and makeup done, she even wears high heels for her walk in the park, thus conforming to the standards of beauty spread by mass media. The park, the location of their stroll, is not trivial as there are few public places where one can go with a newborn. If society glorifies cute and quiet babies, those

FIGURE 6.1   *Happiness Is.*

who scream are banned. Thus, mothers are ghettoized in specific spaces where they can spend time with their babies without bothering others. At the park, loud and dirty children are tolerated, and access is free.

On their stroll, the two protagonists meet a black cat in which they take a lot of interest. A close-up on the mother's face shows she is calm and radiant. A close-up on the baby's face shows he is peaceful and fulfilled. In this silent film, attention to non-verbal speech is crucial. The mother's face is very expressive and displays the wide range of emotions that a woman caring alone for her baby can experience.

The two continue their stroll and meet a priest, engrossed in a large book. Representing a physical incarnation of the divine authority in Catholicism, priests have long been an emblematic figure (in the province of Québec) of morality, righteousness and of acceptable social behaviour. The priest holds a big purple book, most likely breviary. Catholicism, which has had a big influence on Québec's society, had a crucial role in the sexual division of labor by relegating women to the private sphere and unpaid labor, such as childcare. When he crossed paths with the mother, the priest raises his eyes and smiles at her seemingly approving the stay-at-home status of the woman whom he salutes politely.

The mother decides to take a break and sits on a bench. A small white, red and yellow butterfly circles around the stroller. The protagonists are delighted and hypnotized by the butterfly's movements. A medium shot depicts the mother relaxing on a park bench, followed by a change in her expression as she loses her smile. She hurries to her screaming baby. To soothe the baby, the mother gently rocks the stroller, but the baby appears oblivious to his mother's presence at his side, attempting to console him. The mother starts moving the stroller vigorously, but nothing works. The baby remains eyes shut, overwhelmed by his tantrum. The mother then has an idea: she grabs the pacifier from the stroller and places it gently in the baby's mouth. Sat on the bench, full of hope, she watches him. He stops crying and sucks avidly, before spitting it out, leading it to land on the ground. Taken aback, the mother picks it up, and, without cleaning it, places it back in the infant's mouth. Instantly, he spits it out again. The mother grows very frustrated. She jumps up, gestures, her mouth distorted, face tense and hair a mess. Exhausted and defeated, she sits back down on the bench.

Noticing the flash of a camera, the mother pulls herself together. She fixes her hair and smiles. After all, she is in a public sphere. Although the editing initially implies that the mother is the focus of the shots being taken, it ultimately reveals that another woman is the subject of the photographs. Sat next to the mother on the bench, the lady is getting her picture taken. The photographer and his model completely ignore the mother and her crying baby. In the collective imagination, mothers do not exist as sexual objects. In their youth, women define themselves in regard to their beauty; later in regard to motherhood—yet these two states are temporary.

Unsuccessfully, the mother keeps on trying to distract her baby with silly faces. She grows angry again: her expression changing back to distress, her hair tousled again. Ellipsis. If the length of the baby's tantrum is hard to determine, the two following scenes provide time markers. The first shot of a building clock displays the last ten minutes to noon quickly passing by. The second shot then displays a thundering cannon giving way to the formation of a white cloud taking over the screen. Ellipsis.

The mother has another idea. She takes out the bottle from the stroller and offers it to the baby. He calms down and drinks for a few seconds before throwing the bottle to the ground. Shocked, the mother roughly places it back in the baby's mouth. Once more, the bottle lands on the ground. The mother's anger then turns into complete discouragement and she starts to cry.

A man of a respectable age, dressed in a suit and tie, arrives. He walks towards the mother who starts to smile again. He asks about the mother's disarray and introduces her to two other men: a doctor and a military officer. Considering that all of the characters who come to offer advice to the mother are men, this scene perpetuates the stereotype of the tearful woman the male protagonist must "save" and sparks the question of whether there are other women and mothers in *Happiness Is*. As detailed in the following paragraphs, these professionals either seem to promote incorrect knowledge or an expertise that suits them. There are three segments in the film: these variations in the narrative propel the viewers in the universes of the male protagonists. Will they convince the mother that there is such a thing as the maternal instinct? A cloud appears in the middle of the screen. Ellipsis.

In the first scene, the baby is alone in a grey space: he is red and screams in anger. A box falls from the sky and piques his curiosity. A rope comes close to him and a lever appears. The baby rushes to press on it. A colored beach ball comes out of the box. The baby plays with the ball and feels pleasure. He presses on the mechanism multiple times and a variety of objects comes out of the box: a book which he rips in two, a cart that he pushes around, a small blue chair, building blocks, a trumpet, a small car, a pistol, a teddy bear, a doll, a board game, a frog, a rocking horse, etc. The space fills up with toys and the baby is happy. The first scene ends, the cloud explodes and brings the viewers back to the initial narrative universe. In the park, the man offers his business card to the mother who is happy to discover that boredom is probably the cause of her baby's discomfort. The doctor intervenes, visibly disagreeing with the toy retailer. He walks towards the mother and shows her a piece of paper. A cloud forms in the middle of the screen. Ellipsis.

The second segment brings the viewer in a psychiatrist's office. This part of the film could lead to an analysis of desire, jealousy, sexual interest, curiosity about one another, rejection from the source of desire, narcissism, revenge and violence. In a way, the viewer attends the psychoanalytic process in which the patient frees himself of his demons. The segment begins in the doctor's office where a nurse is bringing in the crying baby in a trolley. A trash can rolls by itself next to the trolley. At that moment, the baby splits in two and separates from his body. He imagines himself devouring a multi-layered cake. After eating the whole cake, he starts feeling bad and turns green. Every visual element of this imaginative sequence throws itself in the trash can.

The original baby is still yelling in anger in the office while the doctor takes notes. Another split occurs: the baby separates from his body and holds a red apple. By his side, a taller child steals the apple, hits him on the head and bites into the fruit. Wrought up, the baby starts to cry. The visual elements move and this hypothesis joins the first one in the trash can. On the trolley, the baby keeps on crying. The third split occurs rapidly: the baby changes into a surrealist blue doll which directly goes on its own to join the scraps in the trash can.

In the fourth split, the baby is sitting in front of a blonde-haired lady. Seemingly courting her, he talks to her and tries to look underneath her skirt. The lady hits him on the head. The scene lands in the trash. In the fifth and last split, the baby fights with a brown-haired lady. He grabs a gun and shoots her; she falls on the ground and dies. These ideas also end up in the trash can.

In the psychiatrist's office, a small white cloud explodes from the head of the baby and he feels a lot better: his complexion has regained its normal appearance and he has stopped crying. He externalized repressed thoughts from his unconscious. On its own, the trash can rolls and exits the room carrying all of the baby's externalized aches. Back to the first narrative universe, the doctor gives his business card to the mother who appears delighted to be offered a solution to help her baby. However, the first man walks towards the doctor and the two start arguing. The military officer intervenes and separates them.

The military officer starts talking and a cloud forms in the middle of the screen. Ellipsis. In the third and last scene, the military officer trains seventeen identical babies. The babies take part in various physical exercises, and, like little soldiers, they obey. They follow the same rhythm, they are synchronized, they are robotic. The little soldiers practice showing their emotions: joy, anger, sadness. The babies express their emotions on demand and, once ordered by their leader, instantly stop. They fit the social mould and conform to orders and norms of society. Not only are they being controlled and standardized, but they also learn to manage their emotions on demand. End of the segment.

Back in the first narrative universe, the three specialists are arguing and fighting. The baby's face is red. With his penis perking up, the baby suddenly starts urinating on everybody. All the characters get sprayed with the yellow liquid. Relieved at last, the baby is overjoyed. He has not regained his serenity through the consumption of goods, psychoanalysis, nor training, but he rather solved his problem, by himself, with the satisfaction of a natural need. The priest comes back, salutes everyone and a small angel passes by. All men leave the park. The baby is very happy and the mother is joyous. End of the film.

Research undertaken on this animated film has revealed that the NFB has kept very few elements concerning the film's production in its archives. In his final report to the head of the French animation studio, the film's producer provided more insight on the woman director's objective: "it aimed to highlight the common habit of looking for a solution to a problem based on one's personal preoccupations rather than based on the problem's own data" (Sarault, NFB Archives, 1973, our translation).

Two years of production were necessary to create this film. Although filming begun over the summer of 1971, its final version was only approved on April 27, 1973. "This can seem like an incredibly long time for a cut-out animation project" (Sarault, NFB Archives, 1973, our translation). The production was, in fact, difficult. The animator filmed the animation in its entirety during the summer of 1971 in 16 mm format. Although the animation's quality was good, none of the content could be used due to lighting fluctuations in the recording process. Overexposure affected almost half of the sequences and Clorinda Warny had to start all over again.

In the fall of 1971, the producer Gaston Sarault decided to record the film in 35 mm format. Warny experimented with an unstable 35 mm camera which later required repairs. The technical services of the NFB worked on it during the months of November and December of 1971, which led to more delays. Even if the camera had been fixed, the second filming was difficult. Problems with equipment continued with the voltage regulator functioning poorly. "Despite all these issues, Clorinda Warny makes it through the end of the film." (Sarault, NFB Archives, 1973, our translation). Also, working as an assistant in Bretislay Pojar's *Balalblok* (Pojar, 1972), Warny had to pause her filming repeatedly. At the end of March 1972, Sarault and Warny discovered that the camera was still defective as it let light into the film. Filming stopped. Warny is reassigned to the production of an animated map for one of Marcel Carrière's films, before she took part in the set design for a film of the "*En tant que femmes*" [FR] series.

Between June 21 and July 25, 1972, Clorinda Warny filmed her film in its entirety for the third time. It is rather surprising that she had to start over three times. While it seems unlikely that the NFB would provide poor quality equipment to male directors like Bretislav Pojar or Norman McLaren, it appears that Clorinda Warny was given access to poor quality cameras.

On a different note, at the time, motherhood is often a non-choice for women. Logically, after marriage, the next step is to have children. *The Feminine Mystique*—another seminal book, published approximately 15 years after *The Second Sex* (Beauvoir, 1949)—denounces the social and economic inequalities from which women are victims. In this book, Betty Friedan exposed for the first time the deep distress that tortured stay-at-home mothers. Some were depressed and felt a sense of emptiness and of helplessness regarding their condition. "You wake up in the morning, and you feel there is no point in going on another day like this" (Anonymous woman quoted in Friedan, 1963, p. 20). The author shed light on the impossibility for most women to access credit unless they were endorsed by a man, on the control their husbands had over finances and property, as well as on their exclusion from the labor market and their representation in the media. "There was a strange discrepancy between the reality of our lives as women and the image to which we were trying to conform, the image that I came to call the feminine mystique." (Friedan, 1963, p. XXII). More importantly, the author proposed a theory on the misery affecting American, white, suburban, stay-at-home mothers: the housewife syndrome. Banishing stay-at-home mothers to the private sphere kept them from realizing that this disease stemmed from social origins. They suffered in silence, unsatisfied with the reality of their daily lives and their existence which was limited to cleaning, cooking and childcare. Women were depersonalized, their identities were stolen, as they became "the mother of," "the wife of" or "the daughter-in-law of." "She has no identity except as a wife and mother. She does not know who she is herself" (Sanger, quoted in Friedan, 1963, p. 19). To illustrate Betty Friedan's concept of "queen of the house", focus will be put on *The Spring and fall of Nina Polanski*, directed in 1974 by Joan Hutton and Louise Roy. The six-minute colored animated film was produced by Kathleen Shannon and the executive producer was Wolf Koenig.

THE SPRING AND FALL OF NINA POLANSKI (HUTTON AND ROY, 1974)

This film portrays the life of a young woman, Nina Polanski, who leaves her rural homeland for the traditional destiny of young women of urban origins in the 1970s: get married, have children and become a stay-at-home mother.

Confined to the private sphere, Nina's life beats to the rhythm of her children's needs and of her unpaid domestic work. She is quickly compelled to a life of confinement in her home, where her identity is exclusively reduced to that of a stay-at-home mother. Spending most of her time in the kitchen and in the laundry room, she dedicates her days to cooking, washing dishes, ironing clothes and taking care of her children. She physically turns into the very appliances she uses daily for her housework. At the end of the film, she seems to abandon her family to go back to the forest. *The Spring and Fall of Nina Polanski* (Figure 6.2)[4] raises the problem "that has no name shared by countless women" (Friedan, 1963, p. 7). It is

FIGURE 6.2   *The Spring and Fall of Nina Polanski.*

Source: **Hutton and Roy, 1974, © NFB, all rights reserved.**

an analysis of the oppression in marriage and motherhood that confine them to the golden cage of the "queen of the house."

The animated film begins in a forest where a wide variety of plants and trees are growing—colors remind of summertime. As for the sounds of the scenery, chanting birds and a violoncello classical music make for a relaxing and cozy atmosphere. Three daisy petals slowly fall from the sky. The camera moves to the right to reveal Nina, the protagonist, leisurely walking while tearing the petals from a daisy. She is wearing a mint-green dress and has thick long blond hair that falls to her shoulders. She is wearing a necklace adorned with a red heart. Initially alone in the forest, Nina leaves her homeland for the big city, which represents a duality between the rural and urban lives. The protagonist's journey could also be interpreted as an ecofeminist criticism (exploitation of nature and women) or seen as a change of country for Nina, an immigrant in a new territory where she would be alone without any family.

The second segment of the film is characterized by the transition of colors: initially alone in a colorful forest, Nina is now shown in black and white photographs in a static crowd, dressed as a bride. This second part shows the wedding of Nina Polanski. While it is impossible to know if Polanski was her surname before her wedding, the protagonist's surname might reveal her husband's appropriation of her. For a long time in Québec, married women had to take their husbands' surnames.

Between each picture which displays the unfolding of the ceremony, there are dark moments to suggest the projection of diapositives. It seems like time has stopped. Even if Nina is exclusively shown in black and white in this section, color remains in the backgrounds and in the other elements of the pictures. Many photographs are shown in succession: an official family portrait in which Nina stands in the centre holding a bouquet of roses; a picture of Nina, in front of the church throwing her bouquet to the women gathered to try to catch it; a moment during which Nina holds her husband's hands as they stare into each other's eyes, symbiotic and in love. The projection of slides continues: Nina Polanski holds a brown dog on her lap. Guests have a drink as they chat. The last slide shows the traditional three tier wedding cake with figurines of the two lovers at the top: a close-up shot shows the joint hands of the married couple cutting the cake and sharing it with their guests.

The third segment of the film happens in Nina's home. She is dressed in a pink dress with a white apron and high heels. In her kitchen, she hums and puts colorful flowers, one by one, in the vase on the table, thus creating an immense bouquet. Nina's whole life happens in her home. For the family, the house is the centre of the world. It is the kingdom of the housewife: Nina is the "queen of the house." Symbolically, the house which is often associated to the feminine space, represents the inner self and its feelings. The walls are decorated with a red wallpaper with a colorful pattern of fruits, vegetables and meats. The inner world and the physical space in which Nina lives suggest that she is a nurturing mother. The kitchen is at the centre of most of the action as that is where she must complete the different tasks associated to her motherhood. Nina smells her flowers: she is happy.

Following her wedding, Nina bears a new piece of jewelry: her necklace has been replaced by a watch. She becomes preoccupied with the notion of time which now eludes her. She looks at her watch then walks to the counter, cuts carrots and puts the slices in a bowl. With the mixer, she froths the preparation, then washes the dishes.

Suddenly, a sleeping baby appears in her arms. Surprised, she gasps, "Oh!", which is the only word pronounced throughout the film. Delighted by this apparition, she holds the baby close to her face to hug and holds him lovingly in her arms. She exits the kitchen and places the baby in a cradle. She kisses the sleeping baby on the cheek.

Nina returns to her housewife occupations: she picks up the laundry basket and starts ironing the clothes. When her work is completed, the clothes are neatly folded in the basket. Nina continues her tasks while carrying a big green trash bag. Her baby has grown, he now crawls on the ground. A second school-age child spontaneously appears in the scene. Nina does not seem to notice the arrival of this second child. She shows no emotion and has no reaction. Nina returns to the kitchen where the content of the pot simmers. As she walks in front of the refrigerator, the appliance separates from the background and changes into Nina Polanski's body. She no longer wears her pink dress and white apron: she has changed into the appliance. Her body is a refrigerator. Her fourth dress is under construction: the appliance dress. Her school-age daughter joins her and opens the door of the refrigerator (Nina's body) from which she takes out an apple and bites into it. The clothes are a visible manifestation of her inner self and her feelings. At first, Nina wears a mint-green dress and seems soft, happy, and even naive. If clothes indicate social status or group membership, it is possible to deduce that the beginning of Nina's married life and her first experiences with motherhood are in alignment with the expectations and values of her community and time period. She is dressed in a pretty pink dress, high heels and a white apron. If clothing is seen as a symbol, it exteriorizes the evolution of the protagonist's feelings. Filled with metaphors, Nina Polanski's appliance dress is no stranger to the nature of her distress. This piece of clothing expresses the fundamental reality of the stay-at-home mother: in addition to the dispossession of her individuality, she is crushed by the weight of the domestic tasks she must complete. The appliance dress is tied to the nature and function of housewife. Nina is mechanized, robotic. She turns into those machines that improve housework productivity The capitalist society pushes the population to consume.[5] Not only is overconsumption harmful for the environment, but the undertaking of daily tasks with household appliances puts pressure on women to reach perfection.

With industrialization, stay-at-home mothers were confronted with household consumption, which led to the professionalization of the housekeeper role. Women had to accomplish many chores to meet the standards conveyed in advertising. "The modern technologies that entered the house do not abolish household work, but rather change work methods" (Collectif Clio, 1992, p. 297, our translation). New machines, such as the dishwasher, the washing machine, the electric oven and the vacuum, emerged for an expeditious and facilitated execution of household tasks leading to the automatization, the mechanization and the professionalization of household work. "Although these inventions reduce weariness associated with household tasks, they do not eliminate the tediousness of cleaning and doing laundry and often lead women to clean more often and more thoroughly" (Collectif Clio, 1992, p. 323, our translation). It became increasingly difficult to make choices as a consumer: Which was the best soap quality-wise and price-wise? How could quick homecooked balanced meals be prepared? How could children's education be professionalized by giving them access to the best possible school as well as sports, cultural and artistic activities? It was a true commodification of the housekeeping business. Simply accomplishing chores no longer sufficed, women were required to accomplish them better. The mental load on stay-at-home mothers was increasing as their productivity was expected to be maximal. This "brainwash" generated the perfect image of stay-at-home mothers and their husbands' expectations of them. In that regard, booklets dealing with the husband's return home were published.

Brochures even sometimes advised women to prepare their husband's slippers and newspaper, pour them a glass of their favorite drink, bathe the children and comb their hair while having cooked dinner before their return, wear makeup and most importantly, to not bother them with discussions that could annoy them—their day at work will have put them through enough stress. In a climate where one strives for the American dream, the image of the perfect mother emerged in Québec as the society became emancipated by means of the marketed constructs of happiness that it was being presented.

In the film, when the third child appears, Nina does not notice her. This girl has blonde hair, like her, and is older than the other two. Nina's body continues to change, as the stove has now joined the heavy attire from which the refrigerator was already a part of. She moves towards the dining room table on which her three children's lunchboxes are placed. The table adds itself to the costume. Without paying attention to her, the three children pick up their lunch and leave the house. From her window, Nina waves at her children who are sitting in the school bus. Nina does not exit the house to escort them, nor does she hug them.

The ease with which Nina has her children is fascinating. Did she plan her pregnancies? As her second and third daughter arrive, she no longer reacts. She does not seem to feel any sense of pleasure with her children. She does not express joy; does not play with them. She is completely obsessed with the domestic tasks she must accomplish.

When her children leave for school with clean clothes and the food that she has prepared, she does not obtain any recognition for her work. By not thanking her, her dependent children seem to take their mother's work for granted.

Now home alone, Nina walks towards the ajar door. The dining table, the stove and the refrigerator slowly fall from her body. She returns to the forest, the very place she found herself in at the beginning of the film. However, spring has now changed to fall. Nina seems to give up her domestic life as well as her children to return to the forest. This open-ended conclusion allows for various interpretations. Why did she decide to isolate herself in the forest? Does she suffer from depression? Has she crumbled under the weight of the mental load mothers have to deal with? Will she come back? Without knowing the answers to these questions, it is undeniable that Nina Polanski seems to be an unhappy mother in her domestic life. Sitting on a rock, wearing her pink dress and her housekeeper apron, she watches the autumn leaves fall. The camera gets closer to her face. The short film ends.

At the end of the animation, Nina recovers her physical mobility: she leaves her family home, the place of her domestication and the source of her oppression. Through this action, she reclaims her destiny by crossing these invisible lines that limit her and that "expresses an urgent need to break from the confinement and the immutable reproduction of destiny" (Lord, 2009, p. 34, our translation). Nina needs to change the parameters to her life and wishes to exist outside of her family environment. She transitions from being a passive object to an active subject. Although Nina is of a heteronormative status and her identity was defined by the man she married, she refuses the destiny of the woman who gets married and has a lot of children, such as Disney princesses.

From the 1960s, more and more women, just like Nina Polanski, expressed this sense of emptiness, this lack of accomplishment and this feeling of being incomplete. They were tired, short-tempered and bored at home. They chased the utopia of femininity fabricated by publicity and mass media in order to reproduce the image of what was expected of them. By always being defined by something or someone else, women were no longer themselves. They aspired to other things than a husband, children and a house.

As for the research undertaken in the archives, few elements of the filming were kept at the NFB. The most complete element found was the original storyboard that corresponds to the final version of the film, thus allowing for the assumption that the authors' vision had been abided by.

Two young directors, Louise Roy and Joan Hutton, presented this animated film to producer Wolf Koenig in 1973. Fond of the project, Koenig allowed them to use the NFB's animation camera for free, in addition to supplying them with the necessary artistic material to carry out tests. It is not mentioned in the NFB's archives whether the two women were paid for their work. Hutton spent the summer of 1973 at the NFB working on the animation of the film although she could not complete the whole film before her return at Ryerson University in the fall. There, she then continued her work independently and resumed filming in black and white. Hutton was able to use equipment in Toronto for free. As she perceived no salary for her work, she was granted university credits. She returned to Montréal to show Koenig the initial edit who then considered that the film deserved to be produced at the NFB and filmed in 35 mm format.[6]

The minutes from July 25, 1974 contain the first discussion on the film held by the programming committee: "A short animation film, in which a woman is gradually transformed into a domestic appliance and leaves the house to take stock of her situation in the woods" (NFB Archives, July 25, 1974). The film's directors and the producer Kathleen Shannon were not present at the meeting. Around the table were seated one woman and eight men.[7] The programming committee looked into the whole filming process of the animation: both into the colored animation and its black and white version. The project received heavy criticism and the committee's reaction is rather negative.

> Several members of the committee then took issue with this view of the interest of the idea, finding it an "illustration of the obvious," "a banal statement of a cliché", "very boring" etc. Russ Searle wondered why and how working mothers would be interested in it, and Dorothy Courtois, a working mother herself representing the Director of Production, said that it certainly didn't interest her. No one seemed able to understand what the purpose of the film would serve in the *Working Mothers* series.
>
> (Archives ONF, July 25, 1974)

This quote sparks various questions. Dorothy Courtois was the only women present at the meeting and it appears that all other masculine members of the committee relied on her to approve, or not, of the film's pertinence. The issue with such an intention is that it implies that one woman's opinion (Courtois) would correspond to all other women's opinions. Therefore, if Courtois does not relate to the representation of Nina Polanski, then no other women would, but her opinion is that of one woman, not that of all women. Anyway, some may wonder if that is really Dorothy Courtois' opinion. Could she really express herself freely and think differently than all the men in front of her?

Furthermore, Courtois seemed to hold an atypical professional position. As the representative of the director of production, she held a privileged position of power. In the 1970s, women's place at the NFB was usually outside of positions of decision-making. Although the NFB had, at that time, implemented positive discrimination measures, parity in decision-making and positions of power was still not observed in 1974. Courtois, having a job herself, was not confronted with the same reality as the isolated Nina Polanski whose life was limited to unpaid domestic work. Courtois was an active woman in the public sphere who was part of the labor market and who had a paid—therefore valued—job. The film illustrates what Friedan has written: the unnamed issue, the taboo, this generalized discomfort in women who are required to stay at home to raise their children along with the difficulties they face in adapting to a monotone and repetitive life. That did not seem to be Courtois' reality.

During the meeting, producer John Spotton expressed the opinion that the film only found its value in one single shot. He believed that the sequence during which the woman turns into a refrigerator is the only pertinent part of the movie as he judged the whole message was communicated in this section. Spotton thought there was nothing else to elaborate around this shot. He therefore suggested using it as an introduction logo for each film from the series *Working Mother*, after which executive producer Wolf Koenig concluded the first discussion about the film:

> Wolf said that he felt we had to trust Kathleen's judgment on this: the fact that she felt it would be useful for her was enough for him. It was not the greatest film on earth, but there was much that he admired about it. It was generally regretted that Kathleen had been unable to be present for the discussion and agreed that a recommendation should not be made without hearing from her. The proposal was therefore held over to the next meeting.
>
> (Archives ONF, July 25, 1974)

Kathleen Shannon's role was essential in completing the film in 35 mm format. During the following meeting held on August 1, 1974, Shannon defended the short film in front of the programming committee. Her intervention during that second meeting was crucial for the obtainment of additional funds. The meeting began with a summary of the previous meeting and the negative response expressed towards the film: it was seen to awkwardly state the obvious, that it was similar to another film in production *The Housewife*. "No one could imagine what use it could be in the *Working Mothers* series, except perhaps as a logo, at a shorter length, or why working mothers should be interested in it" (NFB Archives, August 1, 1974). After the negative points were exposed, a progressively more favorable attitude was observed:

> From there, of course, there was nowhere to go but up. Kathleen said that there had been a good reaction from women at home to the

storyboard of the film and explained that it would be used in discussions and workshops with women. The film's open-endedness, which the committee had found feeble and pointless, made it especially good for discussion. This film had been programmed, by Challenge for Change, before *Housewife*, which she had seen and which she considered more a study in repetitive motion and animation technique. *Nina Polanski* was very appropriate as one of the *Working Mothers* films and had always been intended to be part of the series.

(NFB Archives, August 1, 1974)

Shannon then explained that since the film had already been approved for the *Working Mothers* series, there should be no discussion on production viability, the focus should be solely on additional funding to enable shooting in 35mm format. "Somewhat grudgingly, since the film was going to be finished anyways, the committee voted to recommend that it be finished in 35 mm (5 in favour, 1 opposed, 2 abstentions)" (NFB Archives, August 1, 1974). In a memo from August 2, 1974, programming director, Arthur Hammond, signed the recommendation for an additional $5,354. Filming happened quickly, from July 29 to August 26, 1974. Unfortunately, Joan Hutton never got another opportunity to shoot a film at the NFB although her will seemed to have been different. In the minutes from February 24, 1977, the name of Joan Hutton resurfaced as Studio D, located in Winnipeg, offered the director $1,496 to conduct research for an animated film on witches, but she never directed the film.

Happiness Is and *The Spring and Fall of Nina Polanski* illustrate the naivety of some women stepping into motherhood with no idea of the workload that awaits them to raise children. At no time in both films do the mothers show any physical signs of affection towards the children. The protagonist in *Happiness Is* never holds her baby to soothe him, even though the comfort provided by physical proximity with the mother is very real. The affective dimension is often forgotten by radical feminist critics even if it is an essential aspect of the parent-child relationship. The oppression of women must be reimagined to articulate this problematic by "accounting for mother's daily experience in its simultaneously material and affective double component" (Descarries and Corbeil, 1991, p. 347, our translation).

Furthermore, in both films, the father is completely absent. In *Happiness Is*, he is not once shown on screen which suggests that he has abandoned the mother on the emotional front as she is the only person providing care for the baby. Isolated, running out of patience, and lacking confidence, she is unable to succeed. With no support system to help and encourage her, left to her own devices she welcomes without any hesitation the recommendations of perfect strangers that come to help her to soothe her baby's anger. As for Nina, she also has no support system to help her with her children. Her husband is totally absent from their marital life seeing as, after his short appearance during their wedding ceremony, he is nowhere to be found. Nina never communicates with people from the outside world: she is alone, and it can be assumed that she has no access to a daycare.

It is essential to reconsider the parental responsibilities that are automatically appointed to mothers in our said "modern" societies. Society has for a long time legitimized this situation with the argument that procreation consisted in a vocation for women. What does motherhood represent for women at the time of this study: do they really wish to stay home to raise crying children? "Each second of her time—and without hope of seeing this work end at a fixed hour, even at night—she is *absorbed into other individualities*, diverted from the activity which is going on to other activities" (Guillaumin, 1995, p. 188). Nonetheless, society entertains the idea that motherhood represents pure happiness. Childbirth is presented as the ultimate accomplishment of femininity. Indeed, women are submitted to intense pressure to accomplish their biological "duty." Society invites mothers to play this role. However, the idea that all mothers are fulfilled with motherhood is false. It can be difficult to ask for help when everyone speaks of motherhood as this happy emancipating concept and new mothers are often destined to feel lonely and isolated.

Clorinda Warny, Joan Hutton and Louise Roy present a point of view with no rose-colored glasses: they do not show happy mothers in control in accordance with the image that is fabricated in the media. This type of film opens the door for a representation of the plural identity of mothers. According to Friedan, education needs to be reformed: "They learn that truly feminine women do not want careers, higher education, political rights—the independence and the opportunities that the old feminists fought for" (Friedan, 1963, p. 2). The author observes that fewer women attend university after the Second World War and she notices that many pursue higher education only to find a husband. She also notes a considerable increase in feminine press audiences in the 20th century. This type of press glorifies the role of stay-at-home women by representing the home as the only place where they can govern. Such praise of this lifestyle in feminine magazines does not encourage women to emancipate themselves. Friedan wrote of these magazines: "women's world was confined to her own body and beauty, the charming of man, the bearing of babies, and the physical care and serving of husbands, children, and home" (Friedan, 1963, p. 27). The content of this "feminine" press validates the idea that stay-at-home women have no interest in politics, nor for public and international matters, but that their preoccupations are limited by the walls of their home, their appearance and their children's education as they only leave their home to run errands, drive their children to activities or to accompany their husband at professional events.[8]

In the next chapter, the film *The Housewife* furthers the discussion on the difficulties experienced by stay-at-home women and their dream for emancipation. This animation illustrates the notion of sexism and the will for an equal division of household chores between both partners. However, focus will first be put on *Illuminated Lives: A Brief History of Women's Work in the Middle Ages* (Besen, 1989) as this short film exposes the myths regarding the place of women in the labor market throughout History.

NOTES

1. See *The Second Sex, I. Facts and Myths* (Beauvoir, 1953) and *The Second Sex, II. Woman's Life Today.* (Beauvoir, 1953). The first book focuses on the ideas made up by society while the second relates the experiences of women in society. These two books expose the binarism of culture and nature.
2. *Multiplication 1, Multiplication 2* and *Multiplication 3* (Warny, 1971a, 1971b, 1971c).
3. In the French title of the film (*Petit Bonheur*), happiness is qualified as small. Does this adjective represent the lack of prestige associated to motherhood, a minor event, a women's issue?
4. *The Spring and Fall of Nina Polanksi* is a title that offers a double meaning. Here, *Spring* could be interpreted as the season, the awakening of nature: Nina's prepubescent period. On the other hand, *to spring* means "jumping ahead," an action which is the result of a spring. As for *Fall*, to which we can also attribute two meanings, first with that of the season, spring's antonym. Second, it represents the action of falling: *to fall*. These two possible interpretations allow for the observation of a metaphor for the end of a cycle or a life period.
5. *Acid Rain* (Heczko, 1986) is another film that was directed by a woman animator of the NFB and that could be qualified as eco-feminist. Based on a poem of Sean O'Huigin, the film shows the physical disintegration of a

young girl who, after having stepped in a puddle of water polluted by clouds of smoke issued by factories, liquifies into the puddle and eventually evaporates under the sun. A bird which is also cleaning himself in a puddle loses his feathers and dies.

6. Further information will be provided in this section on the difficulties experienced in the obtention of the programming committee's approval as well as Studio D's executive producer Kathleen Shannon's instrumental intervention for the funding of the animated film.

7. Arthur Hammond (programming director), Dorothy Courtois (production director representative), producers John Knight, Don Rennick, John Spotton, and David Wilson, Russ Searle, Tom Bindon (distribution representatives) as well as Marcel Malacket (director of finances), were present at the meeting.

8. Janet Perlman is another animator that focused on mythologies and "feminine" role norms, notably in the films *The Tender Tale of Cinderella Penguin* (Perlman, 1981) and *Lady Fishbourne's Complete Guide to Better Table Manners* (Perlman, 1976).

CHAPTER 7

Women's Labor and the Notion of Sexism

Entering the labor market is an important aspect of women's emancipation. To better understand their reality in the 1970s and the 1980s, periods during which most of the animated films studied in this book were created, it is essential to examine their economic and socioprofessional conditions. Women's entrance into the labor market was inevitably tied to their education[1] as the earliest feminist expressions predate what is known as the "first wave."[2] Indeed, for centuries, women have been cognizant of the restrictions enforced on their freedom.

As previously mentioned, women's labor outside of the household was a matter of concern in the 1970s. Many women questioned their destiny: should they stay at home to raise their children or enter the labor market? Access to employment was very limited for women and they received poor remuneration. Some looked to emancipate themselves from the ghetto of occupations to which they were confined by exploring careers that were not associated to the domestic sphere. Prejudices against women were real as they were under-represented in many prestigious professions, such as law and medicine, while the disparity of wages between sexes was obvious. During the 1960s, some feminists denounced these wage gaps and proclaimed: "Equal pay for equal work!" They objected to the idea that women's labor was only a supplementary income.

One of the misconceptions about women of that period is that they worked to entertain themselves. However, women who entered the labor

DOI: 10.1201/9781032694382-10

market did so due to real financial needs. The fragmentation of the traditional family unit has compelled an increasing number of women to become providers for their families. They represented more than one third of the workforce in Canada and 250,000 were separated from their husbands, widowed or divorced (Shannon, 1974g). Such statistics dispelled the myth implying that mothers had someone else to provide for them, even though the Québec government granted "mothers in need" pensions to those who did not have the financial support of a husband. It was therefore acknowledged that not all mothers had someone to provide for them.

On top of wage discrimination and rather unfavorable policies of career advancement, women who found themselves part of the labor market were often forced to take on a "second shift." These are the consequences of an egalitarian liberal feminism for those who work outside of the household: in addition to their jobs, women also had to complete the unpaid labor that was expected of them in the private sphere which involved cleaning, doing the laundry, cooking, providing care for other members of the family, etc. This easily represented about 50 hours of work a week. To this day, the phenomenon of double workdays constitutes a challenging reality that is difficult to accept.

However, in the Middle Ages, women were active subjects. They could reign, own lands and work as doctors or surgeons. What distinguishes this period is the almost nonexistent separation between the public and the private spheres. Most of the population lived in the countryside where rural production originated from households which led to no clear divisions between paid and unpaid labor. The transition between the Middle Ages (500–1450) and the Renaissance (1450–1600) caused women to be stripped of their autonomy and freedom with the growing influence of the Church which undeniably contributed to the spread of sexist ideas that provoked a significant regression of the condition of women (Federici, 2018). *Illuminated Lives: A Brief History of Women's Work in the Middle Ages* is a short film that portrays the professional lives of women before they were overturned in the Renaissance.

ILLUMINATED LIVES: A BRIEF HISTORY OF WOMEN'S WORK IN THE MIDDLE AGES (BESEN, 1989)

This 1989 five-minute animated film illustrates the condition of women in the labor market. It was directed by Ellen Besen and produced by Margaret Pettigrew along with Kathleen Shannon and Rina Fraticelli as executive producers. This film dismantles the common myth of the poor helpless princess who patiently waits for a strong valiant young man to come save her from her unfortunate situation and provide for the rest of her life. In demonstrating the professional activities in which women participated during the Middle Ages, the animation questions the sexual division of labor and the existing prejudice on women's professional skills.

Born in Toronto, the director, Ellen Besen, is one of the rare directors of her time to have specialized training in film animation having graduated from Sheridan College. After completing multiple freelance contracts in Toronto and being a founding member of Caribou Cartoons (R.R.E.D Studio Ltd.), she was hired at the NFB as a director where she created *Sea Dream* (Besen, 1979).[3] Entirely drawn by hand, this short film is proof of Besen's undeniable talent as an animator in which she repeatedly offers swift movements and sophisticated transitions. In this first project at the NFB, a young girl is seen, in her dreams, playing with an octopus.

Research on this film carried out in NFB archives have revealed that the animator was not properly paid for her creation. Kathleen Shannon, executive producer at Studio D, sounded the alarm: "Ellen's salary had become an embarrassment to the Film Board and the Staff Relations board meetings in Ottawa. Ellen was being paid what she had asked for, but she would now be paid a proper professional rate" (Archives, NFB, October 27, 1977). No additional details were found on this situation, but everything pointed to the fact that Besen represented cheap workforce. Did she suffer from impostor syndrome? Sometimes, due to lack of confidence, women have a hard time demanding a salary that reflects their skills.

The archives also revealed Ellen Besen then tried to direct the film *Simple Hands*. However, after investing in research, the project was abandoned. Besen therefore directed her second project *Illuminated Lives: A Brief History of Women's Work in the Middle Ages* (Figure 7.1) at the NFB more than ten years after directing *Sea Dream*.

The film begins with drums and medieval music playing in the background. On screen, a green three-headed dragon threatens a woman imprisoned in a castle tower. The narrator begins:

> In days of old, when dragons roamed the land, fair maiden spend
> a great deal of time languishing in towers. And devising ways to
> encounter young knights who were eager to rescue them from the
> days of idleness. Or so conventional wisdom would have us believe.
> (Besen, 1989)

FIGURE 7.1 *Illuminated Lives: A Brief History of Women's Work in the Middle Ages.*

Source: Besen, 1989, © NFB, all rights reserved.

In this sequence, the imprisoned woman makes a pulley appear out of nowhere to heave a young man up her window. The two grab onto each other's hands and rest their heads lovingly. The camera moves back allowing the viewer to understand that the image is printed in a book. Then, drawings show women taking part in various agricultural occupations: they transform grains into flour, plow fields, collect wool from sheep, provide care for farm animals and harvest fruit from orchards. The narrator resumes:

> But the records of the time, tax survey and art work, tell a different story. Medieval women in fact worked long and hard, with no immediate rescue in sight. Most belonged to the peasant class. They worked for their father or husband or were indentured to large futile estates. They often did the same back-breaking work as their men, usually for lower wages. Sometimes they formed part of a floating population of workers that roamed the country at harvest time. Or were rented out by their fathers to other households in return for wages and clothing.
>
> (Besen, 1989)

Just like in the Middle Ages, the egalitarian work division was the model on which was based the society that later became Canada. Around 1634, when the first families of settlers came to New France, there was little to no separation of men and women in the work environment: both sexes equally contributed to building houses and clearing lands allowing such jobs to be completed in a complementary fashion.

Contrary to European societies who already favored women's subordination, the people who occupied the territory, such as the Mi'kmaq, Maliseet, Algonquin, Innu, Cree, Atikamekw, Mohawks, Iroquois, Hurons, Seneca, and Inuit nations, just to name a few, lived in relatively egalitarian societies. Although the division of tasks between men and women was quite precise among the First Nations, the worth of said tasks was not placed on a hierarchy. Women were autonomous, free and considered equal to men, both on the political and social front. There was even, among the Iroquois people, a matrilocal society.[4] The arrival of European missionaries and the spread of Catholicism brought changes to the First Nations' relationship model between men and women as a hierarchy of genres was implemented, and spiritual beliefs subordinating women to men emerged.

Illuminated Lives: A Brief History of Women's Work in the Middle Ages continues with a series of drawings of commercial activities and the various occupations in cities of that time in the context of which valuable objects, jewelry, meat, clothing and medicine were sold. Artisans forged metal, fixed shoes and gutted fish. The narrator continues:

> But then, things began to change. The Middle Ages saw the growth of towns and cities and a commercial working class. Now women could become jewellers, shop keepers, tailors and apothecaries. Although class craft guild accepted only men, a woman could gain a foothold in business by apprenticing in her parent's trades or inheriting a shop from her dead husband. And there were some who entered business entirely on their own.
>
> (Besen, 1989)

The film continues with a sequence on the plurality of professional occupations practised by women in the society at that time. They work in the production and transformation of textiles: one woman is seen creating tapestries, another rears silkworms and some weave threads. The director also illustrated women artists creating artwork, a young woman teaching children, nuns praying and studying, as well as caregivers taking care of the sick or assisting women in childbirth.

Men taking control of childbirth was a setback for women. In New France, midwifery was one of the rare occupations women were allowed to practice, in addition to that of being a maid or a wet nurse. Later, the Canadian government took advantage of the rural exodus and industrialization to gradually take charge of childbirth while prioritizing medicalization, as it consisted in a lucrative business: "Childbirth was a matter related to women . . . to which there was no cost, but in the cities men took control, as women generally gave birth with the assistance of a doctor . . . medical intervention slowly discharged women from a profession that was their own" (Collectif Clio, 1992, p. 269, our translation).

Not only was childbirth taken away from women, but with industrialization and urbanization in Canada, the State gradually took ownership of the education system and nursing which, until then, consisted in services mainly offered by religious communities. It was through these communities that women made their mark and built the foundations of the Québec healthcare and education systems. The conclusion of the film contributed to dispelling the myth of the tearful princess:

> far from being pampered, they were expected to entertain and to oversee the preparation and storage of food. Ladies ran huge estates and sometimes ruled whole countries, if only by virtue of birth. And when her lord went out to war, a lady was expected to stay home and hold the fort and keep things in good repair. With so much to be done, there was probably little time left for romantic trysts or dragons. In an age where everyone was bound by class to do certain tasks, women were doubly bound by their sex. But in the course of doing those tasks, they chipped away at the restrictions placed on them for being women. For the benefit of centuries of women to come.
>
> (Besen, 1989)

The Renaissance was a dark period for the condition of women. As a double standard of marital fidelity emerged, husbands were authorized to physically discipline their wives.[5] Women were progressively marginalized by the economic system as they were withdrawn from their professions and confined to the family sphere. Some were persecuted, specifically healers and midwives, for providing knowledge to poor women, therefore presenting a threat to certain interests of the bourgeoisie. Laws were prescribed to allow death sentences for women convicted of witchcraft. For that reason, multiple women were burned at the stake. *Illuminated Lives: A Brief History of Women's Work in the Middle Ages* contributes to a new representation of women's labor by depicting strong and accomplished female role models.

Another essential aspect to consider is the economic recognition of housework, this eminently political matter was at the centre of "second wave" feminist claims. In *Wages for Housework. A History of an International Feminist Movement* (Toupin, 2018), Louise Toupin described housework:

> I am talking about multi-faceted, invisible, and unrecognized labor, indispensable and wealth-producing, the vast majority of which was performed by women within families and in the community. Until then considered from the angle of being "free"—an act supposedly born of the love and generosity inherent to women—this activity was now seen by certain neo-feminist theoreticians as real work and, what is more, work that was being exploited.
>
> (Toupin, 2018, p. 1)

Camille Robert came to the same conclusion in her authoritative book on Québec women's housework which highlights the transition of the issue from the private to the public sphere. In *Toutes les femmes sont d'abord ménagères* [FR] (Robert, 2017), she wrote:

> the housewife progressively emerged as a political subject contributing to historical change through her work of social reproduction. Although the feminist movement initially relied on wives and mothers' work to make claims to the State, this work was then redefined, by the 1970s, as playing a central role in capitalist and patriarchal exploitative relationships, and, consequently, in their objection.
>
> (Robert, 2017, p. 19, our translation)

The liberal system has never taken women's housework into consideration as part of the economic performance and the gross domestic product of the country. Economic theories do not consider the production issued from the private sphere. However, women's housework consists in a work of service which contributes to transforming goods into consumer products.[6] According to the sociologist Christine Delphy, in *L'ennemi principal, Tome 2: Penser le genre* [FR] (2001), the enemy is easy to identify: "Marriage has taken us out of productivity, and out of the market. Attention should not be placed on tasks, but rather on production reports" (Delphy, [2001] 2013, p. 64, our translation). The author criticizes the social contract of marriage which condemns women to the "economic tutelage" of their husband, therefore keeping them from experiencing an egalitarian relationship.

Delphy criticizes the Marxist ideology that has failed to consider women's situation in the private sphere. Marx's analysis focused on factory workers and farmers. By exclusively considering women jobholders as exploited in the capitalist system, the Marxist ideology left out more than half of the adult population, therefore neglecting the value of housework accomplished by women. The exploitation of women happened outside of the capitalist market since they were not paid for their domestic work, while other people benefited from their free labor. Materialist feminists questioned the capitalist system which favored men jobholders who worked outside of their homes while condemning dependent women to the household where they received no salary.

The Marxist ideology did not recognize women as a class which is precisely what would change in radical and materialist feminism. In the private sphere, married women, those who were part of a common-law couple, and single mothers received no salary for the work they completed. For Delphy, this is what makes women part of a group as they all have one thing in common: "They are being extorted free labor; therefore, they are part of specific production reports, which is the definition of a class" (Delphy, [2001] 2013, p. 54, our translation). *The Housewife* (Bennett, 1975) will be at focus as it illustrates the concept of sexism, that is, the free appropriation of women's housework.

THE HOUSEWIFE (BENNETT, 1975)

The Housewife is a six-minute animated short film which was directed in 1975 by Cathy Bennett and produced by Wolf Koenig and Guy Clover that exposes women's free labor. The animation sets in motion a housewife that is completely disconnected from the public sphere, imprisoned in the repetitiveness of domestic chores. The protagonist expresses her desire for emancipation by dreaming of a space where she would be active in the public sphere: she gets lost in her thoughts and imagines herself being somebody else. The artist used a streamlined technique of animation to subtly draw the details of the woman on colored cardboard cutout silhouettes which provided a perfectly fit aesthetic for the exploration of the theme of the ordinary daily life of the housewife.

At the beginning of the film, the housewife wakes up alone in her bed. Naked, she gets up and stretches. Her blanket disappears. She walks towards the right of the screen and her skin color turns red. She puts on a shapeless dress that hides her figure. The fact that she goes against a dominant hegemonic aesthetic immediately strikes the eye.

In the morning, she takes no time to wash up, nor does she look at herself in the mirror and neither does she brush her teeth. Despite having curves, she wears clothes that erase them. She has the body of a woman in the fall season of her life: aged and menopausal. The features of her face are imperceptible: she bears no eyes, nose, nor mouth. Throughout the

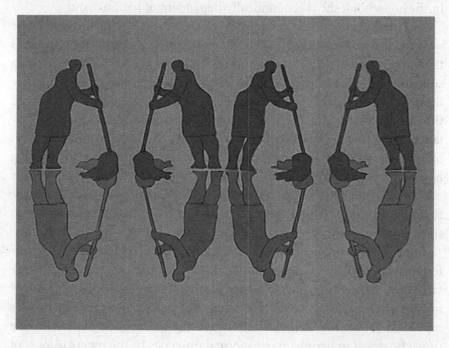

FIGURE 7.2 *The Housewife.*

Source: **Bennett, 1975, © NFB, all rights reserved.**

film, she does not speak, she is anonymous and mute. The housewife has no hair, which is a feature often used in art to represent female sexuality as it sometimes symbolizes women's sexual vitality, seductive power and femininity. Michelle Perrot made connections between women's hair and their body hair as they cover the intimacy of their genitals. In the contrary, "shaving someone, whether a man or a woman, consists in taking possession of them, in anonymizing them" (Perrot, 2006, p. 65, our translation).

The housewife is now in the kitchen. The soundtrack consists of a person repeating technical exercises of musical scales on a piano. The notes resonate mechanically. The housewife cooks breakfast and places the plates on an invisible table. She pours the meal on the plates straight from the pot. A man appears at the table. Too focused on his newspaper, he does not speak to her. The two protagonists eat without communicating. The man disappears. The housewife picks up the dishes and cleans the kitchen. The man reappears at her side as she turns to kiss him on the lips and becomes invisible again. Ellipse. In this segment, it is implied that the man goes to work. The housewife has no salary for the work she completes in the household: she is economically dependent of her husband.

After the husband's departure, the film continues with the housewife who finishes to clean the kitchen. Her orange tone becomes lighter and the background changes: she is now outside. She washes laundry in a big sink and hangs the clothes on the line. Ellipse. As she sweeps the floor, her figure is dark green. Ellipse. In the soundtrack, arpeggios have replaced the musical scales. The housewife stops her work and looks into the distance. Now in a fantasy, her body changes as she imagines herself with blonde hair wearing a splendid dress and a large hat decorated with a big blue feather. Her broom has turned into a golden umbrella. Eyes appear on her face, and she is wearing makeup. Suddenly, she goes back to reality, turns back into her initial anonymous figure and picks up the trash from the ground with the dustpan. Ellipse.

Imprisoned in the private sphere, her desire for emancipation manifests itself when she is daydreaming. When she projects herself in those fantasies, she seems to affirm the singularity of her personality. The director details the protagonist's face when she exteriorizes the character's repressed dream life. Bennett only draws the housewife's hair when she projects herself in her phantasmagorical universe. In the repetitiveness of her daily life, the housewife is never presented as a sexual object, she only bears sexualized characteristics in her fantasy worlds. Without having tied the housewife's hair under a scarf, but rather by hiding it, the director confirms the housewife's loss of seductive power, her desexualisation and the loss of her femininity. Society puts older women aside. The housewife probably feels nostalgic of the beauty of her lost youth since she does no longer look at herself in the mirror.

The reproductive cycle is absent from the narrative arc. The housewife is never in contact with children. This absence is significant. Multiple questions remain unanswered regarding the lack of children: they could have left the household, the couple might have had fertility problems, or they might have voluntarily declined maternity. Among "second wave" feminist claims, the will to reclaim the control of bodies was major. This sexual liberation played out on multiple fronts as women wished to escape policies which had control over their fertility and childbirth cycles. "We shall give birth to the children we want, if we want them and when we want them" (Hirata *et al.*, 2004, p. 3, our translation). Access to contraception and regulation of childbirth was one of the prime issues for women. "In modern occidental societies, sexuality has been highly supervised by the Church which was hegemonic until the 18th century, to which have succeeded, without ever totally dethroning it, medicine as well as civil and criminal law" (Foucault, quoted in Hirata *et al.*, 2004, p. 214, our translation). The *Royal Commission on the Status of Women* (RCSW) recommended better communication of information on contraception throughout Canada and a change in legal measures to provide better access to abortion which led to the decriminalization of the procedure. Women's rights were recognized and took precedence over religious beliefs: women could now choose to end their pregnancy in legal and sanitary conditions.

The film continues and, towards the end of the morning, the housewife is in the kitchen cooking a meal. She sets the table only for herself. She sits down to eat but is very quickly interrupted by lightning. She goes outside as her figure turns blue. She rapidly gathers the clothes she had left to dry on the clothesline. Ellipse. In this sequence, the animator illustrates the impression that women are safer at home. In the film, the outside world is represented as very dangerous with lightning and thunder. For the first time, the background becomes dark, and the woman puts both hands to her head. The director might have also tried to represent the difficult access to the labor market for women and the complexity of their situation when they oppose traditional social roles.

The housewife resumes her day. With repetitive gestures, she irons the clothes and folds laundry. Then, she dusts the empty space around her, thus allowing the viewer to imagine the scenery or representing the emptiness that possesses the character. Her colored figure is bright pink. She stops her work and gets lost in her thoughts: she imagines herself wearing a bikini with blue and green feathers. She resembles a dancer on the stage of a cabaret. Ellipse. The housewife's figure is dark blue. She mops the floor and her silhouette splits in two as its shadow appears on the floor. Another splitting effect is created and there are now four housewives and their reflection cleaning the floor. The events repeat themselves in reverse: from four to two, she is alone again. Ellipse.

As she sweeps the floor, the housewife splits in two and engages in a dance choreography. She might be trying to express her will to be helped through these multiple splits. In any case, this multiplication of her figure highlights the impression of a robotized and repetitive choreography by the woman as she is polishing the floors. Although she is active while completing her tasks, the housewife is passive regarding her fate. She is obedient, compliant, attentive, and only seems to exist to fulfil her partner's needs through meal preparation and house maintenance which are tasks that are expected to be accomplished by the "queen of the house."

Sociologist Colette Guillaumin uses the term *sexage*[7] to define the appropriation of the class of women by that of men and the specific nature of the oppression of women. There are two pillars which constitute the base of her analysis: the first being material (women are objects), while the second is ideological (women pertain to "nature"). If the "feminine nature" is described by the dominant group as compliant, patient, obedient, weak, unintelligent, etc., it is because it makes appropriation easier through subjugation, "sexage," and demand on products of the body, such as sexuality, free workforce and economic gains related to reproduction.[8]

These constructs regarding the qualities and the intelligence of women relegate them to practical matters rather than to prestigious areas. Fundamentally, men take possession of the labor power executed by women for free and Guillaumin, along with Delphy, did not hesitate to compare this situation with slavery since slaves do not sign contracts either.

The film continues and the housewife is in the kitchen. Her figure turns bright orange. The man appears at her side and she leans towards him to kiss him. He disappears. She continues to cook the meal and serves the food the same way she had done it in the morning. The man returns at the table and the two eat without communicating. The man disappears again. The housewife cleans the table and does the dishes. The man returns, but this time, the housewife's figure is dark purple. The housewife turns to the man and absorbs his color. They dance. A series of pictures of the couple taking part in different tasks appear: the man holds a shovel, and the woman holds a broom. Then, he holds a pickaxe while she hangs clothes. He digs, she cooks. He takes the trash out, she folds laundry. He has a jackhammer; she has a duster. The couple is then represented wearing costumes from different periods in time. Next to the well-dressed man holding a cane, the housewife bears blonde hair and is wearing a pretty dress with a golden umbrella. Then, the man is wearing a suit while the woman wears a blue dress, a straw hat and is holding a fan. The man and the woman then appear as cavemen, dressed in cheetah skins. They are both holding the same spear. Then, they are posing in an acrobatic position and wearing skin-tight bodysuits with shoes decorated with long ribbons. The protagonists return to their initial state: two anonymous figures. Ellipse. The housewife is red and takes her clothes off and goes back to bed, alone. She repeats the same actions as those from the beginning of the film, but this time, in a reverse manner. This marks the end of the animation.

In this short film, the protagonist's isolation could be cut with a knife. There are no backgrounds, nor scenery surrounding her. In film animation where everything is built, calculated and drawn, the choice to reduce the number of visual elements is a significant decision. Bennett documented emptiness. The housewife is completely disconnected from the private sphere and confined to the domestic field. Her universe is insular and airtight. She compliantly repeats robotized actions to accomplish domestic chores. As opposed to her husband, she does not read the newspaper, she does not have access to books, nor to magazines and she does not watch television either. This is significant as television was considered a privileged means to reach housewives. The protagonist is alone, without any type of stimulation. Nothing seems to nourish her mind. Apart from the man who comes in and out of the house, nobody communicates with her. She is never in contact with other people. She does not even have a phone.

As for the soundtrack, the first part of the film is accompanied by piano scales and a monotone repetition of technical exercises which are, just like the housewife taking part in daily household tasks, dull and boring. It is not music, but rather an exercise that can be heard. The soundtrack is not that of a piano concert that highlights the pianist's talent in front of an audience: it is recorded in the private sphere and constitutes repetitive scales, arpeggios and patterns. It represents the process of learning a musical skill rather than a performance.

Through her projections in her imaginary world, a glimpse of the protagonist's dissatisfaction as well as her desire for a new identity can be caught. In *L'identité* (Mucchielli, 2009), the author described identity as a set of characteristics and attributes that allow a person or a group of people to perceive themselves as a specific entity while also being perceived as is by others. Identity is never fixed: it is fluid. It is never a reality, but rather a perception. Identity is always built through the eyes of the beholder as well as through the eyes of others. It is plural, in constant transformation. Furthermore, internal identity is not always exhibited to the outside world. Indeed, one may ask:

> What is a domesticated woman? A female of the species. . . . A woman is a woman. She only becomes a domestic, a wife, a chattel, a playboy bunny, a prostitute, or a human dictaphone in certain relations. Torn from these relationships, she is no more the helpmate of man than gold in itself is money . . . , etc. What then are these relationships by which a female becomes an oppressed woman?
>
> (Rubin, 1975, p. 34)

At the end of *The Housewife*, the protagonist imagines what she would like her relationship to be: a space for equal exchanges where the man would participate more in domestic chores. However, the housewife does not have the power to take action. The film maintains the social order between men and women, therefore cementing gender roles and their hierarchy. It fails to go beyond man-woman couple representations due to the housewife's imagination being confined to traditional standards. Cathy Bennett's representations stays within the masculine-feminine dichotomy and they are limited to binary identities. It is a heteronormative representation within the limits of a liberal egalitarian feminism which unrolls at the end of the story. There are no divisions between the sex (the body) and the gender (the social construct). The housewife's fantasies are limited to traditional feminine representations as the author depicts the character in performative "feminine" roles. Bennett never involves her character in emancipatory careers that are usually "reserved" to men, such as writer, police officer, mechanic, firefighter, director, etc. The film does not rethink the sexuality of marginalized women that do not conform to heterosexual norms either. In that sense, the film implies the impossibility to call into question the presumed heterosexuality of women. This normative assignment of femininity idealizes norms and strengthens social dictates without transgressions. Cathy Bennett created a film that is caught in the nets of heteronormativity.

Despite her restricted agency, the housewife still manages to express her desire to be her husband's equal. She attempts to act on the relationship while renegotiating the power balance and the distribution of household chores. Progress in her relationship with the source of her oppression is observed. At the end of the film, the man and the woman communicate throughout their respective transformations. Despite her complete subordination to her husband, the "heroine" projects a new bond on him. The open conclusion could suggest that men, just like women, are trapped by masculine domination.

Cathy Bennett, director of the film, animates a rhythmic choreography of the housewife's life as she unrolls her actions with repetitive gestures in the isolation of her existence. This animation puts in picture a liberal egalitarian feminist discourse on the alienation of women in the context of housework and their loss of identity in the private sphere. The director deals with boredom, economic dependency, invisible labor, and the exploitation of housewives from the perspective of sexism. In the next chapter, animations which question the relationships between men and women and the traditional family unit will be analyzed.

NOTES

1. At the beginning of the 1900s, young Quebecer girls were mostly raised to become wives and mothers. In rural areas, they were usually pulled from the school system early to assist their mother with household chores or help their father with farm work. Although they were not arranged, marriages often served practical purposes to assess the woman's abilities to become a housewife. The only acceptable way for women to escape marriage and motherhood until the 1960s was to become a nun.

2. Although the notion of "waves" is sometimes disputed to qualify feminist movements, this term allows to establish women's fight in a spatiotemporal fashion. The "first wave" was marked by claims for women's equality in the public sphere, so much so in terms of political and civil rights than in terms of economic rights. After earning the right for education, women were then successively given access to the labor market and the right to vote.

3. This five minute animation which was produced by Margaret Pettigrew and Kathleen Shannon illustrates the dream of a young girl that finds herself in the seabed and befriends an octopus. The two friends drink tea, play golf, dance and tell each other stories.

4. This term is used to designate when a man moves into his wife's home. In this semi-sedentary society, agriculture is common practice as opposed to the nomad hunter-gatherer Algonquin societies. For Iroquois people, hunting and fishing consists in secondary practice.

5. From now on, women would always be found responsible for adultery and rape was almost never punished by law.

6. Some jobs from the domestic sphere are paid in the public sphere, such as women and men cleaners, launderers and cooks.

7. Translators' note: In the published translation of Guillaumin's book *Racism, sexism, power and ideology*, the term *sexage* which had been coined by the author was not translated. For the sake of consistency, the term has not either been translated in this book.

8. According to Guillaumin, the four key elements of "*sexage*" relations are the appropriation of time, products of the body, sexual obligation and the physical charge of the members of the group. In the unwritten contract of marriage, the woman's time is being appropriated as she has no schedule. She is required to be available day and night, seven days a week, 24 hours a day. "It is as if the wife is actually owned by the husband, and each man has the enjoyment of the class of women, and particularly each man who has acquired the private use of one of them" (Guillaumin, [1995], p. 182). Wives are not the only ones to work tirelessly for the 'head of the family'. Other women that are not submitted to the contract of marriage with the head of the family, such as daughters, sisters, aunts, cousins, etc. are also victims of this appropriation of time: "[. . .] (the woman, the women) are expected to do the cleaning and arranging, to look after and feed the children, to sweep or to serve the tea, to do the dishes or to answer the telephone, to sew on the button or to listen to the metaphysical and professional ramblings of men, etc." (Guillaumin, 1995, p. 182)

CHAPTER 8

The Reassessment of Social Relations between the Sexes

THE USE OF FILM animation to offer an alternative solution to traditional representations of relations between men and women appears to be a winning narrative strategy. Some directors at the NFB took their distance from traditional imagery and used animation to put forth their personal point of view. Visualizing this internal experience facilitated the conveyance of emotions and fostered a sense of closeness between the protagonists and the spectators.

In that aspect, Francine Desbiens was a pioneer who worked for 34 years in the French department of animation at the NFB as an animator, director and producer.[1] Markedly interested in family, her cinematographic work opened the discussion between feminist creation and film animation. Through her filmography, Desbiens built a unique legacy which, to a certain extent, constitutes the natural prolongation of her private life in her creations. In creating films that way, Desbiens erased the boundary between her life and her artistic work.

Francine Desbiens graduated from the *Institut des arts appliqués de Montréal* and started working at the NFB in 1965 as an attendant at the photo library. She walked the hallways of the cultural agency with her portfolio in hand in hopes to show her creations and be hired as an

DOI: 10.1201/9781032694382-11

artist. In 1965, her encounter with René Jodoin (who was about to create the French animation department) was life-changing, he promised to hire her as soon as the studio opened. Francine Desbiens quit from her permanent position and worked as a freelancer for the studio as an assistant for scholar productions. As previously mentioned, she co-directed *Le corbeau et le renard* [FR] (1969) in collaboration with Pierre Hébert, Yves Leduc and Michèle Pauzé.

Francine Desbiens' first solo directing project, which was produced by Pierre Hébert, stayed close to the theme of Canadian identity quest produced by the NFB. As State employee, Desbiens was aware of her role which consisted in the creation of content for the Canadian population. In that aspect, Jodoin encouraged his recruits to make their debuts with scientific and educational films. With *The Little Men of Chromagnon* (1971) which was an educational film on the range of colors, Desbiens wished to teach the population. However, behind this pedagogical mission, the message of the animator is clear: there existed no pure colors, different cultures were connected vessels and colors were blended. Louise Carrière, feminist historian of Québec film, said of *The Little Men of Chromagnon*: "Our prejudice and our social behaviours favour common denominators and impose norms at the expense of the distinctions and the respect of every individual. Here, intolerance toward a peer's color or shape brings up the question of appearances. Are we all judged based on what we are or rather based on what we come across as?" (Carrière, 1988, p. 348, our translation). There was an eminently feminist question.

A few years later, Desbiens created a more personal film: *Dernier envol* [FR] (Desbiens, 1977). The film was produced by René Jobin and was inspired from a short story by Roch Carrier. Cut-out animation was used to tell the story of a man whose peace was troubled by the arrival of a bird in the spring. The two protagonists became inseparable and time passed so quickly that once fall arrived, the man realized he could not live without the bird's company. Therefore, he did everything in his power to keep the bird with him, but it died from the cold.

THE BREAKDOWN OF THE TRADITIONAL FAMILY UNIT

Variations on: Ah! Vous dirai-je, maman[2] (Desbiens, 1985) was produced by Yves Leduc and is subjectively the strongest work from Francine Desbiens' repertoire. The film consists in a series of picture frames from a family photo album around which the plot unfolds with the cycle of life of the protagonist, from birth to adulthood. Desbiens brought to life the existence of an everyday woman by centering on her day-to-day routines.

The depiction of the household, which is the focus of the film, is associated to the author's private sphere. For the family, the household is at the centre of the world, although the one represented by Desbiens is unlike the traditional family unit. The protagonist is not exclusively destined to the private sphere. As opposed to *The Spring and Fall of Nina Polanski* (Hutton and Roy, 1974), *Variations on: Ah! Vous dirai-je, maman* does not play out in the kitchen, but rather in a multifunctional room which changes and evolves throughout the film.

From the start, the room showcases a big piano. In art, feminist self-representation is often a means for protestation regarding traditional representations. By illustrating her universe, Francine Desbiens emphasizes her musical knowledge and artistic ambitions. Desbiens was not the only one to showcase her knowledge through self-portrait, as some women painters also incorporated elements hinting at their own knowledge in the scenery of their creations.

For instance, Marietta Robusti painted a musical instrument and a partition to show her musical knowledge in her self-portrait (1580) while Angelica Kauffmann emphasized her cultural knowledge with the bust of Minerva as well as her sketchbook in hers (around 1780). Self-portraits offered new methods of representation to woman artists, such as Frida Khalo who used the subject in multiple of her works. In *Henry Ford Hospital* (1932) the artist expressed her pain from a second miscarriage in Detroit.[3] In *The Two Fridas* (1939),[4] Kahlo then communicated the ache she felt from her divorce with artist Diego Rivera. Frida Kahlo created multiple self-portraits throughout her career.

Differentialist feminists[5] encourage women to represent themselves in their creations as subjects since self-representation and agency are notions that are tightly linked to this school of thought. Through a self-portrait, the artist can express her aspiration or her rebellion and, therefore, open a new space to operate a transformation of self-representation. Artist Artemisia Gentileschi created radical interpretations of femininity based on mythology by painting powerful and decisive women. In *Judith Slaying Holofernes* (1611), Gentileschi painted the moment when Judith and her servant violently cut the sleeping captain's head off. The women were strong, decisive and energetic. The emanations of blood intensify the violence of the murder. In *Self-Portrait as the Allegory of Painting* (around

1636–1639), the artist chose an atypical position in which she did not look at the spectator as her head was turned sideways, focused on her painting. As a result, she related to her role of creator (of her art) by showing her deep absorption by her work in the making.

Family evolution is the main theme of *Variations on: Ah! vous dirai-je maman* (Figure 8.1). In this house, we can see multiple photographic portraits on the wall form a family tree. In the middle of the screen, the parent-child relationship is emphasized with a rocking chair placed next to an empty cradle. The characters' absence on screen is subversive. By omitting to show the woman and the child, the author broke the notion of *gaze* (Mulvey, 1975). Ghost-like, the protagonist destroys the function of *to-be-looked-at-ness* (Mulvey, 1975) of the feminine figure in cinema. However, the presence of the mother appears in the soundtrack as she can be heard humming the melody of *Varieties on: Ah! vous dirai-je maman*. The mother's body as she plays the piano is invisible, but the piano notes move as if they were touched by a spirit.

FIGURE 8.1 *Variations on: Ah! vous dirai-je, maman.*

Desbiens used symbols to represent the evolution of the family. For example, cut-out pink and blue hearts meshed together to land on the cradle and give birth to the baby. The first section of the film paints a positive picture of the young family as the photographs on the wall change to illustrate the evolution of the baby near her parents. Multiple gifts are shown under the Christmas tree. The child's toys change as she grows up. Winter comes and the film undergoes a total transformation. The peaceful environment of the family's confinement explodes as lightning and thunder rage. The couple splits and red hearts fall to the ground and break.

The child is now an adult and a white dress placed on a rack and the sound of an organ suggest that her marriage is being celebrated. The inside of the house becomes more modern. A portrait of the newlyweds appears on the wall. The cradle gives way to the marital bed, but blue hearts bring it back. A new baby is born. The cycle of his childhood is represented by multiple photographs and drawings. However, the peaceful family environment is destroyed again as the second couple also splits.

Desbiens staged women who break the holy matrimony and raise their children alone twice. The director created an avant-garde feminine world while leaving room for women viewers to imagine a strong model for themselves to aspire to. The two protagonists free themselves from the constraints of the matrimonial union in favor of the uncertain universe of single mothers. The second protagonist suggests her newly single mother financial struggles when the bills pile up and her to-do list gets longer, but through the symbolism of a typewriter which functions on its own, she seems to emancipate professionally and earn a living.

Desbiens explores the private sphere of her life through her aesthetic choices and her cinematographic discourse. She describes the passing of time and the rupture of the family unit as they transform through memories, presenting "[. . .] a film that is loaded with autobiographical details, a film that is, for Francine Desbiens, some sort of reminiscence of her own existence" (Jean, 2006, p. 118, our translation). Francine Desbiens directed another family-centered film produced by Yves Leduc, *Dessine-moi une chanson* [FR] (Desbiens, 1990). This film depicts a childhood marked by an absent parental figure represented by a working father. Presented through the child's point of view, the film places in his mouth highly touching words. At daycare, the little boy misses his musician dad deeply. He calls him to send him hearts. The dad's absence devastates the child. The director therefore breaks the representation of a perfect and happy childhood.

Desbiens thus shows a man from this new generation of fathers who contribute to the education of their children. Desbiens, being a single mother herself, might have wanted to represent her own son who missed his dad.[6]

Still Point (Gervais, 1983; Figure 8.2) is another film pertaining to a lost family. It is five minutes and thirty seconds and was produced by Robert Forget. Suzanne Gervais, who was trained in drawing, sculpting, and painting at the Montreal School of Fine Arts, is another important artist from the NFB's first women animators. Through her discovery of McLaren's work, she came to understand that film animation did not only consist of cartoons. She started working at the NFB assisting Clorinda Warny with whom she learned to animate. She directed her first animated film *Cycle* [FR] (Gervais, 1971) at the NFB as the studio fostered a favorable environment to her artistic approach. This five-minute film was produced by Pierre Hébert and consisted in lead pencil drawings on white paper. The animation is continuous throughout the film, which justifies the absence of cuts. Pictures are made from a series of transformations of a human body, the universe, nature and the cosmos. Gervais directed many

FIGURE 8.2   *Still Point.*

films at the NFB, such as *La plage* [FR] (Gervais, 1978) and *The Studio* (Gervais, 1988) just to name a few.[7]

Still Point is a mysterious and reflective short film. Its narration focuses on a woman's internal dialogue as she looks back on her existence. Various pictures are hung on the walls of her home, but the relationships which tie the characters together remain unclear. The narrator says: "Sometimes she whispered that the child on the photo was hers, refused to recognize herself. Reflections were blank, were useless. It caused her pain to stand upright. She lived in silence, scarcely moved the air around her. She said she'd lost her voice, her imagination. And sometimes, she screamed, for fear of going dead. And fear, fear was her only luxury" (Gervais, 1983). The pictures seem to represent the portraits of a father, a mother and their three children.

With no clarity on the characters' relationships, the woman's emotional pain is however palpable: "But the wound offers nothing to the eyes or to the fingers' touch, not even an old scar to be felt, to be sued by our breath. And if she still cried, her tears brought no return" (Gervais, 1983). The protagonist's attempts at catching the photographs' subjects fail as they disappear. The woman shrinks. She is tiny. She is crying. A bird comes to grab her with its beak and flies away.

Analyzing this film, Carrière wrote: "the individual breaks free from its shell, looking for a balance between impulses and experience, the repetition of the same movements, the representation of objects and dreams in a way that it lifts the veil on the past and gives way to a calmer imagination. This film is a quest to find rhythm in life, to align and find its way despite anguish, sorrow and memories. To function despite and with it all" (Carrière, 1988, p. 347, our translation).

Still Point makes use of multiple animation techniques: painting, photography and cut-out animation. The choppy imperfect movements which characterize Suzanne Gervais' animated films are manifest. This short film tells the dark family story of a rather anonymous woman. Loneliness accompanies her as she is alone with her cat. The director presents a gloomy and mysterious woman who is trapped in her memories. Isolated, she lives in a closed-off world.

The choice of the theme of sexuality to express a creator's point of view is a means at the centre of the alienation of women. Its use in women's creations often stems from agency as it allows the production of a discourse where directors can criticize, protest and denounce. This narrative strategy allows for the reversal of the social dominance of women and the oppression of their bodies through the identification of certain fantasies and desires. Women animators at the NFB also put forth different representations of relationships between men and women.

RELATIONSHIPS BETWEEN MEN AND WOMEN

Beginnings (Warny, 1980) is a first explorative step on the sexuality of women in an animation at the NFB. Clorinda Warny's posthumous film depicts the theme of sexuality from a feminist point of view, based on the author's personal experiences while criticizing androcentric representations. Subversively, Clorinda Warny explores the sexuality of women differently than in traditional cinema. The animator had the will to act on cinematographic stereotypes, therefore debunking the myth of the heartbreaker, the prostitute, the lesbian, etc. By speaking up, Warny presented herself as a subject rather than an object. The director said of her film:

> In order to direct a film such as the one that we are currently making, it is necessary to truly feel it, to "feel it in your gut." This film links nature and people. Not only does it consist in the four seasons of nature, but also in the four seasons of a couple. It is a visual comparison of what is fundamentally united.
> (Warny, quoted in Champoux, 1977, p. 2, our translation)

In *Beginnings*, the representation of sexuality conforms with the feminine archetype of Mother Earth created for a traditional collective imagination. The sexual heteronormative representation, the driving force of gender divisions and the segregation of women in the private sphere, confines Clorinda Warny's stance to a vision of sexual relationships between men and women. The essentialist version of the woman mother nature results in its ultimate biological destiny: childbirth. However, the director deserves credit for not having hypersexualized sexual relations and the feminine protagonist.

A reversal of the stereotyped representation of the sexes unfolds. The feminine character is not created as a sexual object coveted by the masculine desire, but rather as its equal. The woman is under no circumstances submitted to her partner. In that sense, it is a positive point of view of women's power and agency through their sexuality. "*Beginnings*' biggest strength lies in its ability to reconnect us with primal impulses and energies, the rhythm of the seasons, of the wind, of the sea and of love. It touches on the rampage and the relief of passions and pain, adaptation to life and so many other themes which describe the threads of our hidden existence" (Carrière, 1984a, p. 43, our translation; Figure 8.3).

Erotism complexity is put forward with continuous transformations of intertwined bodies. Different body parts merge, combine into one, then separate as the seasons pass. The approach is poetic while the sometimes abstract and fluidly moving lines are hypnotic. The lines take part in choreography as they transform continuously giving the impression of kissing faces, welded bodies, phallic symbols, feminine curves and metaphors of the life of a fetus. Embraces and arms unite, fire rages behind passionate hugs. Folds and crevices successively take the form of buttocks, thighs and breasts. The way natural elements and human bodies are put in relation allows a red rising sun in the horizon, behind a mountain, to slowly turn into a nipple perked up at the sky. As the point of view rotates, mountains break away from the naked bodies of a man and a woman.

Although the first seasonal sequences of the film present a positive and united vision of the couple from the spring thaw until the summer

FIGURE 8.3 *Beginnings.*

Source: Warny, 1980, © NFB, all rights reserved.

warmth, the short film ends during the winter suggesting painful emotions since a storm, wind, thunder and lightning are shown. The couple's passion is gone. A feeling of distress, sadness and isolation stems from the cold blue color at the end of the film. The protagonists no longer make love. They are seated next to one another, in the sea, drifting away. Does it imply an impossible cohabitation of the couple whose worn out passion has trapped them in silence and solitude? Regardless, as snow appears, the humans have disappeared.

The film's colorization is an essential narrative aspect. The change in colors support the evolution of the dramatic arc as Warny, Gagnon and Gervais used "pastels, stamps and Prismacolor crayons to provide depth to the drawings . . . the colors were animated, they were given life" (Gagnon, quoted in Champoux, 1977, p. 8, our translation). The range of colors establishes the temperature and the precise lighting for each season which intensifies the emotions felt by the audience. In 1981, the film earned the *Special Jury Award* at the Annecy International Animation Film Festival. The mystification of the artist due to her premature death,[8] as well as the film's narrative and aesthetic qualities, had contributed to the public's high interest for the film. *Beginnings* is an essential film. It is an incursion into the director's personal universe and her vision of her inner world with an expertly measured touch of sexuality which, therefore, leaves room for various interpretations. Warny animated feminine desire among a heterosexual androcentric world in a personal manner. "Desire for the masculine Other, but also, through which appears a desire for oneself, a desire to exist on one's own terms and enjoy life as a subject" (Lord, 2009, p. 35, our translation). Harvard professor and filmmaker, Ruth Lingford, highlighted the animators' expression of sexuality in their films:

> There is often a frank and earthy expression of sexuality which is a million miles away from the stereotyped cartoon sexiness. . . . There has been a tendency for women to use animation as an intimate, confessional means of expression . . . an extension of the clarification and projection of the inner world which may be what many women animators find so satisfying.
>
> (Lingford, n.d.)

The difficult relations women have with men is another personal aspect of women's lives shown in the films of women animators at the NFB. The illustration of this theme is explored in the following films: *Climates* (Gervais, 1972), *Oniromance* [FR] (Roy, 1987), *Eye* (Elnécavé, 1972), *Just a Little Love Song* (Elnécavé, 1974) and *La plage* [FR] (Gervais, 1978).

After *Cycle*, Suzanne Gervais directed *Climates* (Gervais, 1972; Figure 8.4), a ten-minute animated film produced by Pierre Moretti. Without narration, the film explores romantic relationships. Gervais adopted a rigid animation technique with watercolors and inks. The film's imagery is fixed. It is the film of a painter looking for the potential purpose of paint in film animation.

> Her work is the expression of a quest, an ongoing reflection on art's ability to get to the bottom of things. This desire to reach the "bottom" of her characters beyond their "shape" has, in fact, important aesthetic repercussions on her films with the most important one undoubtedly being that of the reconsideration of movement.
> (Jean, 2006, p. 27, our translation)

FIGURE 8.4   *Climates.*

Source: Gervais, 1975, © NFB, all rights reserved.

Subjectively, *Climates* resembles a stylistic exercise rather than a cinematographic work due to its visual elements unveiling the process of creating watercolor paintings. *Climates* uses painting as a medium for animation therefore displaying its limits rather than its true artistic potential. Watercolor is harder to transform than acrylic, gouache or oil paint as it dries quickly and is translucent.

Climates is a series of abstract paintings that represent natural Earth sceneries, such as mountains, lakes and the sea. Color tones are varied but are grouped in distinct sections. At the beginning of the film, the colors suggest the action is happening in the fall, later evolving towards winter. In comparison, the last segment of the film put forth bold red colors symbolizing the love between the characters, then bold blue colors symbolizing their breakup. *Climates* is a back and forth between figurative portraits of men, women and couples, and more abstract sceneries as bodies and natural elements sometimes intertwine which explains how a couple lying by the sea could also be seen as a mountain range.

The director mostly represents sad or neutral-looking characters. No smile can be seen throughout the film. Couples seem distant. If they embrace, they barely look at each other or their eyes are closed. Human warmth seems inaccessible outside of the bedroom. The animator's message appears unambiguous; relationships between men and women are conflictual, difficult and disappointing.

Oniromance (Roy, 1987) is another film which explores difficult romantic relationships between men and women. The film was produced by Yves Leduc and was Luce Roy's only project at the NFB. The five-minute animation was drawn with wooden pencils on paper. The film begins with a black and white close-up of a duvet. As the camera backs up, a woman, deeply asleep, is revealed under the covers. Gradually, yellow colorization appears on the bedsheets and becomes an animation of a field of wheat. A red bird hidden in the wheat flies away. A dollhouse moves on the duvet towards the wheat. The wheat disappears. A shot shows a small house's blue door opening on a window that gives onto the blue sky.

A black rotary phone rings and the handset picks up on its own. Multiple identical telephones ring in various rooms of the house. The wires are intertwined. Identical telephones cover the floor in the hallway. A red light vigorously flashes, and the phones ring continuously.

Back in the bedroom, the woman is in bed. The telephones ring again and it seems to slightly wake her up. A man sitting at a table appears on her duvet. Multiple bottles of alcohol surround him. He dials a phone number on a telephone similar to the ones previously illustrated. The woman does not pick up. The man disappears. A phone rings again. The man has re-dialed the number to talk to the woman. Represented by a black silhouette holding the phone up to his ear, he appears with his back facing the viewer on the duvet. The woman wakes up a bit more, but still does not pick up. At last, the man calls the woman from a phone booth that quickly moves across the duvet. The woman finally wakes up and sits in her bed. She gets up, picks up the phone, but no one is at the end of the line.

Several interpretations are possible. The director might have tried to illustrate the domestic violence the woman is victim of. The protagonist is constantly harassed by her spouse who is trying to get in touch with her. The fact that the numerous calls won't wake her up might show she is so used to this violence that she does not notice it anymore. The film might also represent a missed date caused by the woman taking so long to pick up that the man gave up. *Oniromance* animates a couple's communica-tion issues and suggests the two lovers' inability to get in touch, not only over the phone, but also to imply a failure of communication in terms of values, ideals and objectives. The film ends with a shot of the empty bed with its messy sheets. Does this image foreshadow the inevitable break up of a couple who no longer communicates? Only the director can answer this question.

As mentioned in Chapter 2, the first film to be directed by a woman at the French animation studio is *Our Sports Car Days* (Elnécavé, 1969). The animator then directed *Eye* (1972), *Just a Little Love Song* (1974) and *Luna, Luna, Luna* (1981). *Eye* is an experimental eight-minute animation produced by Pierre Moretti that was drawn with wooden pencils and felt markers on paper. The animation begins with large raindrops falling to the ground with one of them transforming into an eye. A character comes out of this eye: a strange blue protagonist with a moon-shaped head who continuously changes into abstract shapes. At first, he crawls, then melts into a swirl before changing into the shape of a sphere with two legs and two wings. The half-human half-animal spherical figure splits into two characters who mirror each other's movements. A third identical but smaller character appears between the first two ones. Here, the director might have represented parents with their child. The three disappear, but the first protagonist quickly reappears crawling before changing into two new entities with one of which being a sphere chasing after him. Another giant eye comes out of the character's hand and it tries to crush the character who represents an obstacle for his stride. The eye then transforms into a ball tied to the protagonist's foot. A group of unhappy men struggle to walk. The eye starts to fly taking the protagonist with him. Both turn into an abstract shape floating on water. Multiple eyes take over the screen before they burst. Hands attempt to catch them as heads and other eyes appear. The film ends. This experimental short film can be seen as a poetic representation of human existence with all its beauty and ugliness. The idea of the domination and monopolization of others is explored through a character who cannot get rid of an eye that turns into its ball and chain keeping him from emancipation. The protagonist is stuck and cannot escape.

Two years later, the director finished *Just a Little Love Song* (Elnécavé, 1974; Figure 8.5), a ten-minute animation produced by Gaston Sarault. Commenting on the title of this film, Carrière wrote: "Voluntarily ironic, the title has nothing to do with the two shapes' ruse, their destructive

FIGURE 8.5 *Just a Little Love Song.*

Source: Elnécavé, 1974, © NFB, all rights reserved.

force, as they mate, flip and suck each other in" (Carrière, 1983, p. 150, our translation). This short film, created with black ink drawings on paper, begins with the initial shape of a rocking chair in movement. A worm comes out of the ground, followed by another. A split happens and there are three worms. They are hit by a baseball bat and change back into the initial shape of the rocking chair. However, the chair moves differently as it now has arms and throws punches. It then plunges its hands into a black square from which it takes out a rooster-sounding parrot. The chair turns into a masculine human figure and attempts to strangle the bird. Of course, the bird tries to break free from its attacker's grip.

A fight ensues between both characters, and the bird is made a prisoner with its wings now tied to ropes. The man reveals pointed teeth. A gun appears in his hands and fires at the bird. Under the violence of the impact, the bird is beheaded. A close-up of the bird's head shows him drawing his last breath. Then, the human character transforms into a woman as breasts appear on the body. The woman plucks the feathers from the dead bird, preparing to cook it. She juggles with the carcass, puts it up on her head and starts to run. The rocking chair returns with threatening pointed teeth and turns into a man chasing the woman bearing a chicken head. The two stop and eagerly devour the bird's flesh.

The two protagonists now appear in the form of two big mouths tied to one another that swallow and devour each other before splitting in two. The woman comes out from one of the mouths and starts to dance. Her stomach grows bigger and bigger. An umbilical cord emerges from her belly button before turning into a lump of soft paste. She vigorously jumps on the mass as it tries to escape. The woman kneads the paste to turn it into dough. The mass then turns into a laughing child. The mother holds the child on her lap, rocks, cuddles and plays with the baby before throwing it to the man who spanks him violently.

The next shot shows the child licking the palm of his father's hand, then licking the top of his mother's foot. The mother presents the child the sole of her other foot which he continues to lick enthusiastically. The mother disappears and the child, terrified, curls up on the floor. The worm from the beginning of the film returns and gets eaten by the child. The foreground shows a hand playing yo-yo with the head of the bird that had been devoured by the parents. The child attempts to catch the head. They succeed and also plays yo-yo with it before throwing it in the air. As the head flies off, the child's arms turn into wings. They start to fly. The bird's head returns near the child and snatches his wings. The bird comes back to life and its body, now whole, allows him to flutter in the sky. The child runs as fast as it can to catch the bird. He manages to jump on the bird's back, and they both fly away, but the child falls off. The parents wait on the ground and the father tries to stab them. The mother holds the child by the wrists and succeeds to immobilize it. The father then kills the child with a knife, thus marking the end of the film.

La plage [FR] (Gervais, 1978; Figure 8.6) is a three minute and thirty-second film created with black pencils on white paper that was directed by Francine Desbiens. This film, an adaptation of Roch Carrier's novel, marked Suzanne Gervais's first attempt at implementing a literary aspect to her work. The silent film offers fluid and abstract animations. A man drinks a glass of water on the beachside while a woman is drowning in the background. She simultaneously appears in the waves and in the man's glass. Alone and dead, she ends up stranded on the shore. At first glance, this film seems to depict the banality of drownings, but it could also be

FIGURE 8.6 *La plage* [FR].

Source: Gervais, 1978, © NFB, all rights reserved.

interpreted as a representation of the difficult communication between a man and a woman, as no one notices the tragedy unfolding nearby.

> The search for harmony remains a demanding quest. In films such as *Cycle*, *Climates*, the trauma presented in *La plage*'s [FR], and the synthesis that represents *Still Point*, the spirit breaks free from its shell, looking for a balance between impulses and experiences. The repetition of the same movements, the representation of objects and dreams until they become part of the individual. These films are a quest to find rhythm in life, to align and find its way despite anguish, sorrow and memories. To function despite and with it all.
>
> (Carrière, 1984a, p. 44, our translation)

In this section, animations presented different models of relationships between men and women as well as modifications to family units. In the next chapter, focus will be put on the professional accomplishment of women in art and on the dangers related to the essentialization of their creations.

NOTES

1. Desbiens produced five movies in the French department of animation: *Chérie, ôte tes raquettes* [FR] (Leduc, 1975), *La plage* [FR] (Gervais, 1978), *Moi je pense* [FR] (Tunis, 1979), *Cogne-dur* [FR] (Daudelin *et al.*, 1979) and *Luna, Luna, Luna* [FR] (Elnécavé, 1981).
2. Translators' note: The title is a clear reference to the children lullaby *Ah! vous dirai-je maman*. The English lullaby *Twinkle, Twinkle Little Star* was created using the melody of *Ah! vous dirai-je, maman*.
3. The background presents the industrial scenery of the city. The artist wrote the name of the hospital on her bed. Six red (umbilical) cords tie her to a fetus and to a pelvis that was damaged by an accident which happened when she was 18 years old that caused her incapacity to complete a full-term pregnancy. The red blood on the sheets conveys the physical, but also the psychological pain of the artist.
4. This painting shows two Fridas sitting and holding hands. The one on the left is fragile and is wearing a bloodstained wedding dress. The one on the right is strong, is wearing a traditional Mexican dress and is holding a tiny portrait of her ex-husband.
5. Differentialist feminists believe that men and women are of different "natures" which, as an indirect result, leads them to be accused of being essentialists.
6. Desbiens's career at the NFB continued in the 1990s with *To See the World* (Desbiens, 1952), an animation which showcases a young man being driven

to the train station by his grandfather in order to travel the world. He is then confronted with socioeconomical struggles from different populations. In *The Tournament* (Desbiens, 1995), the author tells the story of a young deaf girl who manages to ignore her opponent's foolishness during a chess tournament. Finally, her last film at the NFB, *My Child, My Land* (Desbiens, 1998), is a commissioned piece of work which discusses antipersonnel landmines.

7. More information on *La plage* [FR] (Gervais, 1978) is available at the end of this chapter and for *The Studio* (Gervais, 1978), it is provided in the next section.

8. Clorinda Warny passed on March 4, 1978, at the age of 39 years old from a heart attack, during the production of *Beginnings*. As the film's animation had been completed, the French department of the animation studio decided to salvage it and hire Lina Gagnon and Suzanne Gervais to finish the colorizing process.

CHAPTER 9

Professional Accomplishment and the Trap of Essentialism

ACCESS TO THE LABOR market and socioprofessional accomplishment consist in important stakes to improve the condition of women, not only because this environment allows them to feel a sense of accomplishment that is different from the traditional roles of marriage and motherhood, but also because of the financial autonomy provided by their salary. Nonetheless, prestigious professional careers remain harder to reach for women, especially in filmmaking.

Speaking up and representing their perception of their surroundings are often a major achievement for women artists as there are multiple obstacles for them to overcome: lack of moral and financial support, exclusion from the select masculine artistic domain, and prejudice on their qualities and creative skills. As shown in the critical essay "Why have there been no great women artists?" (Nochlin, [1971] 1998) which was considered by many as the founding article of the feminist history of art, artists of a same period often had more in common than artists who were categorized by genre.

With this essential denunciatory text, Nochlin "analyses the representation of power relationships which she refers to as 'the work of ideology' in works of art" (Dumont and Sofio, 2007, p. 28, our translation). Her political stance questions the multiple reasons invoked to exclude women from

DOI: 10.1201/9781032694382-12

the arts. Instead of rethinking the concept of author, Nochlin criticized the absences and the silences of the history of art. Seeing as the solution does not reside in the addition of a plethora of women artists' names, she suggests looking at the way the discipline was established, in other words, to question its pretension to a universal documentation. To speak of a typically feminine art only exacerbates the essentialism of the dominant position. Therefore, the author suggests multiple avenues explaining the causes for the exclusion of women in the world of arts: the sexualization of the labor market, the man-woman domination, sociocultural prejudices, the myth of the artistic genius, access for women to education, and the filiation of fathers. For Nochlin, access to the status of artist somewhat depended on family education: "What if Picasso had been born a girl? Would Señor Ruiz have paid as much attention or stimulated as much ambition for achievement in a little Pablita" (Nochlin, [1971] 1998, p. 155)? What would have been Pablita Picasso's destiny? Would Pablo's father, an artist himself, have encouraged and educated his child the same way if he hadn't been a boy?

The opportunity to access patriarchal education establishments to receive artistic training similar to the one provided to men was a priority for women artists. This lack of access to education for women painters and sculptors was for a long time the cause to their exclusion from the artistic community. This segregation kept them from reaching the top of the discipline. For example, in the hierarchy of classic arts, nude art long represented the quintessence of beauty. However, until the 1900s, women could not participate in sittings with nude models. They practised with farm animals and plants. Not fully trained, women were relegated to works that were considered of minor importance, such as portraits and still life paintings. Women's only role in nude art consisted in posing.

The Studio (Gervais, 1988) is a short film in which the animator completely reversed the traditional view of artists and their models. Produced by Yves Leduc, the ten-minute film was made with various animation techniques, including drawings, cut-out paper, sculptures and painting. The animation puts forth a different perspective on the relationships between men and women in the context of artistic production. In The Studio, a fully dressed woman plays the role of the artist while the masculine model poses naked, showcasing a feminine creation and a masculine muse. The conversation between both characters and the protagonist's internal dialogue pertain to existential questionings. The Studio deals with how we see ourselves, how we perceive others and how others perceive us.

THE STUDIO (GERVAIS, 1988)

The Studio is a leading film of Suzanne Gervais' corpus (see Figure 9.1). This short film begins in an artist's studio where various blurry drawings are displayed on the wall and a sculpture covered in bandages stands in the foreground. Footsteps are heard. A masculine voice says: "Hello." A warm and reassuring feminine voice responds: "Come in. You can leave your clothes here." He answers: "Thank you." The title of the film appears in white letters: *The Studio*.

The camera moves to reveal the studio where multiple grey clay human figures are placed haphazardly on the table. The necessary tools are displayed on the wall in the background. The woman gently talks to her model: "Sit any way you like." In a choppy movement, the camera backs up and moves to the right to reveal the naked man. His back is facing the camera. The woman studies him carefully. He looks down modestly and covers his genitals with his hands. The camera moves towards the sheet of paper highlighting the pencil held in the artist's hand. A quick and abstract transition ensues on a mirror allowing the viewer to see the model from the woman's point of view. She draws and thinks: "He was there, motionless,

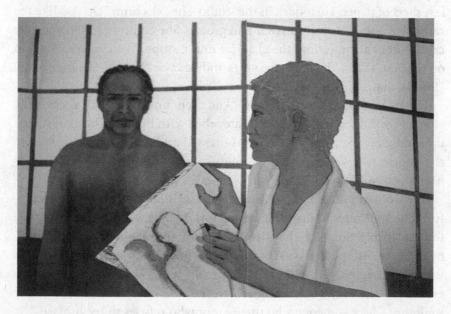

FIGURE 9.1 *The Studio.*

posing in the light of the studio." The timid man closes his eyes while the woman continues to work on different sketches. The camera closes in on the model's face. She continues: "Only his glance, his intense gaze revealed the life within." Again, the model closes his eyes. The artist thinks: "In the studio, I've noticed time is different, slower. An interior world, a place to find oneself, it takes time to learn to trust, discover the face of a stranger."

The work session is over. Now dressed, the man walks towards the artist. The camera closes in on the woman's face: "Suddenly, he was there in front of me." She places her hand in front of her mouth as to protect it. A close-up shows the man's hand as he takes the money from the woman's hand. The man says: "Thank you." She answers: "See you next week." The model leaves the studio.

Now alone in her studio, the artist takes off the fabric covering her sculpture. She looks at it from different angles. "A face, like a landscape suddenly revealed to us, which now we must explore. A landscape thirsting for rain." She puts the fabric back on the sculpture.

A series of charcoal sketches of the naked man appear on screen. Introspectively, she continues her reflection: "Once again, I'm searching." She moves a last drawing which reveals the naked masculine model on the last sheet of paper. He is back in the studio. She asks him: "Do you like the rain?" He does not really answer and groans. She continues: "Do you ever cry?" After this question, the classical music stops. The camera closes in on the man's face. The music resumes and he says: "Never." She carries on: "I think that. . . . No, nothing."

Her internal narration resumes: "And then, unsure, we fall silent." The woman continues her work. She is absorbed with her art. The man stands up and leaves the frame. He returns dressed and reaches his hand out to the woman. She says, internally: "I didn't realize it was so late." She hands him money and says: "Thank you." He leaves the studio.

The woman pins her new sketch to the wall and returns to her sculpture. She continues to shape it, turning towards the wall from time to time to draw inspiration from her drawing. "We can imagine anything. Little by little, we feel the approach of something like a color which overwhelms us, and we begin to grasp this landscape which had escaped us. . . . Do you ever cry?" The man's voice echoes: "Never." The artist works on another sculpture. "Like someone who turns away, who refuses to see himself."

A black and white photograph of Pablo Picasso is displayed on the wall. Pablo Picasso looks at the camera and, in the background, his back reflects in a mirror. The woman places her hand on the picture and takes it off the wall to examine it. The film cuts to a wider shot of the studio where the woman props up a large mirror on the wall. The naked man is standing and his reflection appears in the mirror. He says: "Like this? In front of the mirror?" She answers: "Yes, yes. In front of the mirror." The model looks at himself and objects: "But. . . ." He turns to her. The woman remains silent. He looks at his reflection. She begins to draw him and tells him: "You're worried, but I won't see anything in you that isn't a part of you. What I'm looking for is already there, in you." She adds touches of red on the charcoal portrait she is working on. With this new color, she draws the outline of another character meant to be a copy of the man. She compares her drawing to her model. "I'm waiting from one word from you, one gesture that will reveal this otherness, you." The model looks at his reflection in the mirror as it transforms into a mummified body. Then, the illusion disappears. He turns to the woman and says: "Shall we stop?" She responds: "Oh, of course. Would you like a coffee? Come." The man who has put on a white robe continues his introspection and stares at his reflection in the mirror. The artist returns: "You're not coming?" The two look at each other intensely. The man says: "But what is it you're really trying to do?" She answers: "I'm searching."

The model walks towards the sculpture. The artist continues: "I'm trying to find out who we are, inside." He questions her: "Inside?" Now naked, the man is standing in front of the mirror again, looking at himself. His reflection now in black and white gives the impression of having been sketched by the artist with lead pencil on white paper. The woman says: "You look at yourself. Who comes to meet you? The person you were or the one you will become?" Different portraits of the man appear in the mirror. The music is dramatic. There is tension. The man looks at the woman harshly. He snatches the artist's drawing, examines it and drops it. He gets dressed and leaves the room. The woman tries to catch up to him with money in her hand: "Wait!" But it is too late, the man has disappeared.

Standing in her studio, she unwraps the sculpture, revealing two men turning their backs to each other. "Are we so fragile inside? Must a part of us always remain broken?" She touches her own reflection in the mirror. The model comes back. She turns to face him. Silent, they look at each other, then at the sculpture. The man says: "Shall we continue?" The film ends.

Interview (Leaf and Soul, 1979) is another creation produced at the NFB that focuses on women's professional accomplishment. This film is an incursion in two women's experience with the creation of a short film at the NFB. This animated film inside another animation is a *mise en abyme* of the creation process. The protagonists' art, work, and personal life intertwine, blurring the limits between documentary and fiction.

Mises en abyme rarely appear in commercial cinema, but they can be showcased in auteur cinema. "The concept of 'film in a film' can, depending on the director, fulfil different objectives, but each time, a questioning on the nature of cinema is at the center of the work" (Hamel, 2011, p. 48, our translation). Multiple directors have illustrated the reflective narrative in cinema, such as Frederico Fellini (*8^{1/2}*, 1963) or François Truffaut (*Day for Night*, 1973). They both used a fictive double to illustrate their point of view on film directing. In the context of Hollywood cinema, the reflective narrative usually criticizes the American cinematographic production system with films such as *The Player* (Altman, 1992) or *Mulholland Drive* (2001) and *Inland Empire* (2006), two films by David Lynch.

> Although these cineast's approaches are fundamentally different, their films show a common preoccupation: the relationship between the artist and their work. The process of mise en abyme allows them to reflect on this issue, to theorize it while including it in a dramatic narrative structure.
>
> (Hamel, 2011, p. 51, our translation)

Interview offers a self-portrait of the working filmmakers as the creation process is put into picture. The characters tied to the making of the film are the directors themselves. They are not playing a role; they are playing their role as they make film animation. The directors present the story of their creation by depicting themselves, revealing their desires and values.[1]

Interview is a 13-minute film produced by David Verrall with Derek Lamb as executive producer. For the NFB this film is atypical, since it presents an intimate and open discussion between Caroline Leaf and Veronika Soul. Their narration puts forth their existential questionings regarding identity and the profession of director. Not only is *Interview* a self-portrait, but it is also the portrait of one director by another. The women inquire, reply and compare each other. Seen working on an animation, they offer a rare perspective in NFB's cinema with a *mise en abyme* of what the work of animator consists in as well as feminist questionings. More than just an anecdotal conversation, the film touches on a universal subject—women's experience—from an internal point of view. Strong themes of the film are autobiography, reflexivity, feminine creation and the professional emancipation of women.

INTERVIEW (LEAF AND SOUL, 1979)

The two directors were born in the United States. Caroline Leaf directed her first animated film, *Sand or Peter and the Wolf* (Leaf, 1969), as part of her degree in visual arts at Radcliffe College. She was already demonstrating great talent. With this film, she was granted a scholarship from Harvard University and completed two films: *Orfeo* (Leaf, 1970) and *How Beaver Stole Fire* (Leaf, 1971). Norman McLaren discovered her work when he visited Derek Lamb in Boston. Leaf was invited to work at the NFB in 1972 where she directed multiple films[2] before setting aside film animation to focus on her painting career. In the 1970s, Caroline Leaf was the animator at the NFB who reached the greatest notoriety internationally. As for Veronika Soul, she worked for American magazines and arrived in Montréal in 1970. She created her first film at McGill University. At the NFB, she directed multiple animations[3] before leaving Canada to pursue a prolific career in the United States.

Interview is a clever mix between reality and fantasy (see Figure 9.2). The animation techniques highlight the contrastive and unique personalities of the animators; the combination of Leaf and Soul's respective talents is the one of this work's biggest strengths. Both animators leave a distinct mark on the film, since their styles of animation are different. When Leaf's segments are rhythmic, Soul's are slow. Veronika Soul mainly made her animations from cut-out images found in photographs and newspapers, while Caroline Leaf specialized in animations painted under the camera, a time-consuming and laborious process.

The film begins with a series of black and white photographs on which Caroline Leaf and Veronika Soul are seen sitting at a kitchen table. While Caroline holds the switch to take photographs, the directors give the viewer the impression of witnessing the recording of the film. Caroline says: "This is a film about two people who make movies, usually not about themselves." Veronika answers: "That's Caroline, screen right. And I am Veronika, screen left." Caroline: "Hollywood, Hollywood! Ho, that could be our title." Veronika: "No, our film is called *Interview*."

The narration highlights the directors' relationship with each other and with the film they are creating. The audience can identify Caroline and Veronika based on their appearances and their voices. This *mise en abyme* is an atypical narrative approach that allows viewers to witness both the

FIGURE 9.2 *Interview.*

Source: **Leaf et Soul, 1979, © ONF, tous droits réservés.**

creation process and the recording of the film. The film itself becomes a third character due to the emphasis on its technical device. Being the visual echo of the directors' internal worlds and personalities, animation is the third protagonist in *Interview*.

The film continues in Veronika's apartment as she wakes up. The animated light added to the photograph gives the impression of a sunrise. The protagonist is sitting in her bed and yawns. Time passes by, yet Soul remains still. The animation technique used in this shot is mixed since it turns into the recording of live action during which Veronika touches her hair. Veronika: "I should look like my ideal person. I should look like David Bowie and act like Lauren Bacall. I always wanted to be a man but now I don't because I would have to lose too much. There could never be a man like me." This intriguing narration could hold multiple meanings: she might be transgender, have a masculine mind trapped in a feminine body, highlight creative possibilities limited by gender or that creations are not limited by gender.

The film continues with a photograph of Caroline's naked shoulder on which is written: "location change—Caroline's apartment." Contrary to Veronika, Caroline lives in a modest apartment. Multiple colored photographs are shown to unveil her morning routine: she takes a shower, makes coffee, and gets dressed. Caroline says: "I like to be alone in the morning. I like to do things slowly, but it makes me late for work." At that moment, Leaf is completely still although the soundtrack suggests otherwise. In the same shot, she appears multiple times coming in and out of the frame under various animated representations. Pixilation is used to document Leaf as she puts her coat on and turns into an animated character. She turns back into her human form when she opens her front door and takes the elevator. Veronika compares her own personal situation: "I am never late. I work at home."

Caroline looks directly into the camera and then looks at her reflection in the mirror. She says:

> I love adulation. Oh Caroline! I want to kiss you. . . . On the snout! People like my films and it makes me like myself more than I used to. But I think people see my films and they don't see me. I don't think very many people see me.

An abstract double exposure of multiple Veronikas in her workshop shows her working, picking up the phone and drinking coffee. The camera's point of view unveils her creation.

In her workshop at the NFB, Caroline Leaf is working under the Oxberry animation camera and is painting her film. The room is completely dark, there are no windows, and the director is only lit by the lights directed towards the animation table. Leaf is animating a sequence while she describes her creative process. She says:

> I love what my hands are doing. I would never sacrifice my own life now for anybody. My work is like finger-painting on glass. I draw a new shape in the paint with a wood stick and fill it in with my fingers. Then I wipe away the old image with a wet cloth, so when I'm finished there's nothing left except the film. Drawing and re-drawing the image makes it move.

The camera moves closer to Leaf's workspace to reveal the complexity of the animation process. The artist's hand is seen in action: it draws, paints, erases and records images. Caroline says of her creative process:

> My work is so slow. But I don't have to redraw each image completely. I'm only careful with shapes I know the eye will follow.

> I work in a dark dark room without windows, all day. It's calm and it's cut off from the excitement of daily life. I love it! But my work would be more powerful if I didn't hide from life. I feel I'm losing my life. I feel trapped by my own personality.

In comparison with Veronika, Caroline is rather reserved. She works alone all day without talking to anyone and suffers from isolation. These creation conditions are the cause of her discomfort. In the animation room, an enormous character painted on the real shots comes out from the background and walks around Caroline before stopping near her. He whispers in her ear:

"Trapped!" He disappears and Leaf continues to work. Caroline: "When you make movies, you are your own anesthesiologist."

In the window of her apartment, Veronika is looking out, standing still: it is daytime. Slowly, the lighting changes. Initially shown against the light, the inside of the apartment is revealed when the lights turn on and the city turns dark. A whole day goes by without Veronika moving away from her window.

The last segment of the film unfolds in the lively environment of a restaurant. Similar to the beginning of the film, Leaf and Soul are sitting next to each other, but their bodies are painted and their photographed faces have been reworked with a photocopy machine. The two protagonists stare at a plate questioningly: a blue and green fish. A large white hand appears and takes the plate from the table. "I want to eat and drink." Multiple plates with different meals are carried above Soul's head and she looks at them with envy. "I would like to get thinner." This last segment of the film immerses the protagonists in an eclectic universe where they self-represent in an imaginary world. The painted characters, humans and animals, come from the animated sequence Caroline had previously been painting earlier in the film. The two animators devour their meal, socialize, enjoy themselves, then return to the solitude of their apartments. This marks the end of the film.

The two friends show creativity by compressing both of their personalities in one day while simultaneously working on the creation of their film and the one being watched by the audience. They are therefore directing a documentary without using traditional documentary techniques. The filmmakers' individual journeys resonate with that of other animators. They are in the margins of the traditional roles associated to women. The animators, wishing to make women's experience in film animation visible, reveal their creation conditions at the NFB. It is an artistic approach supported with a feminist discourse that revalues the profession of women animator directors. The directors take over the position of the discursive authority with the chosen genre (animated autobiographical documentary), the narrative mode combining personal statements and discussions between both creators, and the film structure. Both protagonists are free and independent women who refuse to opt for the constraints of married life.

Interview is a film in which the directors speak up. The animation presents a political position resisting to traditional "feminine" models, making its subversive potential real. The protagonists' agency is also remarkable. In addition to the creation of a work of art, they place themselves outside of social dictates limiting women to the private sphere, reproduction and sexism. Leaf and Soul accomplish themselves professionally while creating films that are different from the institution's usual productions. They portray themselves as "feminine figures who craft and assert their identities as subjects and actors" (Lord, 2009, p. 26, our translation). Therefore, Leaf and Soul hold an autonomous status that is never defined by another person. The directors also break traditional cinematographic conventions by integrating animation techniques in narration when films tend to hide cinematographic production devices.

NOTES

1. A wide variety of films in which directors self-represent themselves at work exists: *Aprile* (Moretti, 1998), *Tomorrow and Tomorrow Again* (Cabrera, 1998), *Bologna Centrale* (Dieutre, 2003) and *Panic Bodies* (Hoolboom, 1998) (Tinel, 2004).
2. *The Owl Who Married a Goose: An Eskimo Legend* (Leaf, 1974), *The Street* (Leaf, 1976), *The Metamorphosis of Mr. Samsa* (Leaf, 1977) and *Two Sisters* (Leaf, 1991).
3. *Tax: The Outcome of Income* (Soul, 1975) and *Poets on Film No. 2* (Soul, 1977).

Conclusion

THIS NEW READING OF film animation history in the province of Québec and in Canada touched on the condition and the visual representations of women, the NFB as an institution, the socioprofessional insertion of women directors as well as the corpus of feminist animated films produced by the NFB. It was proven that these pioneer animators were active agents of their destiny and that their works revealed the true oppression of women within the limits of an institutional liberal egalitarian feminism that is neither intersectional, nor representative outside of heteronormativity. The directors of this corpus have contributed to the evolution of the representation of gender relations in cinema by presenting protagonists as thoughtful and attentive subjects who are oppressed in the private and public sphere.

However, it should be acknowledged that there are still multiple stereotypes on the competencies attributed to women. "Anne-Claire Poirier, pionneer of the new wave of women directors at the NFB, says that she once wanted to complete an internship to work cameras, but that she was ridiculed for aspiring to a masculine profession" (Véronneau, 1980, p. 3, our translation). Questioning women's professional qualities and "their aptitude to create, generally associated to the larger question of 'art sex,' was, in history, always subordinated to the conscience of a double standard regarding arts" (Dumont and Sofio, 2007, p. 17, our translation). Louise Beaudet, a film animation historian, came to a similar conclusion as she noticed that women animators seemed less tempted to use new technologies to direct their films compared to their masculine counterparts:

> Would they be instinctively protecting themselves from often alienating exterior forces by preferring to work directly under the camera using nearly artisanal methods that only require a small circle of collaborators, thus keeping complete control over their productions?
>
> (Beaudet, 1983, p. 218, our translation)

DOI: 10.1201/9781032694382-13

Bélanger and Migner-Laurin (2012),[1] come to the same conclusion in their study *Les réalisatrices du petit écran* [FR] pertaining to the situation of women directors in the television world. Although the authors observe that women use more and more technical methods that were once men's prerogative, the fact remains that they are victims of preconceived ideas regarding their qualities. "If women directors now claim to possess technical competencies and knowledge, the same cannot be affirmed for the trust granted to them in their workplace regarding those aptitudes" (Bélanger and Migner-Laurin, 2012, p. 72, our translation). Women in film direction experience similar situations because their technical abilities are discredited. The authors bring up another important issue: the absence of feminine models to whom women directors can identify.

> This absence is not only linked to the limited number of women in the profession, but also to the lack of recognition. Often limited and part of a minority among a profession that is already little known and recognized by the general public, it remains of a high importance for women to be surrounded by examples of success.
>
> (Bélanger and Migner-Laurin, 2012, p. 75, our translation)

If there exists a mental and political space where men keep dominating, it is in cinema. For example, in May 2018, at the prestigious Cannes Film Festival, 82 women walked up the steps of the Palais des Festivals to denounce the inequalities in the field. These women symbolized the 82 female directors that have had their film nominated as part of the official competition since the inauguration of the festival in 1939 against 1,688 masculine directors. The following year (2019), the festival nominated a record number of women-directed films: 4 out of a total of 21. Until very recently, *The Piano* (Campion, 1993) was the only women-directed film to have won the Palme d'or. However, Campion shared this prize with a man, the director of *Farewell My Concubine* (Kaige, 1993). It was only in 2021 that a Palme d'or was awarded to a sole female director: Julie Ducournau with *Titane* (Ducournau, 2021). In 2023, another woman received the prestigious award: Justine Triet with *Anatomy of a Fall* (Triet, 2023).

In the United States, few women were ever nominated at the Oscars for fiction feature film direction.[2] It was only in 2010 that Kathryn Bigelow became the first woman to be awarded the prize with *The Hurt Locker* (2008), followed by Chloe Zhao with *Nomadland* (Zhao, 2020) and Jane Campion with *The Power of the Dog* (Campion, 2021). As for animated feature films, out of the women to have been nominated,[3] only two[4] have been awarded an Oscar for best animation, but they have always shared their prize with male co-directors.

These observations are not trivial since recognition is an important factor for film promotion and conservation. Prestigious prizes set artists on the international stage and contribute to the progress of their career, but it appears that women are still excluded from these acknowledgments.

Within the National Film Board of Canada, the collaboration between Norman McLaren and Evelyn Lambart exemplifies the discredit of women's labor and the anonymization of their contribution. Norman McLaren received many honours and has marked history whereas Lambart long remained anonymous. Nowadays, she is being rediscovered and revalued, but mainly for her contribution to McLaren's work and not her personal art. Having worked on many of McLaren's films, she remained in the shadows, unknown and almost absent from historical documentation.

The lack of consideration brought to contemporary female directors' works is another form of oppression within an artistic field that is marginal and marginalized. Torill Kove,[5] Martine Chartrand,[6] Amanda Forbis and Wendy Tilby[7] remain virtually unknown by the general public although they have been awarded prestigious and coveted prizes.[8] Considering all the means and funds needed, filmmaking is practically a privilege. The weight of traditions, the persistent idea of the profession as masculine and the investors' omnipresence is unfavorable to women. The questioning of their professional qualities and their creative aptitudes is proof of the double standard in the appreciation of their work. However, there are now more and more women-made films. Every form of media is calling loud and clear for parity in film direction. For more than ten years, the group Réalisatrices Équitables (RÉ) has been doing activist work to raise awareness and denounce the gender disparity in Québec cultural productions. They have published multiple studies[9] and their conclusions are worrying. RÉ notices a surprising disparity between the number of women in educational institutions and their true presence on the labor market. If 43 to 60% of students in film production are women, they only represent 31% of the members of the Association des Réalisateurs et Réalisatrices du Québec (ARRQ). Therefore, gender relations in student cohorts do not reflect the reality of the labor market. What happens between the time they graduate and enter the labor market?

Women in cinema remain victims of inequalities and discrimination: "lower budgets, lower pay, restricted film genres, limited range of roles, lower on-screen longevity, reduced film broadcasting, lack or absence of longevity" (Rollet, 2017, p. 7, our translation). It is essential to keep implementing positive discrimination measures, not only at the NFB, but also in all film financing organizations, such as the SODEC and Telefilm Canada to encourage the emergence of a new wave of women-made productions. It should be noted that there is a certain resistance regarding equality measures since funding diversity leaves experimented filmmakers with the impression of paying for such measures and being victims of agism.

At the end of July 2019, RÉ used the media to criticize how granting agencies entertained the illusion that parity was practically reached by claiming that "half" of their financed works were produced by women. RÉ blamed these agencies for using terms such as "almost," "nearly," or "near half of the chosen projects" to report on equality measures when, in reality, women did not benefit from half of the available funds, but rather from a third. Without minimizing the efforts made to reach parity, much still has to be done. Based on the numbers compiled by RÉ, during Telefilm's 2017–2018 financial year, only 28% of the 73 million dollars allocated for fiction feature films went to female directors. Statistics only tell half the story. There are often more women working on low-budget films, such as documentaries.

The NFB's official and temporary solutions to this difficult issue have been proven effective in the 1970s when critical feminist films influenced society by succeeding to resonate among the population (especially isolated women) by introducing in the public sphere issues experienced by women of the private sphere. Live-action productions have raised awareness among women by specifically focusing on their issues (abortion, labor market, day care, etc.). By favoring the spread of women's voice, the NFB has not only become active in the discussion, it also provided a space for that discussion to take place. Nonetheless, the cuts in the subsidies granted by the federal government to the institution have largely toned down the frenzy over animated creations in Canada both for men and women creators. Their consequences have revealed to be devastating for film production. This was not limited to animation seeing as the abolition of Studio D in 1996 now keeps Canadian women directors from an internationally unique and essential production vessel to put contemporary feminist claims into picture.

Animation, being closely related to fantasy, is more easily freed from the narrative conventions limiting the representation of women. Women directors' contribution to film animation at the NFB has allowed them to put into picture the plurality of women's lives in their daily experiences therefore breaking the essentialist representations of feminine figures in cinema. In broadening their cultural practices to include the feminist thought, the NFB's institutional animation holds new representations. This programming integrates political, social, economic, and historical dimensions in cultural productions as well as in broadcasts of innovative and personal animated films and generates a new aesthetic of animation contributing to raising awareness and making social change.

To account for women's daily experience using animation cinema offers the unique opportunity to revisit history under the lens of feminism and understand the realities and challenges of society. Being submitted to a similar oppression in the field of film production, women should work together to develop a collective project for the betterment of their creation conditions. In cinema, the feminist fight is not held against men: they are needed as allies in order to build an egalitarian and equal society. The solution does not reside in replacing a power structure with another, but rather in allowing the collectivity—by making social gender relations more egalitarian—to experience relationships that are freed from the grip of domination.

NOTES

1. This study was jointly funded by the Association des réalisateurs et réalisatrices du Québec (ARRQ) and the Community Services department at Université du Québec à Montréal (UQAM).
2. *Seven Beauties* (Lina Wertmüller, 1975), *The Piano* (Jane Campion, 1993), *Lost in Translation* (Sofia Coppola, 2003), *The Hurt Locker* (Kathryn Bigelow, 2008), *Lady Bird* (Greta Gerwig, 2017), *Nomadland* (Chloe Zhao, 2020), *Promising Young Woman* (Emerald Fennell, 2020) and *The Power of the Dog* (Jane Campion, 2021)
3. *Persepolis* (Paronnaud and Satrapi, 2007), *Kung Fu Panda II* (Jennifer Yuh Nelson, 2011), *How to Train Your Dragon 2* (Arnold and DeBlois, 2014), *Frozen* (Buck and Lee, 2013), *Brave* (Andrews and Chapman, 2012), *Loving Vincent* (Kobiela and Welchman, 2017), *The Breadwinner* (Twomey, 2017) and *Turning Red* (Shi, 2023).

4. Brenda Chapman (2012) and Jennifer Lee (2013).
5. Oscar for the Best Animated Short Film with *The Danish Poet* (Kove, 2006).
6. Golden Bear for the Best Short Film at the Berlin International Film Festival with *Black Soul* (Chartrand, 2001).
7. Palme d'or for the Best Short Film at the Cannes Film Festival with *When the Day Breaks* (Forbis and Tilby, 1999).
8. It could be argued that a similar problem with the recognition of talented male directors' works, such as Paul Driessen, Cordell Barker, or Chris Landreth, but to this day, there are no female equivalents to Norman Mclaren and Theodore Ushev.
9. *Encore Pionnières. Parcours des réalisatrices québécoises en long-métrage de fiction* (Lupien *et al.*, 2011), *La Place des réalisatrices dans le financement public du cinéma et de la télévision, mise à jour des statistiques* (Lupien, 2012), *L'avant et l'arrière de l'écran. L'influence du sexe des cinéastes sur la représentation des hommes et des femmes dans le cinéma québécois récent* (Lupien *et al.*, 2013) and *La place des créatrices dans les postes clés de création de la culture au Québec* (Réalisatrices équitables, 2016).

Appendix A: Short Films Directed by Marie-Josée Saint-Pierre

Bertrand, M. and Perrier, J. (producers) and Saint-Pierre, M.-J. (producer and director). (2016). *Oscar* [animated film]. Canada: MJSTP Films and National Film Board of Canada.

Bertrand, M. (producer) and Saint-Pierre, M.-J. (producer and director). (2014). *Jutra* [animated film]. Canada: MJSTP Films and National Film Board of Canada.

Létourneau, Y. (producer) and Saint-Pierre, M.-J. (director). (2022). *Lauzon's Theory* [animated film]. Canada: Périphéria Productions.

Saint-Pierre, M.-J. (producer and director). (2004). *Post-Partum* [documentary film]. Canada: MJSTP Films.

_____ (2006). *McLaren's Negatives* [animated film]. Canada: MJSTP Films.

_____ (2008). *Passages* [FR] [animated film]. Canada: MJSTP Films.

_____ (2010). *The Sapporo Project* [animated film]. Canada and Japan: MJSTP Films and S-Air Artist Center.

_____ (2012). *Femelles* [FR] [animated film]. Canada: MJSTP Films.

_____ (2014). *Flocons* [FR] [animated film]. Canada: MJSTP Films.

_____ (2018). *Your Mother Is a Thief!* [animated film]. Canada: MJSTP Films.

Appendix B: Short, Animated Films Directed by Women at the National Film Board of Canada (1939–1989)

Arioli, D., McGregor, J. and Koenig, W. (producers) and Lanctôt, M. (director). (1975). *A Token Gesture*.

Besen, E. (director). (1979). *Sea Dream*.

Desbiens, F. (producer) and Daudelin, M., Lebel, E. and Saint-Pierre, R. (directors). (1979). *Cogne-dur* [FR].

Desbiens, F. (producer) and Gervais, S. (director). (1978). *La plage* [FR].

Desbiens, F. and Moretti, P. (producers) and Elnécavé, V. (director). (1981). *Luna, Luna, Luna*.

Duncan, A. and McLaren, A. (directors). (1951). *Folksong Fantasy*.

Forget, R. (producer) and Gervais, S. (director). (1981). *Still Point*.

Forget, R. and Leduc, Y. (producers) and Gervais, S. (director). (1988). *The Studio*.

Glover, G. (producer) and Bennett, C. (director). (1975). *The Housewife*.

Glover, G. (producer) and Borenstein, J., Cohen, S., Perlman, J. and Soul, V. (directors). (1977). *Poets on Film No. 2*.

Glover, G. (producer) and Doucet, R. and Hartmann, F. (directors). (1977). *Poets on Film No. 3*.

Glover, G. (producer) and Heczko, B., Lewis, E., Perlman, J. and Thomas, G. (directors). (1977). *Poets on Film No. 1*.

Glover, G. (producer) and Leaf, C. (director). (1976). *The Street*.

Glover, G. (producer) and Reiniger, L. (director). (1976). *Aucassin and Nicolette*.

Glover, R. (producer) and Soul, V. (director). (1975). *Tax: The Outcome of Income*.

Jodoin, R. (producer) and Desbiens, F. (director). (1977). *Dernier envol* [FR].

Jodoin, R. (producer) and Desbiens, F., Hébert, P., Leduc, Y. and Pauzé, M. (directors). (1969). *Le corbeau et le renard* [FR].

Jodoin, R. (producer) and Elnécavé, V. (director). (1969). *Our Sports Car Days*.

Jodoin, R. (producer) and Warny, C. (director). (1971a). *Multiplication 1*.

_____ (1971b). *Multiplication 2*.

_____ (1971c). *Multiplication 3*.

Johnson, G. (producer) and Maylone, B. (director). (1979). *The Magic Quilt*.

Hébert, P. (producer) and Desbiens, F. (director). (1971). *The Little Men of Chromagnon*.

Hébert, P. (producer) and Gervais, S. (director). (1971). *Cycle*.

Hébert, P. (producer) and Klein, J. (director). (1970). *Catuor*.

Hébert, P. (producer) and Olivier, S. (director). (1971). *Des ensembles* [FR].

Koenig, W. (producer) and Heczko, B. (director). (1973). *Pictures Out of My Life*.

_____ (1986). *Acid Rain*.

Koenig, W. and Lamb, D. (producers) and Perlman, J. (director). (1976). *Lady Fishbourne's Complete Guide to Better Table Manners*.

Koenig, W. (producer) and Lambart, E. (director). (1976). *The Lion and the Mouse*.

Koenig, W. (producer) and Michailidis, A. (director). (1974). *We*.

Koenig, W. (producer) and Smith, L. (director). (1974a). *Purple Hat*.

_____ (1974b). *Happy Birthday*.

_____ (1974c). *In the Center Ring*.

Koenig, J. and Verrall, R. (producers) and Szasz, E. (director). (1968). *Cosmic Zoom*.

Lamb, D. (producer) and Thomas, G. (director). (1977). *The Magic Flute*.

Lambart, E. (director). (1947). *The Impossible Map*.

_____ (1957). *O Canada*.

_____ (1968). *Fine Feathers*.

_____ (1969). *The Hoarder*.

_____ (1970). *Paradise Lost*.

_____ (1973). *The Story of Christmas*.

_____ (1974). *Mr. Frog Went A-Courting*.

_____ (1976). *The Lion and the Mouse*.

_____ (1980). *The Town Mouse and the Country Mouse*.

Leaf, C. (director). (1977). *The Metamorphosis of Mr. Samsa*.

Leduc, Y. (producer) and Desbiens, F. (director). (1985). *Variations on Ah! vous dirai-je, maman*.

Leduc, Y. (producer) and Roy, L. (director). (1987). *Oniromance*.

Long, J. (producer) and Maylone, B. (director). (1979). *The Hometown*.

_____ (producer) and Maylone, B. (director). (1981). *Distant Island*.

Moretti, P. (producer) and Elnécavé, V. (director). (1972). *Eye*.

Moretti, P. (producer) and Gervais, S. (director). (1972). *Climates*.

Moretti, P. (producer) and Klein, J. (director). (1972). *Modulations*.

Moretti, P. (producer) and Leaf, C. (director). (1974). *The Owl Who Married a Goose: An Eskimo Legend*.

Moretti, P. (producer) and Warny, C. (director). (1971). *The Egg*.

Patel, I., Smith, L. and Verrall, D. (producers) et Smith, L. (director). (1982). *The Sound Collector*.

Perlman, J. (producer and director). (1981). *The Tender Tale of Cinderella Penguin*.

Pettigrew, M. (producer) and Besen, E. (director). (1989). *Illuminated Lives: A Brief History of Women's Work in the Middle Ages*.

Pettigrew, M. (producer) and Borenstein, J. (director). (1987). *The Man Who Stole Dreams*.

Sarault, G. (producer) and Elnécavé, V. (director). (1974). *Just a Little Love Song*.

Sarault, G. (producer) and Klein, J. (director). (1973). *Sports Challenge*.

Sarault, G. (producer) and Warny, C. (director). (1972). *Happiness Is*.

_____ (1980). *Beginnings*.

Shannon, K. and Chatwin, L. (producers) and Hutton, J. and Roy, L. (directors). (1974). *The Spring and Fall of Nina Polanski*.

Thomas, G. (director). (1972). *It's Snow*.

_____ (1980). *A Sufi Tale*.

_____ (1984). *The Boy and the Snow Goose*.

Verrall, D. (producer) and Borenstein, J. (director). (1981). *Five Billion Years*.

Verrall, D. (producer) and Leaf, C. and Soul, V. (directors). (1979). *Interview*.

Verrall, D. (producer) and Leyer, R. (director). (1969). *Little Red Riding Hood*.

Verrall, D. (producer) and Smith, L. (director). (1979). *This Is Your Museum Speaking*.

Verrall, D. (producer) and Soul, V. (director). (1981). *Countdown Vignette*.

Filmography

Alexeïeff, A. and Parker, C. (producers and directors). (1933). *Night on Bald Mountain* [animated film]. France: Alexeïeff -Parker.

Alexeïeff, A. and Parker, C. (producers and directors). (1963). *The Nose* [animated film]. France: Alexeïeff-Parker.

Alexeïeff, A. and Parker, C. (producers and directors). (1972). *Pictures at an Exhibition* [animated film]. France: Films Roger Leenhardt.

Alexeïeff, A. and Parker, C. (producers and directors). (1980). *Three Themes* [animated film]. France: Alexeïeff-Parker.

Anderson, D.K. (producer) and Unkrich, L. (director). (2017). *Coco* [animated film]. United States: Pixar Animation Studios et Walt Disney Pictures.

Arnold, B., Sanders, C. and DeBlois, D. (producers) and Arnold, B. and DeBlois, D. (directors). (2014). *How to Train Your Dragon II* [animated film]. United States: DreamWorks Animation.

Asher, M., Janvey, D., McDormand, F. and Spears, P. (producers) and Zhao, C. (producer and director). (2020). *Nomadland.* [film]. United States: Searchlight Pictures, Cor Cordium Productions, Hear/Say Productions and Highwayman Films.

Askénazi, A., Lesage, B. and Garret, F. (producers) and Luciani, F. (director). (2006). *Le Procès de Bobigny* [film]. [FR] France: Mascaret Films and Danos, société de production.

Avril, P. and Mutu, O. (producers) and Mungiu, C. (producer and director). (2007). *4 Months, 3 Weeks and 2 Days* [film]. Romania and Belgium: Mobra Films Productions.

Barbagallo, A. and Labadie, J. (producers) and Moretti, N. (director and producer). (1998). *Aprile* [film]. Italy.

Bartosch, B. (producer and director). (1932). *The Idea* [animated film]. France: Théâtre du Vieux-Colombier.

Batchelor, J. and Halas, J. (producers and directors). (1954). *Animal Farm* [animated film]. United Kingdom and United States: Halas and Batchelor.

Beaudet, J. (producer) and Lepage, M. (director). (1995). *The Lost Garden: The Life and Cinema of Alice Guy-Blaché* [documentary]. Canada: National Film Board of Canada.

Beaudry, D. (producer and director) and Shannon, K. (producer). (1978). *An Unremarkable Birth* [documentary]. Canada: National Film Board of Canada.

Beech, E. and Patullo, C. (producers and directors) and Beecherl, E. (director). (2018). *Lotte That Silhouette Girl* [short documentary]. United States: EP Trick Studio.

Berbert, M. (producer) and Truffaut, F. (1973). *Day for Night 2* [film]. France: Les Films du Carrosse, PECF et PIC.

Bergeron, G. (producer) and Dansereau, M. (director). (1972). *La vie rêvée* [film]. [FR] Canada: Association coopérative de productions audiovisuelles.

Beveridge, J. (producer) and Marsh, J. (director). (1942). *Inside Fighting Canada* [documentary]. [FR] Canada: National Film Board of Canada.

Bigelow, K., Boal, M., Chartier, N., Mark, T., McCusker, D., Shapiro, G. and Ladjimi, K. (producers) and Bigelow, K. (director). (2008). *The Hurt Locker* [film]. United States: First Light Production et Kingsgate Films.

Bigras, J.-Y. and Delacroix, R. (directors). (1949). *Le gros Bill* [film]. [FR] Canada: Les productions Renaissance.

Birnbaum, R., Moore, D. and Todd, S. (producers) and Scott, R. (producer and director). (1997). *G.I. Jane* [film]. United States: Hollywood Pictures, Caravan Pictures, Roger Birnnhaum Productions, Largo Entertainment and Scott Free Productions.

Blackton, J.S. (producer and director). (1906). *Humorous Phases of Funny Faces* [animated film]. United States: American Vitagraph.

_____ (producer and director). (1907). *The Haunted Hotel* [animated film]. United States: American Vitagraph.

Blum, S. (producer) and Cabrera, D. (director). (1997). *Tomorrow and Tomorrow Again* [film]. France: Institut National de l'Audiovisuel.

Bobbitt, S.M., Mactaggart, I. and Welchman, H. (producers) and Kobiela, D. and Welchman, H. (directors). (2017). *Loving Vincent* [animated film]. United Kingdom and Poland: BreakThru Films and Trademark Films.

Bobet, J. (producer) and Carle, G. (director). (1964). *Solange dans nos campagnes* [short film]. Canada: National Film Board of Canada.

Borremans, G. (director and producer). (1960). *La femme-image* [film] [FR]. Canada.

Brakhage, S. (producer and director). (1959). *Window Water Baby Moving* [experimental film]. United States.

Brakhage, S. (producer and director). (1963). *Mothlight* [experimental film]. United States.

Brault, M. and Groulx, G. (directors). (1958). *Les raquetteurs* [documentary]. Canada: National Film Board of Canada.

Bray, J.R. (producer) and Fleischer, M. (producer and director). (1918). *Out of the Inkwell* [animated series]. United States: Paramount Pictures and Fleischer Studios.

Brossard, N., Guilbeault, L. and Wescott, M. (directors). (1978). *Some American Feminists* [documentary]. Canada: National Film Board of Canada.

Brown, D., Tolkin, M. and Wechsler, N. (producers) and Altman, R. (director). (1992). *The Player* [film]. United-States: Avenue Pictures, Spelling Entertainment, David Brown Productions and Addis-Wechsler.

Brüning, J. and Zirn, J.-P. (producers) and Jouvet, E. (director and producer). (2010). *Too Much Pussy! Feminist Sluts, a Queer X Show* [documentary]. France: Womart Productions, La Seine Productions and Jürgen Brüning Filmproduktion.

Bush, E., O'Neill, E. and Rudin, S. (producers) and Gerwig, G. (director). (2017). *Lady Bird*. [film]. United States: IAC Films, Scott Rudin Productions et Management 360.

Bute, M.E. (director). (1952). *Abstronic* [animated film]. United States: Ted Nemeth Studio Production.

Carmody, D. (producer) and Villeneuve, D. (director). (2009). *Polytechnique* [film]. Canada: Remstar Productions.

Chamson, N., Garand, J.M. and Poirier, A.C. (producers) and Danis, A. (director). (1973). *Souris, tu m'inquiètes* [film] [FR]. Canada: National Film Board of Canada.

Chapman, J. (producer) and Campion, J. (director). (1993). *The Piano* [film]. Australia, France and New Zealand: CiBy 2000 and Jan Chapman Productions.

Cobb, M. and Del Toro, G. (producers) and Yuh Nelson, J. (director). (2011). *Kung Fu Panda II* [animated film]. United States: DreamWorks Animation.

Cohl, É. (producer and director). (1908). *Fantasmagorie* [animated film]. France.

Colombo, A. (producer) and Wertmüller, L. (producer and director). (1975). *Seven Beauties* [film]. Italy and Yugoslavia: Medusa Produzione et Jadran Film.

Coté, G.L. (producer) and Poirier, A.C. (director). (1968). *Mother-to-Be* [documentary]. Canada: National Film Board of Canada.

Couëlle, M. and Godbout, C. (producers) and Mankiewicz, F. (réalisateur). (1980). *Les Bons Débarras* [film] [FR]. Canada: Productions Prisma.

Dansereau, F. (producer) and Brault, M. and Perrault, P. (directors). (1963). *Pour la suite du mode* [*Of Whales, the Moon, and Men*] [documentary]. Canada: National Film Board of Canada.

Dansereau, F. and Jobin, V. (producers) and Groulx, G. (director). (1961). *Golden Gloves* [documentary]. Canada: National Film Board of Canada.

Dauman, A. and Halfon, S. (producers) and Renais, A. (director). (1959). *Hiroshima mon amour*. France: Argos Films, Como Films, Daiei Studio et Pathé Entertainment.

De Chomón, S. (producer and director). (1908). *The Electric Hotel* [animated film]. France: Pathé Frères.

Derode, J., Pevsner, T. and Roth, R. (producers) and Zinnemann, F. (director). (1977). *Julia* [film]. United States: 20th Century Fox.

Desbiens, F. (producer) and Leduc, A. (director). (1975). *Chérie, ôte tes raquettes* [animated film]. Canada: Office national du film du Canada.

Desbiens, F. (producer) and Tunis, R. (director). (1979). *Moi je pense* [short film]. Canada: Office national du film du Canada.

Descaries, T. (producer) and Desbiens, F. (director). (1992). *To See the World* [animated film]. Canada: Office national du film du Canada.

_____ (1995). *The Tournament* [animated film]. Canada: Office national du film du Canada.

Disney, W. (producer and director). (1924–1927). *Alice Comedies* [short animated film series]. United States: Walt Disney Studios.

Disney, W. (producer) and Alger, J., Armstrong, S., Beebe, F., Ferguson, N., Handley, J., Hee, T., Jackson, W., Luske, H., Roberts, B. and Satterfield, P. (directors). (1940). *Fantasia* [animated film]. United States: Walt Disney Studios.

Disney, W. (producer) and Disney, W. and Iwerks, U. (directors). (1928). *Steamboat Willie* [animated film]. United States: Walt Disney Studios.

Disney, W. (producer) and Disney, W. and Iwerks, U. (directors). (1929–1939). *Silly Symphonies* [short animated film series]. United States: Walt Disney Studios.

Disney, W. (producer) and Geronimi, C, Luske, H. and Reitherman, W. (directors). (1961). *One Hundred and One Dalmatians* [animated film]. United States: Walt Disney Studios.

Disney, W. (producer) and Hand, D. (director). (1937). *Snow White and the Seven Dwarfs* [animated film]. United States: Walt Disney Studios.

Disney, W. (producer) and Hand, D.D. (director). (1942). *Bambi* [animated film]. United States: Walt Disney Studios.

Disney, W. (producer) and Kinney, J. (director). (1943). *Der Füehrer's Face* [animated film]. United States: Walt Disney Studios.

Disney, W. (producer) and Luske, H. and Sharpsteen, B. (directors). (1940). *Pinocchio* [animated film]. United States: Walt Disney Studios.

Disney, W. (producer) and Sharpsteen, B. (director). (1941). *Dumbo* [animated film]. United States: Walt Disney Studios.

Dufaux, G. and Perron, C. (directors and producers). (1964). *Solange dans nos campagnes* [short film]. Canada: National Film Board of Canada.

Dunning, G. and Low, C. (producers and directors). (1947). *Cadet Rousselle* [animated film]. Canada: National Film Board of Canada.

Dunning, J. and Link, A. (producers) and Héroux, D. (director). (1969). *Valérie* [film] [FR]. Canada: Cinépix Film Properties (CFP).

_____ (1970). *L'initiation* [film] [FR]. Canada: Cinépix et Productions Héroux.

Duparc, M. (producer) and Lefebvre, J.-P. (director). (1970). *Q-bec My Love—Un succès commercial* [FR]. Canada: Cinak Compagnie Cinématographique.

Eggelin, V. (producer and director). (1925). *Diagonal Symphony* [animated film]. Germany.

Fearnley, L. and Page, M. (producers) and Kove, T. (director). (2006). *The Danish Poet* [animated film]. Norway and Canada: Mikrofilms AS and National Film Board of Canada.

Fischinger, O. (producer and director). (1947). *Motion Painting No.1* [animated film]. Germany: Metro Goldwyn Mayer.

Flaherty, R.J. (producer and director). (1922). *Nanook of the North* [documentary]. United States: Pathé.

Forget, R., Leduc, Y., Dagmar, T. and Vallée, J. (producers) and Leaf, C. (director). (1976). *Two Sisters* [animation film]. Canada: Office national du film du Canada.

Frappier, R. and Malo, R. (producers) and Arcand, D. (1986). *Le déclin de l'empire américain* [film] [FR]. Canada: Films René Malo and National Film Board of Canada.

Garand, J.M. and Poirier, A.C. (producers) and Blackburn, M., Huycke, S., Morazain, J., Saïa, F. and Warny, C. (directors). (1973). *À qui appartient ce gage?* [documentary] [FR]. Canada: National Film Board of Canada.

Garand, J.M. and Poirier, A.C. (producers) and Dansereau, M. (1973). *J'me marie, j'me marie pas* [film] [FR]. Canada: National Film Board of Canada.

Garand, J.M. and Poirier, A.C. (producers) and Poirier, A.C. (director). (1974). *They Called Us 'Les filles du Roy'* [documentary]. Canada: National Film Board of Canada.

Garand, J.-M. (producer) and Favreau, R. (director). (1975). *Le soleil a pas d'chance* [documentary]. Canada: Office national du film du Canada.

Garand, R. (producer) and Bigras, J.-Y. (director). (1952). *La petite Aurore, l'enfant martyre* [film] [FR]. Canada: L'Alliance cinématographique canadienne, Inc.

Gélinas, G. (producer and director) and Delacroix, R. (director). (1953). *Tit-Coq* [film] [FR]. Canada: Les productions Gratien Gélinas (Québec).

Giraud, E. (producer) and Dieutre, V. (director and producer) (2003). *Bologna Centrale* [film]. France: Les Films de la Croisade.

Gitlin, M.P., Khouri, C. and O'Brien, D. (producers) and Scott, R. (producer and director). (1991). *Thelma and Louise* [film]. United States: MGM and Pathé Entertainment.

Green, P.B. (producer and director). (2018). *Be Natural: The Untold Story of Alice Guy-Blaché* [documentary]. United States: Be Natural Productions.

Grierson, J. (producer and director). (1929). *Drifters* [documentary]. England: New Era.

_____ (1934). *Granton Trawler* [documentary]. England: McGraw-Hill Contemporary Films.

Grierson, J. (producer) and Lye, L. (director). (1935). *Colour Box* [animated film]. England: GPO Film Unit.

Grierson, J. (producer) and McLaren, N. (director). (1938). *Love on the Wing* [animated film]. England: GPO Film Unit.

Guèvremont, P. and Poitevin, J.-M. (directors). (1943). *À la croisée des chemins* [film] [FR]. Canada: La société des missions étrangères de la province de Québec.

Guy-Blaché, A. (director). (1896). *The Fairy of the Cabbages* [film]. France: Gaumont Studio.

Guy-Blaché, A. (director). (1906). *The Birth, the Life and the Death of the Christ* [film]. France: Gaumont Studio.

Guy-Blaché, A. (director). (1914). *The Lure* [film]. United States: Solax Studio.

Hébert, P. (producer and director). (1966). *Op hop—Hop op* [animated film]. Canada: National Film Board of Canada.

Hébert, P. and Jean, M., Leduc, Y. (producers) and Chartrand, M. (director). (2001). *Black Soul* [animated film]. Canada: National Film Board of Canada.

Héroux, C. and Kemeny, J. (producers) and Héroux, D. (director). (1971). *7 fois . . . par jour* [film] [FR]. Canada: Minotaur Film Productions, Production Héroux and Steiner Films.

Héroux, D. and Héroux, J. (producers) and Carle, G. (director). (1981). *Les Plouffe* [film]. Canada: International Cinema Corporation.

Hagen, L. (producer) and Isaacs, J. (director). (1970). *The Art of Lotte Reiniger* [short documentary]. United Kingdom: Primrose Productions.

Hoolboom, M. (director and producer). (1998). *Panic Bodies* [film]. Canada.

Hsu, B., Hsu, F., Hsu, J., Ranvaud, D and Xia, Z. (producers) and Kaige, C. (director). (1993). *Farewell My Concubine* [film]. China: Beijing Film Studio and China Film Co-Production Corporation.

Jarvis, R.J. (producer) and Delacroix, R. (director). (1952). *Le rossignol et les cloches* [film] [FR]. Canada: Québec Productions.

_____ (1953). *Cœur de maman* [film] [FR]. Canada: Québec Productions.

Jodoin, R. (producer and director). (1961). *Ronde carrée* [animated film] [FR]. Canada: National Film Board of Canada.

_____ (1966). *Notes on a Triangle* [animated film]. Canada: National Film Board of Canada.

Jodoin, R. and McLaren, N. (producers and directors). (1944). *Alouette* [animated film]. Canada: National Film Board of Canada.

_____ (1969). *Spheres* [animated film]. Canada: National Film Board of Canada.

Johansson, S., Shannon, K. (producers) and Singer, G. (producer and director). (1984). *Abortion: Stories from North and South* [documentary]. Canada: National Film Board of Canada.

Johansson, S. (producer) and Signer, G. (producer and director). (1987). *A Mother and Daughter on Abortion* [documentary]. Canada: National Film Board of Canada.

Jousset, M., Kennedy, K., Rigault, X. and Robert, M.-A. (producers) and Paronnaud, V. and Satrapi, M. (directors). (2007). *Persepolis* [animated film]. France: TF1 Vidéo.

Jutra, C. and McLaren, N. (producers and directors). (1957). *A Chairy Tale* [animated film]. Canada: National Film Board of Canada.

Karmitz, M. (producer) and Chabrol, C. (director). (1988). *Une Affaire de femmes* [film] [FR]. France: Les Films du Camélia, Les Films A2, MK2 Productions et La Sept.

Kemeny, J. (producer) and Ballantyne, T. (director). (1967). *The Things I Cannot Change* [documentary]. Canada: National Film Board of Canada.

Koenig, W. and Kroitor, R. (producers) and Nelson, B. (director). (1974). *Propaganda Message* [animated film]. Canada: National Film Board of Canada.

Lamy, P. (producer) and Fournier, C. (director). (1970). *Deux femmes en or* [film] [FR]. Canada: Films Claude Fournier.

L'Anglais, P. (producer) and Gury, P. (director). (1949a). *Le curé de village* [film] [FR]. Canada: Québec Productions Corporation.

_____ (1949b). *Un homme et son péché* [film] [FR]. Canada: Québec Productions Corporation.

Larkin, R. (producer and director). (1965). *Syrinx* [animated film]. Canada: National Film Board of Canada.

_____ (1966a). *Cityscape* [animated film]. Canada: National Film Board of Canada.

_____ (1968). *Walking* [animated film]. Canada: National Film Board of Canada.

Lasseter, J., Del Vecho, P. and Scribner, A. (producers) and Buck, C. and Lee, J. (directors). (2013). *Frozen* [animated film]. United States: Walt Disney Animation Studios.

Lasseter, J. and Sarafian, K. (producers) and Andrews, M. and Chapman, B. (directors). (2012). *Brave* [animated film]. United States: Walt Disney Animation Studios.

Leaf, C. (director and producer). *Sand or Peter the Wolf* [animation film]. United States.

_____ *Orfeo* [animation film]. United States.

_____ *How Beaver Stole Fire* [animation film]. United States.

Leduc, Y. (producer) and Desbiens, F. (director). (1990). *Dessine-moi une chanson* [animated film]. Canada: National Film Board of Canada.

Lefebvre, J.-P. (producer) and Chabot, J. (director). (1970). *Mon enfance à Montréal* [film] [FR]. Canada: National Film Board of Canada.

Lefebvre, J.-P. (producer) and Patry, Y. (director). (1970). *Ainsi soient-ils* [film] [FR]. Canada: National Film Board of Canada.

Léger, F. and Murphy, D. (producers and directors). (1924). *Ballet mécanique* [film]. France: Synchro-Ciné.

Legg, S. (producer and director). (1942). *Inside Fighting Russia*. [documentary]. Canada: National Film Board of Canada.

Le Lorrain, E. (producer) and Nash, T. (director). (1982). *If You Love This Planet*. Canada: Office National du Film du Canada.

Leo, A., Moore, T., Rosen, A. and Young, P. (producers) and Twomey, N. (director). (2017). *The Breadwinner* [animated film]. Ireland, Canada, and Luxemburg: Cartoon Saloon.

Lindsey, C. (producer) and Shi, D. (director). (2023). *Turning Red* [animated film]. United States: Walt Disney Pictures and Pixar Animation Studios.

Low, C. (producer and director). (1952). *The Romance of Transportation in Canada* [animated film]. Canada: National Film Board of Canada.

Luciani, M.-A. and Harari, A. (producers) and Triet, J. (director). (2023). *Anatomy of a Fall* [film]. France: Les Films Pelléas et Les Films de Pierre.

Lye, L. (producer and director). (1958). *Free Radicals* [animated film]. United States: Len Lye Foundation.

_____ (1966). *Particles in Space* [animated film]. United States: Len Lye Foundation.

Malo, R. (producer) and Lanctôt, M. (director). (1980). *L'Homme à tout faire* [film] [FR]. Canada: Films René Malo.

Marsh, J. (director). (1942). *Women Are Warriors* [documentary]. Canada: National Film Board of Canada.

_____ (1943a). *Proudly She Marches* [documentary] [FR]. Canada: National Film Board of Canada.

_____ (1943b). *Wings on Her Shoulder* [documentary] [FR]. Canada: National Film Board of Canada.

_____ (1943c). *Alexis Tremblay: Habitant* [documentary] [FR]. Canada: National Film Board of Canada.

Martin, M. (producer) and Fortier, M. (director). (1964). *La Beauté même* [film] [FR]. Canada: National Film Board of Canada.

McCay, W. (producer and director). (1914). *Gertie the Dinosaure* [animated film]. United States: The Box Office Attraction Company.

_____ (1918). *The Sinking of the Lusitania* [animated documentary]. United States: Universal Films and Transatlantic Films.

McDormand, F., Spears, P., Asher, M. and Janvet, D. (producers) and Zhao, C. (director and producer). (2020). *Nomadland* [film]. United States: Highwayman, Hear/Say Productions and Cor Cordium Productions.

McLaren, N. (producer and director). (1941a). *Mail Early for Christmas* [animated film]. Canada: National Film Board of Canada.

_____ (1941b). *V for Victory* [animated film]. Canada: National Film Board of Canada.

_____ (1942a). *Hen Hop* [animated film]. Canada: National Film Board of Canada.

_____ (1942b). *Five for Four* [animated film]. Canada: National Film Board of Canada.

_____ (1944a). *Keep Your Mouth Shut* [animated film]. Canada: National Film Board of Canada.

_____ (1944b). *C'est l'aviron* [animated film]. Canada: National Film Board of Canada.

_____ (1947). *La poulette grise* [animated film] [FR]. Canada: National Film Board of Canada.

_____ (1949). *Experiments in Animated Sound* [animated film]. Canada: National Film Board of Canada.

_____ (1951). *Pen Point Percussion* [documentary]. Canada: National Film Board of Canada.

_____ (1952). *Neighbours* [animated film]. Canada: National Film Board of Canada.

_____ (1955). *Blinkity Blank* [animated film]. Canada: National Film Board of Canada.

_____ (1959). *Le merle* [animated film] [FR]. Canada: National Film Board of Canada.

_____ (1967). *Pas de deux* [animated film] [FR]. Canada: National Film Board of Canada.

_____ (1972). *Ballet adagio* [animated film]. Canada: National Film Board of Canada.

_____ (1983). *Narcissus* [animated film]. Canada: National Film Board of Canada.

McLaren, N. and Lambart, E. (directors). (1949). *Begone Dull Care* [animated film]. Canada: National Film Board of Canada.

_____ (1956). *Rythmetic* [animated film]. Canada: National Film Board of Canada.

_____ (1960). *Lines Vertical* [animated film]. Canada: National Film Board of Canada.

_____ (1962). *Lines Horizontal* [animated film]. Canada: National Film Board of Canada.

_____ (1965). *Mosaic* [animated film]. Canada: National Film Board of Canada.

McLaren, N. and Munro, G. (producers and directors). (1976a). *Animated Motion: Part 1* [documentary]. Canada: National Film Board of Canada.

_____ (1976b). *Animated Motion: Part 2* [documentary]. Canada: National Film Board of Canada.

_____ (1977). *Animated Motion: Part 3* [Animated Motion: Part 3]. Canada: National Film Board of Canada.

_____ (1978a). *Animated Motion: Part 4* [documentary]. Canada: National Film Board of Canada.

_____ (1978b). *Animated Motion: Part 5* [documentary]. Canada: National Film Board of Canada.

Méliès, G. (producer and director). (1902). *A Trip to the Moon* [film]. France: Star Film.

Menken, M. (director). (1945). *Visual Variations on Noguchi* [animated film]. United States.

Mohammadian, M. (producer) and McWilliams, D. (director). (2017). *Eleven Moving Moments with Evelyn Lambart* [documentary]. Canada: National Film Board of Canada.

Moretti, P. (producer) and Hoedeman, C. (director). (1972). *Tchou-tchou* [animated film]. Canada: National Film Board of Canada.

Oken, S. and Sherkow, D. (producers) and Lapine, J. (director). (1991). *Impromptu* [film]. United Kingdom and United States: Ariane Films.

Panahi, J. (producer and director). (2006). *Offside* [film] [FR]. Iran: Jafar Panahi Film Productions.

Panahi, J. (producer and director) and Atebbai, M. (producer). (2001). *The Circle* [film] [FR]. Iran and Italy: Jafar Panahi Film Productions, Lumière & Company, Mikado et Tele +.

Paré, L. (producer) and Bélanger, F. (director). (1971). *Ty-Peupe* [film] [FR]. Canada: National Film Board of Canada.

Patry, P. (producer and director). (1964). *Il y eut un soir, il y eut un matin* [short film] [FR]. Canada: National Film Board of Canada.

Pojar, B. (producer and director). (1972). *Balablok* [animated film]. Canada: National Film Board of Canada.

_____ (producer and director). (1981). *E* [animated film]. Canada: National Film Board of Canada.

Poirier, A.C. (producer and director). (1975). *Before the time Comes* [film]. Canada: National Film Board of Canada.

Poirier, A.C. (producer) and Girard, H. (director). (1974). *Les filles, c'est pas pareil* [documentary] [FR]. Canada: National Film Board of Canada.

Raymond, M.-J. (producer) and Fournier, C. (director). (1974). *La pomme, la queue . . . et les pépins!* [film] [FR]. Canada: Rose Films Inc.

Reiniger, L. (producer and director). (1926). *The Adventures of Prince Achmed* [animated film]. Germany: Comenius-Film G.m.b.H.

Reymond, C. (producer) and Ducournau, J. (director). (2021). *Titane* [film]. France: Arte France Cinema, Frakas Production and Kazak Productions.

Reynaud, É. (producer and director). (1892). *Un bon bock* [pantomime lumineuse]. France.

_____ (1892a). *Pauvre Pierrot!* [pantomime lumineuse]. [FR].

_____ (1892b). *Le clown et ses chiens* [pantomime lumineuse]. [FR].

_____ (1894a). *Un rêve au coin du feu* [pantomime lumineuse]. [FR].

_____ (1894b). *Autour d'une cabine* [pantomime lumineuse]. [FR].

Richter, H. (producer and director). (1921). *Rhythmus 21* [animated film]. Allemagne.

Rizzoli, A. (producer) and Fellini, F. (director). (1963). *8^{1/2}* [film]. Italy and France: Cineriz and Francinex.

Robbie, M., McNamara, J., Ackerley, T., Browning, B. and Fox, A. (producers) and Fennell (producer and director). (2020). *Promising Young Woman* [film]. United States and United Kingdom: FilmNation Entertainment and LuckyChap Entertainment.

Rudin, S., Bush, E. and O'Neil, E. (producers) and Gerwig, G. (producer, director, and scriptwriter). (2017). *Lady Bird* [film]. United States: IAC Films, Scott Rudin Productions and Management 360.

Ruttmann, W. (producer and director). (1921). *Lichtspiel Opus 1* [animated film]. Germany: Ruttmann Film G.m.b.H.

Schlesinger, L. (producer) and King, J. (director). (1935). *A Cartoonist's Nightmare* [animated film]. United States: Leon Schlesinger Studios.

Schneemann, C. (producer and director). (1964). *Meat Joy* [performance/video]. United States: Carolee Schneemann.

_____ (1967). *Fuses* [performance/video]. United States: Carolee Schneemann.

Shannon, K. (producer and director). (1974a). *Extensions of the Family* [documentary]. Canada: National Film Board of Canada.

_____ (1974b). *It's Not Enough* [documentary]. Canada: National Film Board of Canada.

_____ (1974c). *Like the Trees* [documentary]. Canada: National Film Board of Canada.

_____ (1974d). *Luckily I Need Little Sleep* [documentary]. Canada: National Film Board of Canada.

_____ (1974e). *Mothers Are People* [documentary]. Canada: National Film Board of Canada.

_____ (1974f). *They Appreciate You More* [documentary]. Canada: National Film Board of Canada.

_____ (1974g). *Tiger on a Tight Leash* [documentary]. Canada: National Film Board of Canada.

_____ (1974h). *Would I Ever Like to Work* [documentary]. Canada: National Film Board of Canada.

_____ (1975). *Our Dear Sisters* [documentary]. Canada: National Film Board of Canada.

Shannon, K. (producer and director) and Angelico, I. and Henderson, A. (directors). (1975). *And They Lived Happily Ever After* [documentary]. Canada: National Film Board of Canada.

Sherman, E., Canning, I., Frappier, R. and Seghatchian, T. (producers) and Campion, J. (director and producer). (2021). *The Power of the Dog* [film]. New Zealand, United Kingdom, Canada and Australia: New Zealand Film Commission, BBC Film, Max Films, See-Saw Films, Bad Girl Creek and Cross City Films.

Sprinkle, A. (producer and director). (1992). *Slut And Goddesses* [video]. United States: Annie Sprinkle.

Sullivan, P. (producer) and Messmer, O. (director). (1919). *Felix the Cat* [short animated film series]. United States: Paramount Pictures.

Sweeny, M. (producer) and Lynch, D. (director and producer) (2006). *Inland Empire* [film]. France, Poland, and United-States: Absurda, Studio Canal, Fundacja Kultury and Camerimage Festival.

Sweeney, M., Sarde, A, Edelstein, N., Polaire, M. and Krantz, T. (producers) and Lynch, D. (director). (2001) *Mulholland Drive* [film]. France and United-States: Les Films Alain Sarde, Asymmetrical Productions, Babbo Inc., Le Studio Canal+ and The Picture Factory.

Todd Hénaut, D. and Rosen, M.L. (producers) and Sherr-Klein, B. (director). (1981). *Not a Love Story: A Film About Pornography* [documentary]. Canada: National Film Board of Canada.

Trnka, J. (director). (1959). *A Midsummer Night's Dream* [animated film]. Czechoslovakia: Czechoslovakian Film, Studio of Animation and Puppet Film and Marionettes Film Prague.

―――― (1965). *The Hand* [animated film]. Czechoslovakia: Ústřední Pujcovna Filmu, Loutkovy Film Praha and Studio Kresleného a Loutkového Filmu.

Trnka, J. (producer) and Krejcik, J. and Trnka, J. (directors). (1946). *The Gift* [animated film]. Czechoslovakia: KF a.s. and Studio Brati v triku.

Tunstell, D. (director and producer). (1958). *Women on the March* [documentary]. Canada: National Film Board of Canada.

Verall, D. (producer) and Forbis, A. and Tilby, W. (directors). (1999). *When the Day Breaks* [animated film]. Canada: National Film Board of Canada.

Verrall, D. (producer) and McWilliams, D. (director and video editor). (1991). *Creative Process: Norman McLaren* [documentary]. Canada: National Film Board of Canada.

Bibliography

Anderson, B. (1983). *Imagined Communities*. New York: Verso.

Arbour, R.M. (dir.). (1982). *Art et féminisme* [catalogue]. [FR] Québec: Ministère des Affaires Culturelles.

Aspler Burnett, M. (1980). Des cinéastes québécoises anglophones. [FR] *Les dossiers de la cinémathèque*, (6), 32–34.

Beaudet, L. (1979). L'animation à l'ONF. [FR] *Copie Zéro, 1* (2), 3–4.

———— (1983). Une brèche dans le fief. [FR] In D.L. Carrière (dir.), *Femmes et cinéma québécois* (pp. 212–224). Montréal: Boréal Express.

Beauvoir, S. de [1949] (2016a). *Le deuxième sexe, I: Les faits et les mythes* [*The Second Sex, I. Facts and Myths*]. Paris: Gallimard.

———— [1949] (2016b). *Le deuxième sexe, II: L'expérience vécue.* [*The Second Sex, II. Woman's Life Today*]. Paris: Gallimard.

———— (1953a). *The Second Sex, I. Facts and Myths*. London: Lowe and Brydone.

———— (1953b). *The Second Sex, II. Woman's Life Today*. London: Lowe and Brydone.

Beckman, K. (2014). *Animating Film Theory*. Durham (NC): Duke University Press.

Bélanger, A. et Migner-Laurin, A. (2012). *Les réalisatrices du petit écran*. [FR] Montréal: Université du Québec à Montréal.

Bendazzi, G. (2016a). *Animation: A World History, Volume 1: Foundations—The Golden Age*. Boca Raton (FL): Focal Press.

———— (2016b). *Animation: A World History, Volume 2: The Birth of a Style—The Three Markets*. Boca Raton (FL): Focal Press.

———— (2016c). *Animation: A World History, Volume 3: Contemporary Times*. Boca Raton (FL): Focal Press.

Bilodeau, A. (2016). Art féministe. Le corps, outil de transgression, de contestation et de décolonisation. [FR] *Nouveaux Cahiers du Socialisme*, (15), 161–166.

Blais, D. (1983). Des femmes à l'Office national du film. [FR] In L. Carrière (dir.), *Femmes et cinéma québécois* (pp. 201–207). Montréal: Boréal Express.

Bocke, K. (1957). *Cosmic View*. New York: The John Day Company.

BoiLeau, J. (1983). Images récentes dans les films à succès. [FR] In L. Carrière (dir.), *Femmes et cinéma québécois* (pp. 113–129). Montréal: Boréal Express.

Booker, K. (2010). *Disney, Pixar, and the Hidden Messages of Children's Films*. California: Greenwood Publishing Group.

Bourdieu, P. (1992). *Les règles de l'art: Genèse et structure du champ littéraire* [*The Rules of Art: Genesis and Structure of the Literary Field*]. Paris: Éditions du Seuil.

Braidotti, R. (2015). Penser avec un accent: Françoise Collin, Les Cahiers du Grif et le féminisme français. [FR] Dans D. Fougeyrollas-Schwebel and F. Rochefort (dir.), *Penser avec Françoise Collin: Le féminisme et l'exercice de la liberté* (pp. 13–32). Dontilly: Éditions iXe.

Burnett, M. (1980). Des cinéastes québécoises anglophones. [FR] *Les dossiers de la cinémathèque*, (6), 32–34.

Carrière, L. (1981). À propos des films faits par des femmes au Québec. [FR] *Les dossiers de la cinémathèque*, 1 (11), 44–51.

—— (dir.). (1983a). *Femmes et cinéma québécois*. [FR] Montréal: Boréal Express.

—— (1983b). *La série de films Société Nouvelle dans un Québec en changement (1969–1979)* (M.A. thesis). [FR] Université du Québec à Montréal.

—— (1984a). Et si on changeait la vie? (animation ONF: 1968–1984). [FR] *Les dossiers de la cinémathèque*, 1 (14), 42–47.

—— (1984b). 25 ans plus tard: Où êtes-vous donc? [FR] *Les dossiers de la cinémathèque*, 2 (14), 20–47.

—— (1988). *Les films d'animation à l'O.N.F. (1950–1984) et la protestation sociale* [FR] (unpublished doctoral dissertation). McGill University.

Champoux, L. (1977). *Clorinda et Lina ont choisi le film d'animation*. [FR] Montréal: Photo-Journal.

Clarens, B. (2000). *André Martin, écrits sur l'animation 1*. [FR] Paris: Dreamland.

Collectif Clio. (1992). *L'histoire des femmes au Québec depuis quatre siècles*. [*Quebec women: A History*]. Montréal (QC): Le Jour.

Coulangeon, P. (2004). Classes sociales, pratiques culturelles et styles de vie. Le modèle de la distinction est-il (vraiment) obsolète? [FR] *Sociologie et Sociétés*, 36 (1), 59–85.

Crafton, D. (1982). *Before Mickey: The Animated Film*. Chicago: The University of Chicago Press.

—— (2013). *Shadow of a Mouse: Performance, Belief, and World-Making in Animation*. Berkeley (CA): University of California Press.

DaudeLin, R. (1980). Attention . . . cinéastes au travail! [FR] *Les dossiers de la cinémathèque*, (6), 7–17.

Davis, A.M. (2006). *Good Girls and Wicked Witches: Women in Disney's Feature Animation*. New Barnet: John Libbey.

De Blois, M. (2006). La première mort de l'animation. In M. Jean (dir.), *Quand le cinéma d'animation rencontre le vivant*. [FR] (pp. 27–32). Montréal: Les 400 coups.

Delphy, C. [2001] (2013). *L'Ennemi Principal, Tome 2: Penser le Genre*. [FR] Paris: Éditions Syllepse.

Denault, J. (1981). Le cinéma féminin au Québec. [FR] *Les dossiers de la cinémathèque*, 1 (11), 36–44.

—— (1993). Des femmes devant et derrière la caméra: le cas de l'Office national du film du Canada, 1941–1945. [FR] *Recherches féministes*, 6 (1), 113–118.

_____ (1996). *Dans l'ombre des projecteurs. Les Québécoises et le cinéma.* [FR] Sainte-Foy: Presses de l'Université du Québec.

Denis, S. (2017). *Le cinéma d'animation. Techniques, esthétiques, imaginaires* (3e éd.). [FR] Paris: Armand Collin.

Descarries, F. et Corbeil, C. (1991). Penser la maternité: les courants d'idées au sein du mouvement contemporain des femmes. [FR] *Recherches sociographiques, 32* (2), 347–366.

Descarries, F. et Poulin, R. (coord.). (2010a). Présentation: socialismes, féminismes et émancipation humaine. [FR] In *Nouveaux Cahiers du Socialisme* (pp. 6–21). Montréal: Écosociété.

Descarries, F. et Poulin, R. (2010b). Présentation: Socialismes, féminismes et émancipation humaine. [FR] *Nouveaux Cahiers du Socialisme, 4.*

Des Rivières, M. et Saint-Martin, L. (1994). Des images et des représentations renouvelées? [FR] *Recherches féministes, 7* (2), 1–5.

Dumont, F. et Sofio, S. (2007). Esquisse d'une épistémologie de la théorisation féministe en art. [FR] *Cahiers du Genre, 2* (43), 17–43.

Edera, B. (1983). L'animation au féminin. [FR] *La Revue du Cinéma*, (389), 73–86.

Evans, G. (1979). John Grierson et l'esprit totalitaire: la propagande et la Deuxième Guerre mondiale. [FR] *Copie Zéro, 1* (2), 5–7.

Faludi, S. (2013). Death of a revolutionary. *The New Yorker.* Retrieved from https://www.newyorker.com/magazine/2013/04/15/death-of-a-revolutionary.

Federici, S. (2018). *Witches, Witch-Hunting and Women.* Toronto: Between the Lines.

Field, R.D. (1942). *The Art of Walt Disney.* London: Collins.

Finch, C. (1973). *The Art of Walt Disney: From Mickey Mouse to the Magic Kingdom.* Columbia: Mullen Books.

Firestone, S. [1970] (2003). *The Dialectic of Sex: The Case for Feminist Revolution.* New York: Straus and Giroux.

Friedan, B. [1963]. *The Feminine Mystique.* New York: W. W. Norton & Company.

Froger, M. (2009). *Le cinéma à l'épreuve de la communauté. Le cinéma francophone de l'Office national du film 1960–1985.* [FR] Montréal (QC): Les Presses de l'Université de Montréal.

Furniss, M. (dir.). (2009). *Animation: Art and Industry.* New Barnet: John Libbey Publishing Ltd.

Furniss, M. (2016). *A New History of Animation.* New York: Thames and Hudson.

Giguère, N. et Pérusse, M. (1980). Vidéo Femmes. [FR] *Les dossiers de la cinémathèque*, (6), 35–36.

Glover, G. (1975). Une influence libératrice. [FR] *Séquences, 1* (82), 133–134.

Gouvernement du Canada (1939). *Loi nationale sur le cinématographe (extraits).* [FR]. Retrieved from http://collections.cinematheque.qc.ca/articles/loi-pour-creer-un-office-national-du-film-loi-nationale-sur-le-cinematographe-extraits/.

_____ (1951). *Canada. Report on the Royal Commission on National Development in the Arts, Letters and Sciences (1949–1951).* Report. Ottawa, Massey, V. Retrieved from https://www.collectionscanada.gc.ca/massey/h5-400-e.html.

_____ (1970). *Report of the Royal Commission on the Status of Women in Canada*. Retrieved from https://publications.gc.ca/collections/collection_2014/priv/CP32-96-1970-1-eng.pdf.

Grierson, J. (1938). *Rapport sur les activités cinématographiques du gouvernement canadien*. [*Report on Canadian government film activities*]. Retrieved from http://collections.cinematheque.qc.ca/wp-content/uploads/2013/06/DCQ_1978_01w2.pdf.

Guévin, R. (2000). Le cinéma québécois à l'ombre de Duplessis. [FR] *Histoire Québec*, 5 (3), 9–14.

Guillaumin, C. (1978a). Pratique du pouvoir et idée de la nature (1): L'appropriation des femmes. [FR] *Questions Féministes*, (2), 5–30.

_____ (1978b). Pratique du pouvoir et idée de la Nature (2): Le discours de la Nature. [FR] *Questions Féministes*, (3), 5–28.

_____ (1979). Question de différence. [FR] *Questions féministes*, (6), 3–21.

_____ (1995). *Racism, Sexism, Power, and Ideology*. London: Routledge.

Hamel, J.F. (2011). Lorsque le récit devient autoréflexif: mises en abyme. [FR] *Ciné-Bulles*, 29 (4), 48–51.

Hébert, P. (2006). *Corps, langage, technologie*. [FR] Montréal (QC): Les 400 coups.

Hirata, H., Laborie, F., Le Doaré, H. et Senotier, D. (2004). *Dictionnaire critique du féminisme* (2e éd. augm.). [FR] Paris: Presses universitaires de France.

Houle, M. et Julien, A. (1978). *Dictionnaire du cinéma Québécois*. [FR] Montréal: Fides.

Jankovic, J. (2015). Teaching Canadian identity, nationhood and media literacy with Shameless Propaganda. *NFB Blog*. Retrieved from https://blog.nfb.ca/blog/2015/12/15/teaching-canadian-identity-nationhood-media-literacy-shameless-propaganda/.

Jean, M. (dir.). (2006). *Quand le cinéma d'animation rencontre le vivant*. [FR] Montréal (QC): Les 400 coups.

Lamartine, T. (1980). Du cinéma et, de-ci de-là, des femmes. [FR] *Les dossiers de la ciné- mathèque, Copie Zéro*, (6), 30–32.

_____ (2010). *Le féminin au cinéma*. [FR] Montréal (QC): Sisyphe.

Lambart, E. (1975). Un inventeur. [FR] *Séquences*, 1 (82), 130–132.

Lamoureux, D. (1986). *Fragments et collages. Essai sur le féminisme québécois des années 70*. [FR] Montréal (QC): Éditions du remue-ménage.

Levitin, C. (1992). Caroline Leaf et le Cinéma d'Animation. [FR] *ASIFA Canada*, 19 (2), no page.

Lingford, R. (SD), Women animators with a distinctive feminine and/or feminist perspective. Retrieved from www.screenonline.org.uk/film/id/468226/index.html

Lord, V. (2009). *Une voix féminine contestataire des années 1930: agentivité et écriture dans Dans les ombres d'Éva Sénécal* (M.A. thesis). [FR] Université du Québec à Montréal.

Lupien, A., Descarries, F. et Réalisatrices Équitables. (2011). *Encore Pionnières. Parcours des réalisatrices québécoises en long-métrage de fiction*. [FR] Montréal: Réalisatrices Équitables. Retrieved from https://sac.uqam.ca/upload/files/publications/femmes/Encore%20pionnieres.pdf.

_____ (2013). *L'avant et l'arrière de l'écran*. [FR] Montréal: Réalisatrices Équitables. Retrieved from https://realisatrices-equitables.com/wp-content/uploads/2016/02/etude-avant-arriere-ecran-2012.pdf.

Lupien, L. (2012). *La Place des réalisatrices dans le financement public du cinéma et de la télévision, mise à jour des statistiques*. [FR] Montréal: Université du Québec à Montréal. Retrieved from https://realisatrices-equitables.com/wp-content/uploads/2016/01/Etude-place-realisatrices-financement-public-2012.pdf.

Maltin, L. (1973). *The Disney Films*. New York: Crown.

Morazain, J., Larocque, M. et Poirier, A.C. (1971). *"En tant que femmes", rapport de recherches*. [FR] Montréal: Office national du film du Canada.

Mucchielli, A. [1986] (2009). *L'identité*. Paris: Presses Universitaires de France.

Mulvey, L. [1975] (2009). Visual pleasure and narrative cinema. In D.L. MuLvey (dir.), *Visual and Other Pleasures* (2nd ed., pp. 14–27). London: Palgrave Macmillan.

_____ [1981] (2009). Afterthoughts on "Visual pleasure and narrative cinema " inspired by King Vidor's *Duel in the Sun* (1946). In D.L. MuLvey (dir.), *Visual and Other Pleasures* (2nd ed., pp. 31–40). London: Palgrave Macmillan.

_____ (dir.). (2009). *Visual and Other Pleasures* (2nd ed.). London: Palgrave Macmillan.

Nochlin, L. (dir.). [1971] (1998). Why have there been no great women artists? In D.L. Nochlin (dir.). *Woman, Art, and Power and Other Essays* (pp. 145–178). Boulder (CO): Westview Press.

_____ [1988] (1998). Woman, art, and power. In D.L. NochLin (dir.), *Woman, Art, and Power and Other Essays* (pp. 1–36). Boulder (CO): Westview Press.

Orwell, G. (1945). *Animal Farm*. England: Secker and Warburg.

Ouvrard, H. (1974). "En tant que femmes ". [FR] *Le Nouvelliste*, s. p.

Perrot, M. (2006). *Mon Histoire des femmes*. [FR] Paris: Éditions du Seuil.

Pilling, J. (dir.) (1992). *Women and Animatiom: A Compendium*. Suffolk: St. Edmundsbury Press Ltd.

Poirier, A.C. (1980). Je suis née femme, je suis devenue cinéaste. [FR] *Les dossiers de la cinémathèque*, (6), 18–19.

Poncet, M.-H. (1952a). *Étude comparative des illustrations du Moyen Âge et du dessin animé*. [FR] Paris: Nizet.

_____ (1952b). *L'esthétique du dessin animé*. [FR] Paris: Nizet.

Ravary-PiLon, J. (2018). *Femmes, nation et nature dans le cinéma québécois*. [FR] Montréal: Presses de l'Université de Montréal.

Réalisatrices Équitables. (2016). *La place des créatrices dans les postes clés de création de la culture au Québec*. [FR] Montréal: Réalisatrices Équitables. Retrieved from https://realisatrices-equitables.com/wp-content/uploads/2016/06/rapport-la-place-des-creatrices-12-juin-2016.pdf.

Robert, C. (2017). *Toutes les femmes sont d'abord ménagères. Histoire d'un combat féministe pour la reconnaissance du travail ménager: Québec 1968–1985*. [FR] Montréal: Éditions Somme Toute.

Rollet, B. (2017). *Femmes et cinéma, sois belle et tais-toi!* [FR] Paris: Belin/Humenis.

Roy, J. (2007). Les Femmes et le cinéma d'animation au Québec: Un cinéma de l'intimité. [FR] *Nouvelles vues sur e cinéma, 1* (7), 1–15.

Rubin, G. (1975), *The Traffic in Women: Notes on the "Political Economy" of Sex* (pp. 33–65). Duke University Press.

Ryohashi, A. (1995). *The progressive philosophy of Studio D of the National Film Board of Canada: a case study of to a safer place* (1987) (M.A. thesis). Université McGill.

Sellier, G. (2005). Gender studies et études filmiques. [FR] *Cahiers du Genre, 1* (38), 63–85.

Smith, S. (1998). *The Film 100: A Ranking of the Most Influential People in the History of the Movies.* New York: Citadel Press.

Solomon, C. [1998] (2009). The Disney Studio at War. In Furniss DM (dir.), *Animation: Art and Industry* (pp. 145–150). New Barnet: John Libbey Publishing Ltd.

Spivak, G.C. (2009). *Les subalternes peuvent-elles parler?* [*Can the Suballtern Speak?*] Paris: Amsterdam.

Starr, C. [1997] (2009). Fine art animation. The art of the animated image: An anthology. In Furniss DM (dir.), *Animation: Art and Industry* (pp. 9–12). New Barnet: John Libbey Publishing Ltd.

Thébaud, F. (2007). *Écrire l'histoire des femmes et du genre.* [FR] Lyon: ENS Éditions.

Tinel, M. (2004). L'autoportrait du cinéaste au travail. [FR] *ETC*, (68), 25–28.

Toupin, L. (2018). *Wages for Housework. A History of an International Feminist Movement, 1972–77.* Vancouver: UBC Press.

TrembLay-DaviauLt, C. (1983). Avant la Révolution tranquille: Une Terre-Mère en perdition. [FR] In D.L. Carrière (dir.), *Femmes et cinéma québécois* [FR] (pp. 21–52). Montréal: Boréal Express.

Van Enis, N. (2012). *Féminismes pluriels.* [FR] Bruxelles: Aden.

Vanstone, G.E. (2003). *Documenting D: Studio D of the NFB and Its Representation of Women's Lives in Canada, 1974–1996* (Doctoral thesis). York University.

Véronneau, P. (1979). L'ONF et Maurice Dupessis. [FR] *Les dossiers de la cinémathèque,* (5), 9–10.

———— (1980). Plus lourd que la caméra, le poids des préjugés. [FR] *Les dossiers de la Cinématheque,* (6), 3–6.

Walt Disney Productions Ltd. (1938). *Mary V. Ford's letter from Mary V. Ford's personal archives.* Retrieved from https://news.lettersofnote.com/p/women-do-not-do-any-of-the-creative.

Zapperi, G. (2016). Regard et culture visuelle. [FR] In D.J. Rennes (dir.), *Encyclopédie critique du genre* [FR] (pp. 549–558). Paris: La Découverte.

Zéau, C. (2008). Cinéaste ou propagandiste? John Grierson et "l'idée documentaire". [FR] *Revue de l'Association française de recherche sur l'histoire du cinéma, 1* (55), 53–74.

———— (2015). Du devenir de la notion de documentaire à l'ONF: des discours aux formes. [FR] *Revue d'études interculturelles de l'image.* Retrieved from https://imaginationsjournal.ca/index.php/imaginations/article/view/25966.

Archives

The following documents were obtained from the National Film Board of Canada's archives, Archives and Records Management Department, NFB.

(December 1st 1971). *Note from the programming committee "Petit bonheur/Happiness Is".*

(April 11th 1975). *Micheline Lanctôt's service contract for the production of "A Token Gesture".*

(August 12th 1975). *Memo for Julie McGregor's title as producer on "A Token Gesture".*

(November 7th 1975). *Micheline Lanctôt's service contract for the production of "A Token Gesture".*

Bishop, L. (April 22nd 1976). *Letter sent to Julie McGregor confirming the distribution of "A Token Gesture" by Columbia.*

———— (January 7th 1977). *Memo on the French translation of "A Token Gesture".*

Production budgets for "Cogne-Dur"; "The Housewife"; "Petit bonheur/Happiness Is"; "The Spring and Fall of Nina Polanski" and "A Token Gesture"

Charrette, Y. (January 26th 1977). *Memo on the translation of "A Token Gesture".*

Dennie, H. (April 22nd 1976). *Letter sent to Nancy Lawand regarding the distribution statistics of "A Token Gesture" by Columbia.*

Distribution sheets: "À qui appartient ce gage?"; "Cogne-dur"; "Countdown Vignette"; "Extensions of the Family"; "Interview"; "It's not enough"; "The Housewife"; "Like the Trees"; "Mothers are People"; "Our Dear Sisters"; "Petit bonheur/Happiness Is"; "Before the Time Comes"; "Luckily

I Need Little Sleep"; "*Souris, tu m'inquiètes*"; "*The Spring and Fall of Nina Polanski*"; "*They Appreciate You More*"; "*Tiger on a Tight Leash*"; "*A Token Gesture*" and "*Would I Ever Like to Work*".

Findlay, S. (September 16th 1974). *Memo: Proposed film on women for 1975.*

Hammond, A. (August 2nd 1974). Memo: *Recommended addition to the English program, "The Spring and Fall of Nina Polanski".*

Hammond, A. (March 12th 1975). *Memo for the storyboard of "A Token Gesture".*

Koenig, W. (April 3rd 1975). *Micheline Lanctôt's hiring letter for the production of "A Token Gesture".*

Leaf, C. and Soul, V. (without date) *A Film proposal.*

McGregor, J. (September 24th 1974). *Memo: Proposed animated film on women.*

_____ (October 31st 1974). *Memo: Film on women.*

_____ (March 21st 1975). *Memo on the storyboard of "A Token Gesture".*

Biographical notice on Cathy Bennett.

Biographical notice on Veronika Soul.

Program committee reports: October 3rd 1969; November 18th 1970; January 30th 1970, November 9th 1972; January 20th 1972; February 9th 1972; August 10th 1973; February 21st 1974; June 6th 1974; June 13th 1974; July 25th 1974; August 1st 1974; November 14th 1974; November 28th 1974; January 30th 1975; February 13th 1975; February 20th 1975; June 19th 1975; April 15th 1976; December 9th 1976; August 11th 1977, and July 28th 1977.

Qui sont les femmes qui travaillent à l'ONF? (1973). *Médium Média, 2,* 11.

Sarault, G. (May 17th 1973). Report from the producer to the Studio Manager, Production: "Happiness Is"—72 019.

Storyboard of the film "The Spring and Fall of Nina Polanski" by Joan Hutton and Louise Roy.

Storyboard of the film "A Token Gesture" by Don Arioli.

Shannon, K. (July 25th 1974). *Letter to the programming committee about the film "The Spring and Fall of Nina Polanski" (to finish as a theatrical short).*

Vanasse, J.P. (March 4th 1977). *Memo on the translation of "A Token Gesture".*

Index

Note: Page numbers in *italic* indicate a figure on the corresponding page.

Printed in the United States
by Baker & Taylor Publisher Services